The Wow Boys

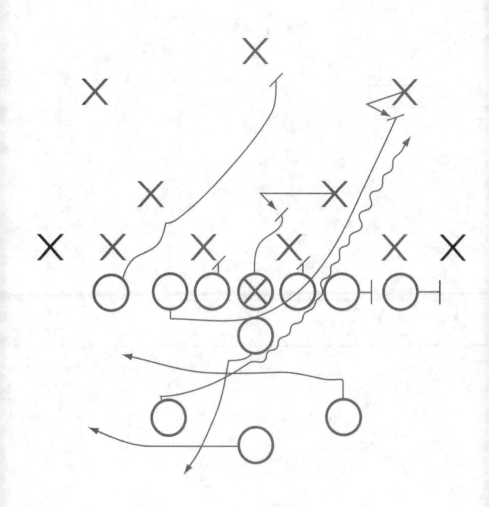

THE WOW BOYS

A Coach, a Team, and a Turning Point in College Football

James W. Johnson

University of Nebraska Press   Lincoln & London

Library of Congress Cataloging-
in-Publication Data
Johnson, James W.
The wow boys : a coach, a team,
and a turning point in college
football / James W. Johnson.
p. cm.
Includes bibliographical
references.
ISBN-13: 978-0-8032-7632-1
(pbk. : alk. paper)
ISBN-10: 0-8032-7632-X (pbk. :
alk. paper)
1. Stanford University—
Football—History. 2. Stanford
Cardinal (Football team)—
History. 3. Shaughnessy, Clark
Daniel, 1892– . 4. Football—
Offense. I. Title.
GV958.S7J64 2006
796.332'630979473—dc22
2006010696

*To my father, who loved
Stanford University.*

Shaughnessy's meeting with these players stands as one of those rare instances in life when time, place and personalities join in perfect union, when disparate and formerly malfunctioning parts mesh into a precision instrument. American football has never had a moment like it.

RON FIMRITE in a 1977
Sports Illustrated article

Contents

Illustrations

Preface

The period between 1936 and 1941 was one of the most remarkable in the history of the United States—economically, politically, artistically, and athletically.

Franklin Delano Roosevelt beat Alf Landon in the November 3, 1936, election, as Americans gave him a mandate to continue his New Deal program designed to lift the country from the throes of a long Depression. The airship *Hindenburg* exploded at Lakehurst, New Jersey, a catastrophe that brought an end to lighter-than-air transportation on May 6, 1937.

Adolph Hilter's Nazis were marching through Europe. They took over Austria on April 10, 1938. On June 25 Roosevelt signed legislation raising the minimum wage from twenty-five cents to forty cents an hour. On September 3, 1939, France and Great Britain declared war on Germany, but Roosevelt said the United States would remain neutral. On October 12 four hundred Londoners were killed by a heavy German air raid. In 1940 Winston Churchill became prime minister of Great Britain.

Congress passed the Selective Service Act on September 16, 1940, requiring men between the ages of twenty and thirty-six to register for the military draft. Roosevelt won an unprecedented third term on November 5, 1940, over Republican Wendell Willkie. Congress passed the forty-hour workweek into law. On December 7, 1941, the Japanese bombed Pearl Harbor, killing three thousand U.S. sailors and sinking most of the navy's Pacific fleet. The next day the United States declared war on Japan. Three days after that Germany and Italy declared war on the United States.

Our Town by Thornton Wilder won the Pulitzer Prize for drama on May 2, 1938. Orson Welles's *War of the Worlds* panicked radio listeners who thought aliens from outer space were invading America on October 30, 1938. *Gone with the Wind,* acclaimed as one of the best movies ever, was released in 1939. Tickets were thirty cents (equivalent to four dollars in 2006). John Steinbeck won the Pulitzer Prize for his book *The Grapes of Wrath* on May 6, 1940. Walt Disney's *Fantasia* opened in movie theaters in 1940 while the nation was rocking to the Glenn Miller orchestra's "Tuxedo Junction," "In the Mood," "Careless," and "The Woodpecker Song," and crooner Frank Sinatra belted out "I'll Never Smile Again." The women danced while wearing nylon stockings, which went on sale for the first time.

Jesse Owens won four gold medals in track at the 1936 Olympics in Berlin, embarrassing Nazi leader Adolph Hitler and his notion of the "Aryan Master Race." War Admiral won the Triple Crown of horse racing on June 5, 1937, by winning the Belmont Stakes. Heavyweight boxing champion Joe Louis knocked out Germany's Max Schmeling in the first round of their June 27, 1938, fight, again a setback to Hilter's claims of white superiority. An amazing racehorse, Seabiscuit, was named Horse of the Year in 1938. 'Biscuit received more newspaper column inches of coverage that year than did President Roosevelt, Hitler, or Mussolini. On December 8, 1940, the Chicago Bears ran over the Washington Redskins 73–0, the most lopsided score in a professional football championship game then and since.

In baseball two remarkable milestones were set: The New York Yankees' Joe DiMaggio had a fifty-six-game hitting streak, a major league record that still stands. It ended on July 17, 1941, and the Boston Red Sox's Ted Williams hit .406, the last player to bat above .400. He achieved the mark on the last day of the season by getting six hits in a doubleheader.

College football ruled the day, however, with the game drawing more fans than Major League Baseball—ten million fans attended games each year by the start of the 1930s.

None of the world events escaped the attention of the community at Leland Stanford Junior University in Palo Alto, California. Nor did the excitement of football. Despite the unsettling news of the world, life carried on at the eighty-eight-hundred-acre university, known as "the Farm." The private school was ranked among the top universities in the nation for its academics. It called itself the "Harvard of the West." Some students referred to Harvard as the "Stanford of the East." The Farm attracted a diverse number of top scholars and students to its campus.

Students and faculty strolled the campus watching construction of the 274-foot-tall, six-hundred-thousand-dollar Hoover War Library—"the Libe," they called it—named for the school's most famous alumnus, Herbert Hoover. Stanford's goal was to be one of the top academic schools in the country, but it also sought to be among the best athletically. In recent years Stanford consistently has been No. 1 in the Sears Directors' Cup, which began in 1993 as the reward for being the nation's best athletic department. Striving for excellence on the playing field was no different during that period.

In 1936 Stanford's Angelo "Hank" Luisetti revolutionized basketball by abandoning the two-handed set shot for the one-handed shot. The shot came to the basketball world's attention when the Indians played Long Island University in New York's Madison Square Garden and made Luisetti a national figure. "That night changed the game around," he said. "I got credit for the one-handed shot. I'm sure someone else did it before me, but I did it in Madison Square Garden. Anything you do something in New York, everyone hears about it."

In 1938 Stanford's golf team began a five-year run of dominating college golf by winning four NCAA titles. Its track team finished second in the NCAA track championships in 1939. It included Clyde Jeffrey, who tied the world record for the one-hundred-yard dash.

Perhaps no year on the campus was bigger than 1940. While war and the economy were on everyone's mind, they didn't captivate the imagination of the student body like the football team. And while Stanford president Ray Lyman Wilbur became caught up in the preoccupation with football, he cautioned students and faculty the day before Stanford's game with USF that Americans were becoming "an amusement-minded nation that hates to face the disagreeable facts of today's upheaval."

Stanford students, as well as millions of Americans, needed their escape from world events, and sports provided that interlude. They were no different from millions of other fans who loved their football. Right alongside the front-page story of Wilbur's speech in the *Stanford Daily*, editors ran four pictures of Stanford football players and an "ear" alongside the masthead that said, "Good Luck, Coach Shaughnessy . . . Beat U.S.F." That game launched a remarkable season. Not only did the Wow Boys provide a season of thrills, with a complicated T-formation offense that Shaughnessy brought with him to the Farm, they changed forever the game of football. In 2002 ESPN, the TV sports network, rated the shift to the modern T formation as the No. 2 sports innovation of all time, right behind baseball's free agency.

This is the story of Stanford's memorable season about how a new coach, Clark Shaughnessy, introduced the modern T that dramatically changed college football.

Acknowledgments

The editors on the *Arizona Daily Star* sports desk probably aren't aware of it, but they inspired me to write this chronicle of a football season that changed college football. One night when working on the desk while moonlighting away from my full-time job as a journalism professor at the University of Arizona, I noted that the College Football Hall of Famer Frankie Albert had died a week or so before. But I had not seen a story in the *Star* in Tucson about his passing.

When I asked editors why they had failed to run an obituary on Albert, who quarterbacked and coached the San Francisco 49ers, the answer was, "Never heard of him." Granted, nobody on the desk was over the age of fifty—I was long past that point; I had watched Albert play with the 49ers—but surely they had heard about a man who carried out the T formation that changed football. "Nope," came back the reply. Wasn't he worthy of at least a couple of paragraphs in the "Sport Shorts"? I asked. But I just got blank stares.

With that, I told two or three of them that Albert was an important figure in football and that his memory should be preserved. Hence this book. So indirectly, those editors were responsible for this piece of work. To them I say, "Thanks for the inspiration."

Many thanks go to four of my extraordinary students—Tiffany Keller, Ty Young, Joe Mazzeo, and Lindsey Stockton. They spent countless hours poring through microfilm of papers from that period. Not once did I hear any complaints; Mazzeo, in fact, said he learned a great deal by reading the front pages of the newspapers during the year before the United States entered World War II.

I couldn't have written this book without the help of Cyclone Covey, a Professor Emeritus of history at Wake Forest University. His 1957 book, *The Wow Boys: The Story of Stanford's Historic 1940 Football Season, Game by Game*, was invaluable. He and his wife watched hours of game films, most of which no longer exist, to put together a readable book. I found him via the Internet and asked if he had any copies of the long out-of-print book. He might have a publisher's copy in his basement, he said. A week later the copy showed up in my mailbox. Thanks, Cyclone.

Scott Leykam, who was assigned to media relations for Stanford football, also was extremely helpful. He let me pore unimpeded through file cabinets looking for newspaper and magazine articles as well as pictures of the players. He also e-mailed me pictures of several players. He always was patient with my pestering e-mails.

Special thanks also go to Maggie Kimball, a librarian in the Special Collections Department at the Stanford Library. When I visited Stanford during the summer of 2003, she suggested I look at microfilm of the *Stanford Daily*. I decided to pass because I didn't have much time and I didn't think the papers would be useful. Several weeks later I realized that I needed to get a feel for what the campus was like during 1940, so I asked Maggie if there was any way I could peruse the microfilm without traveling from Tucson to Stanford. Another trip would be expensive and take too long. Sound impossible? Not to Maggie. She said she could get copies of microfilm made and mailed to me. All she asked is that they be mailed back. When I viewed the microfilm, I found it invaluable. Never doubt a librarian's help. And she has the microfilm back in her safekeeping.

Former teaching colleagues Don Carson and Jim Patten, and

gym workout buddies Ron Navarette and Bill Dallman offered good ideas and criticism. I appreciate their efforts.

Thanks also go to the former players whom I interviewed. They were all more than willing to share their memories—all of them sharp—of what it was like to play with the Wow Boys.

I found Milt Vucinich extremely helpful. He told me how to reach some players and which players were no longer living. He and his wife graciously welcomed my wife and me into their beautiful home in San Mateo, California. And thanks also go to his teammates Ray Hammett, Ed Stamm, Chick Orme, and Bill Mannon. I only wish I had started this book years earlier to record the memories of players now deceased.

Many thanks to my editors, Rob Taylor and Jeanée Ledoux, who offered revisions that made this book far better than I could have hoped.

Introduction

The New Coach

On April 3, 1940, more than one hundred Stanford football players were summoned to a history classroom in the campus quadrangle to meet their new coach. They had read about him in the school newspaper, but this was their first meeting. They didn't know what to expect; they knew their new coach's won-loss record at the University of Chicago the previous year was almost as bad as Stanford's.

"We'd been reading about all those beatings Shaughnessy's men had taken," said sophomore fullback Milt Vucinich, who moved up from the freshman squad to the varsity, "so we were joking among ourselves that wasn't it just like Stanford to hire somebody like this to coach us." Senior guard Jack Warnecke said, "We felt [the new coach] was only what we deserved."

Just then, a tall, slim man with gray hair and a stoic look walked into the room. The first thing he said was, "Boys, I am not to be addressed as 'Clark' or, especially, 'Soup' [a nickname one of the sportswriters gave him because that was what he was going to find himself in]. To you, I am 'Mr. Shaughnessy' or 'Coach.' Nothing else. I am a professor of football."

Then Clark Shaughnessy, late of the University of Chicago's hapless football team, startled the curious players. "Now, I have a formation for you that if you learn it well will take you to the Rose Bowl," he said. Shaughnessy told them they would score a dozen touchdowns with one play, which astonished the men. "We all snickered," junior Frankie Albert said years later. "The guy sounded like a goof. . . . I didn't know whether to laugh or walk out."

The diagram showed a back hitting a hole in the line in a direct handoff from the quarterback. "Whoever heard of a back charging into a line without a blocker ahead of him? It looked like suicide," Albert said. He remembered the first chalk talk that Shaughnessy gave. "He told us that particular play he was drawing would produce ten to twelve touchdowns that season. We hadn't made that many the whole 1939 season."

Other players were skeptical as well. Senior halfback Hugh Gallarneau said Shaughnessy's prediction of a dozen touchdowns sounded good to him, but "I thought he was crazy. I was a halfback and when Shaughnessy diagrammed a play which sent the halfback into the line without a blocker ahead of him, I laughed."

Stanford had played the single wing the year before, where the center snapped the ball directly to the runner, who would follow other backfield men as blockers and power straight ahead.

But the players knew matters couldn't be any worse than the previous year, when the Indians won one, lost seven, and tied one. They were taking a wait-and-see attitude, but they were willing to give it a chance. They liked Shaughnessy's attitude almost right away. "Shaughnessy was a most refreshing person," Albert said. "He was a very positive thinker and had a job to do. After all, we were a bunch of losers, more or less."

What Shaughnessy had discovered was that Stanford players had enormous talent but had been misused with the single wing. The changes he brought to the team with the modern T formation revolutionized football to the point that within the next decade, most of the major football powers across the country used the formation. In 1943 Shaughnessy ranked the backfield he assembled as the best in football history. More than sixty-five years later, that still may be true.

Although Shaughnessy's prediction of scoring a dozen touchdowns on a single play never came to fruition, the T formation so befuddled Stanford's opponents that the Indians did indeed go to the Rose Bowl.

And it all became possible following a chance meeting Clark Shaughnessy had with the coach of the Chicago Bears in the struggling National Football League in the mid-1930s.

1

From Power to Finesse

One evening in 1935 Clark Shaughnessy, the frustrated coach from a mediocre University of Chicago football team, attended a civic dinner in Chicago, where he ran into George Halas, the founder and head coach of the Chicago Bears.

Shaughnessy told Halas that he had attended several of the Bears' games, observing that Halas had been using the T formation without much luck. After a loss to Green Bay, Shaughnessy said, he noticed Halas sitting dejected on the bench. Years later Shaughnessy would say about that incident, "I made up my mind right then that I was going to try and help him."

Would Halas like to hear what he had in mind? Shaughnessy asked. Halas was more than happy to hear him out. Halas, who would go on to become a legend in the National Football League, asked Shaughnessy to join him for dinner. They rearranged place cards so they could sit together. Shaughnessy told Halas he too had been dabbling with the T and he thought he might be able to help Halas improve the Bears' offensive attack. In essence he told

Halas that he had worked up a new offense that featured "hidden ball stuff, but with power." But, he said, he had not used the formation at the University of Chicago because he lacked the players to make it work.

During dinner Shaughnessy whipped out a pen and began sketching plays with Xs and Os on napkins and tablecloths. Waiters after the dinner must have thought a mad scientist had been drawing plans for a weapon of mass destruction. He was, of course, drawing plays to destroy defenses.

"We passed the evening," Halas said, "talking about the formation. We merely touched basic principles."

Halas was well aware that the NFL had struggled since its inception in 1922 as an industrial and milltown league. It took a backseat in every aspect to college football. The league had attracted little attention from the press and fans except for a brief flurry when the "Galloping Ghost" Red Grange, the Illinois All-American, joined the NFL. But even that illustrious star couldn't draw enough people to the games. The play was just too dull. It lacked the pageantry of the college game as well as the built-in loyalty of alumni, students, and hometown fans.

Halas recognized that the single-wing and double-wing offenses were boring spectators. During the 1932 season neither the Chicago Bears nor their opponents scored a single touchdown through four games—the Bears tied three 0–0 and lost one 2–0—behind the "three yards and a cloud of dust" offense run by standouts Grange and Bronko Nagurski.

That was not the kind of football that would attract legions of fans to professional football, and Halas knew it. He wanted to liven up the game and began experimenting with the T formation. The T had been used until the turn of the twentieth century but abandoned by teams that preferred the single wing.

Halas had first come across the T formation in 1914 as a freshman at the University of Illinois, where his coach and later mentor Bob Zuppke used it in its most rudimentary form. Zuppke's T became a model that Halas and Shaughnessy would improve with extraordinary success. Zuppke's freshman coach that year was Ralph Jones, who Halas later would hire to put the T into the Bears' offense.

What Jones brought to the Bears in the late 1920s set the stage for the dramatic changes Halas and Shaughnessy would bring to the formation. Jones's T spread the line and backfield a little farther apart to give them more operating room. The quarterback crouched behind the center with two halfbacks and a fullback lined up behind him in a row horizontal to the line of scrimmage. Jones added a man in motion to Zuppke's T.

Jones took advantage of a rule that allowed one backfield man to move before the center snapped the ball. The quarterback would take a direct snap from the center and whirl around to hand off the ball to one of the backs. Or the quarterback had the option of dropping back to pass to a halfback who ran parallel to the line of scrimmage toward the sideline, or the quarterback could hand off the ball to the fullback or the other halfback. It was that formation that Halas and Shaughnessy would further refine.

After dinner Halas invited Shaughnessy to drop by his office and learn more about the Bears' plans for the T. Shaughnessy and Halas often would meet in Halas's office four nights a week from 8 until midnight discussing strategies.

"I did a good bit of the inventing, but George did the selecting and correcting. I'd come along with something and say: 'You know football; you pick this to pieces and take what you like.' That's the way it was done, gradually, experimentally," Shaughnessy said.

In 1937 Shaughnessy joined the Bears in an advisory capacity, helping Halas with terminology and analyzing game-scouting reports. In a collaboration rarely seen today, Shaughnessy continued to coach his team while being paid two thousand dollars a year by the Bears.

That same year Halas began hearing reports of a shifty runner and accurate passer at Columbia University in New York by the name of Sid Luckman. When Shaughnessy watched game films of Luckman, he knew right away that Luckman could be the quarterback the Bears needed to make the T formation go. In 1938 the Bears drafted Luckman, and Shaughnessy went to work drawing up plays especially for him. But Luckman wasn't sold on the formation.

Shaughnessy proposed brush blocking to keep the defense off balance. In brush blocking, linemen would initiate contact with defensive linemen, but instead of holding their blocks, they slid off them to charge ahead for a second block. Quick backfield men without backs to block for them would hit holes created by the brush block and skip through into the secondary before the defensive linemen had an opportunity to react.

When Shaughnessy began instituting the formation for the Bears, Luckman remarked, "You're nuts. How can you send a halfback into the line alone, without a back to block for him? You'll get him killed." Halas told him, "You worry about the signals. We'll worry about our halfbacks."

In a 1942 *Esquire* article—football coaches in those days picked up extra money on a regular basis by writing magazine articles for a football-crazed readership—Shaughnessy wrote:

"[The T] is simply, clearly, definitely and completely a breakaway from the old power game based on blocking, power blocking. That is the key point that is never, or seldom ever brought up. Concealment of the ball by the quarterback turning around instantly, as in the early days, sets the stage for a finesse, deceptive, speed type of attack. The direct pass to the back of the other systems instantly reveals where the ball is, and that fact forced the spinner and fake spinner to be developed in those attacks.

"Speed or deception football, whether worked from the T formation or any other formation, is a complete breakaway from the old power game; it is based on an entirely different strategy, and an entirely different philosophy. This type of play literally opens up the play, just as the swiftness of the airplane and light tanks has opened up the threat of attack in war, making it very difficult, if not impossible, for a wide front of fixed positions to be held effectively.

"The big heavy ponderous slow-moving men in the power offensive could move only relatively forward along a very limited sector of the field. Our quick, shifty, feinting, speedy men with their fast getaway and quick turns and side thrusts can threaten the defensive line from sideline to sideline constantly, thus opening up a wider territory for attack, and consequently, of course, a wider territory to be defended. Instead of threatening a segment of ground scarcely wider than from end to end, we threaten continually the entire width of the playing field."

Shaughnessy also compared the T to boxing: "The quick opening plays can be compared to the left jab of a boxer, the man-in-motion and the faking of the backs to the feints, and the fullback plays to the real punch. The pass plays should be used as the unexpected sock."

By using the man in motion, Shaughnessy sent a halfback running parallel to the line of scrimmage, thereby forcing a defensive player to follow him and stretch the defense.

Through the T, Shaughnessy introduced the specialist. For example, the quarterback's main duty was to pass and direct the offense. Two backs were the primary ball carriers. The third was mostly a receiver, adding a third pass catcher to the team.

Halas described Shaughnessy as "a man with a decided flair for the technical side of football, [who] played a leading role in working out the numbering system which is still the basis of the Bears' signal system today [in 1953]. Shaughnessy also was a leader in staff planning on the development of the 'counter plan.'"

Shaughnessy persuaded Halas to throw more passes than he had in previous uses of the T. Quarterbacks would fake handoffs to backs, thereby "freezing" the defense, and then step back to throw to one of the three receivers.

"Before we began collaborating," Halas recalled, "our T formation had two major weaknesses which enabled other clubs in the league to get too familiar with our ball carriers. One trouble was, we had only two end runs. . . . Thanks to Shaughnessy, we have twenty-two maneuvers around the ends—touchdown plays. Second, the majority of our plays went to the side of the line of the man in motion. Shaughnessy designed ground gainers that run to the side opposite the man in motion. Those counter plays were honeys."

During the first game of the 1940 season, the Bears, using the wide-open T formation, walloped the Green Bay Packers, 41–10. The T was here to stay. And Luckman was a believer.

"Football is a science to me," Shaughnessy wrote in 1942, "the maneuvering of men to attain an objective. It is very comparable to military strategy. So when George Halas didn't laugh at me or my theories I naturally warmed up to him. He didn't make fun of me and he was willing to listen. So when I'd make a suggestion he'd listen and we'd discuss it. So as I propounded some of these pet theories of mine, he would take them, try them out. Some results were apparent."

As well as things were going with the Bears, all was not so smooth at the University of Chicago. After the 1939 season the school abandoned football, opting to focus more of its efforts on academics. Shaughnessy no longer had a team to lead, and his future as a football coach was up in the air.

2

A Surprise Choice

It came as no surprise when Stanford fired football coach Tiny Thornhill after the Indians' 1-7-1 season in 1939, but what did surprise most Stanford backers was that the school hired a new coach whose record was almost as bad. "We just got the only coach in the world who had a worse record than Tiny Thornhill," said Hugh Gallarneau. Actually, Shaughnessy's record was a half game better than Thornhill's. He had won two games and lost six.

Claude "Tiny" Thornhill's team had fallen on hard times in the late 1930s after three consecutive trips to the Rose Bowl between 1934 and 1936, a team that became known as the "Vow Boys," because they vowed never to lose to Southern California, and they never did.

The Indians' success was a big accomplishment for Thornhill, who replaced the legendary Pop Warner, for whom Thornhill had played tackle at Pittsburgh in 1916. He served as Warner's line coach at Stanford beginning in 1922. He replaced Warner in 1934 and in his first three seasons, Stanford went 25-4-2, winning one Rose Bowl when it really was the "Granddaddy of All Bowl Games."

After the Vow Boys graduated, the team slipped considerably, posting a 10-25-1 record. Thornhill became lax in his coaching responsibilities. Halfback Pete Kmetovic said Thornhill "was a hang loose, old-time coach who didn't utilize his material." Gallarneau, who went on to play with the Chicago Bears, said "Thornhill, a hail fellow, well met type of individual, exerted no discipline nor provided any constructive leadership for his squad."

Bud Spencer of the now defunct *San Francisco News* wrote, "In days gone by, the Stanford men were known as laughing boys, who flaunted their sass and vinegar in a dizzy state of a football circus. Every day was a waltz, every coach a waltzing partner, and there were times when the boys in a good spirit of fun, even tackled their coach [Thornhill] and ruptured a muscle in his leg, while the boys rolled on the ground and hee-hawed. They thought it the vogue to clean out a tavern the night before a game; then waking up to find themselves with a cut eye or a sprained shoulder, they'd go into games injured with hiccoughs of hangovers echoing across the greensward."

Critics began calling for Thornhill to be fired early in 1939. A November 13 editorial in the student newspaper, the *Stanford Daily*, noted that it had refrained from criticizing the coach. That was beginning to change. The editorial commented, "But there are experts who will tell you that no Stanford team ever looked any worse than the one which bowed so easily to a not-too-great Santa Clara eleven." The editorial noted "that probably less than a half dozen of the whole squad would not fight for Tiny as a man if any issue ever arose. But don't ask them too many questions about his coaching technique. A good majority of them draw the line there."

During Thornhill's final season the Indians—they did not become the Cardinal until 1981—were able to beat only Dartmouth, and they managed to score only 54 points, the lowest of any Stanford team since 1919.

Dartmouth coach Earl "Red" Blaik, who later went on to coach the Army team with its great backs Doc Blanchard and Glenn Davis, recognized that Stanford wasn't living up to its potential. "None of us can understand what has happened to Stanford this year," he said. "They headed into the season with what we all thought to be great prospects. Most of us doped them next to Southern California out there. But they simply haven't clicked. They have the stuff; we know that. We've seen some of these boys of theirs play and we know about others. They are big and fast and they know how to play football. If they turn it on against us on Saturday, we are in for a very touch afternoon."

During the Dartmouth game, played in New York in a driving rain and a muddy field, neither Thornhill nor his coaches knew what to say to the players at halftime when they were losing 3–0. So Thornhill called on former halfback Bones Hamilton, a star on the Vow Boys who had traveled with the team to the game. Hamilton was less than kind: "You are by far and large the worst group of players who have ever worn the Stanford red." The stunned Indians rallied with two touchdowns to win 14–3 and salvage an otherwise miserable year. But the win also gave hope for next year. Tackle Jack Warnecke said later, "That was the making of the 1940 team."

As the players, coaches, and alumni took the three-day and four-night train trip home, everyone knew Thornhill's reign was over. When he arrived back in Palo Alto, Thornhill found his critics complaining that he lacked leadership. But he wasn't entirely to blame, said some. Alumni, they said, who did the bulk of the recruiting in those years, had grown complacent with success and had slacked off on their duties. Also, other schools had stepped up their recruiting, making good players more difficult to come by. Nor could many good athletes meet Stanford's rigorous academic requirements.

Thornhill may have known his time was up even before the USC game on November 11, which Stanford lost 33–0. The *San Fran-*

cisco Chronicle that day reported that Thornhill had confided in one of his players that his contract would not be renewed. Names of successors began popping up: Harry Stuhldreher of Wisconsin, Clipper Smith of Villanova, Carl Snavely of Cornell, Tex Oliver of Oregon, Dud DeGroot of San Jose State, and Buck Shaw of Santa Clara. Nowhere did the name Clark Shaughnessy of the University of Chicago surface.

Frankie Albert showed some promise for the coming year after he led the comeback against Dartmouth. In fact, of the seven touchdowns the Indians scored that year, Albert had passed for four and run for two. But Albert was disheartened. He told his brother Ward, "I guess I'm just another of those high school players who can't develop enough for college football."

Before the Big Game against California on November 25, 1939, one former football standout at Cal tabbed Albert for the star he was to become. Writing in the *San Francisco Chronicle*, Brick Morse picked stardom for Albert long before anyone else realized his potential, perhaps even Thornhill. "No coach wants to risk his reputation on an inexperienced boy," he wrote about Albert. "Far be it from me to criticize [not playing Albert very much]. The coaches know their business far better than I do. However, if I were again a football coach I'd get reckless; I'd stick Albert ... in there and let [him] stay till [he] dropped. ... Remember the names Albert and Orville Hatcher [a Cal player] and watch these two phenoms in the Big Games of 1940–41." How right he was, although Stanford lost the Big Game 32–14 in 1939 with Albert engineering the Indians' two touchdowns.

Sportswriters had high hopes for Stanford's success the next year, provided that Stanford rid itself of Thornhill. Dick Friendlich of the *Chronicle* wrote that Thornhill's "successor will fall heir to a number of good football players, but the matter of organizing them into a winning combination is something else again."

Thornhill refused to resign, and on December 15 Stanford's Board of Athletic Control voted 7–2 not to renew his contract.

Discussion leading up to the vote took twenty minutes. The board spent the next two and a half hours discussing the process of hiring a new coach, perhaps by January 7.

Shaughnessy, a coach without a team, spent a depressing holiday season with his family, waiting for the American Football Coaches Association to hold its annual convention in Los Angeles. Perhaps, he thought, he could find a coaching job there.

The search for a new Stanford coach began almost immediately. A poll of students indicated they favored Santa Clara's Buck Shaw, or Dud DeGroot of San Jose State, but that was probably because they were familiar with them. Not a single student had mentioned the name of Clark Daniel Shaughnessy.

Shaw had taken two teams to the Sugar Bowl and had always given Stanford all it could handle on the football field. He would later become the San Francisco 49ers' head coach.

DeGroot's undefeated 1939 Spartans team outscored its opponents 324 to 29. He had the backing of coaching legend Pop Warner. The old coach said, "Dud conducts his practice in a much more efficient manner than I ever did, and I doubt if there is a head coach in the country who is his equal in developing inexperienced material." DeGroot was a Stanford graduate and a Phi Beta Kappa and possessed a PhD. There was speculation that if DeGroot were selected as head coach, Warner would join him in an advisory capacity, perhaps mapping out the offensive scheme. That would have appealed to Stanford alumni who remembered Warner's glory days at the Farm.

Sportswriters added Oregon's Tex Oliver to the list with DeGroot as their No. 1 choice. Fifteen other names were bandied about, including a brief mention of Clark Shaughnessy, whose school, the University of Chicago, had just abandoned football.

Not long after the search for a new coach began, the American Football Coaches Association began its annual convention in Los Angeles. The gathering was often a fertile ground for finding new coaches, and Stanford sent its entire Board of Athletic Control to take part. The name that kept surfacing during the session was Shaughnessy, who had been Chicago's head coach since 1933. Among his losses in 1939 were to Michigan 85–0, Harvard 61–0, and Virginia 47–0. Illinois, which to date that season had scored 29 points while giving up 74, beat the Maroons 46–0. Opponents had scored 308 points while Chicago had managed just 37—"one of the most disastrous seasons in gridiron history of a major institution."

Shaughnessy was set up to lose after the University of Chicago named him to replace the legendary Amos Alonzo Stagg. Almost immediately, president Robert Hutchins raised academic standards and told Shaughnessy football would take a backseat to academics. Despite his well-earned reputation as a shrewd tactician, his new team had little talent with the exception of Jay Berwanger, the greatest halfback in the school's history and the nation's first Heisman Trophy winner. Shaughnessy gave Berwanger jersey number 99 "because that was as close to a perfect 100 as I could get." Despite his heroics, the Maroons never won more than half their games. After Berwanger left, Chicago's football fortunes fell into even deeper despair.

In trying to field a competitive team, Shaughnessy presented a list of forty-six prospects to the university's Committee on Eligibility in his final year. Twenty-three of those players were turned down, leaving him with twenty-three players to suit up. He noted that half the players on the university squad had not even played high school football. "One of the reasons for the big scores against Chicago was the university policy of letting every player who wanted to play get into the game. We were hopelessly outclassed, anyway, and it made no particular difference," Shaughnessy said.

On October 24 the University of Chicago newspaper, the *Daily Maroon*, editorialized that the football team was "getting to be a joke in the eyes of the American public and a sore spot to the alumni." Shaughnessy recognized he wasn't getting the job done.

"I was . . . teaching boys to go in there and fight against hopeless odds," Shaughnessy said. "And I want to tell you that takes guts. It isn't so bad to fight a man when you have an even chance to win but to get into that ring when you're outclassed as much as if you were facing Joe Louis takes what it takes in this man's game. I wasn't winning much, and a football coach who isn't winning is just a joke to the public."

Shaughnessy became the fall guy for the movement to abolish football. One alumnus, Jasper King, wrote to Hutchins, "I'm tired of all this pussyfooting and statistics. There is not a football man here but thinks the coaching at Chicago was bad—bad, lousy, rotten—and that Chicago could get enough men and get them on the level to have a good winning team if it had a new coach."

At the end of the year, Hutchins and board trustees explored the possibility of dropping football, not only because of the woeful performance of past teams but also to maintain the lofty academic tradition the school had attained. He had shown his hand when he wrote in the December 3, 1938, *Saturday Evening Post* that "since the primary task of colleges and universities is the development of the mind, young people who are more interested in their bodies than their minds, should not go to college." Hutchins was able to convince trustees and influential alumni to drop football. "I did not de-emphasize football at the University of Chicago," Hutchins said. "I abolished it."

The *Daily Maroon* editor editorialized that "if this school's football has been dead for years, we can only breathe a sigh of relief now that it has its burial." The decision failed to please everyone. An alumnus wrote that he was sending his son to Northwestern because Chicago abolished football. "For the first time I have felt an overstressing of academic life on campus. Red-blooded young men and women demand a well-balanced environment for study. . . . Football has it[s] place in college athletics. In the eyes of the collegiate world Chicago has quit."

Hutchins was steadfast. "It's [abolishing football] the best thing I ever did," he said in 1951.

Although Shaughnessy was no longer football coach, the school offered to allow him to stay on as a tenured professor of physical education with a lifetime job and salary of nine thousand dollars a year, at a time when the top professional football players earned six thousand dollars a year. Shaughnessy, who believed passionately in collegiate football, tried to talk with Hutchins about the folly of his move, but to no avail. The move shocked, angered, and deeply hurt Shaughnessy, and he had no intention of staying at a school that had no team. "I'm not going to sit around here and watch a great game go to hell," Shaughnessy told his wife.

Football was Shaughnessy's life. At the age of forty-seven, he wasn't about to sit back and reap the benefits of academia, no matter how lucrative. "I couldn't have done that," he said. "Football is my hobby. I live it and I love it."

Almost three years later Shaughnessy said, "Someone has written that I've put the death touch on football everywhere I've been. That is untrue. Football at Loyola of the South was at its peak when I went to Chicago. And the coaches who followed me there were not responsible for its death.

"Everyone should know that at the University of Chicago, football was dead before I went there. It was dead before Coach [Amos Alonzo] Stagg went there."

Shaughnessy was born in St. Cloud, Minnesota, on March 6, 1892. He had never even seen a football game let alone played one when he entered the University of Minnesota in 1908. All he knew about football was what he read in the newspapers. He decided to take in his first game at Minnesota's Northrup Field. Lacking the price of admission, he peeked over a fence to watch the Carlisle Indians, coached by Pop Warner, take on the Minnesota Gophers, coached by Henry Williams.

Liking what he saw, he turned out for freshman football. The coaches asked him if he had ever played before. When he said no, he was refused a uniform. Undaunted, Shaughnessy returned ten days later and was given a uniform. Failing to attract the coaches' attention, he never even got into a scrimmage.

The following year he made the team as a third-string tackle but never got into a game. During practice before the team's final game against Michigan, Williams told Shaughnessy to take over the guard position with the first team. He was to pull out of the line to lead interference for ball carriers.

"I was scared stiff," Shaughnessy recalled, "so I came out so fast that I ran away from the rest of the interference every time. In the dressing room, later, someone said my name was on the list for the trip to Ann Arbor. I edged over to the bulletin board. Sure enough, Doctor Williams had scrawled my name in pencil on the typewritten list. I felt great."

Although Shaughnessy traveled with the squad to Ann Arbor to play Michigan, he didn't get into the game. He sat on the bench to watch what the two coaches—Williams and the Wolverines' Fielding Yost—called the greatest game they had ever seen. Michigan prevailed 6–0. Shaughnessy agreed with that assessment. In 1943 he listed it as one of the twelve greatest games in football history. "That game eventually caused me to be a football coach," Shaughnessy said. "It was that great."

In the summer of 1911, he had heard of young men in Canada who were throwing spiral passes with a football. As he was driving a team of horses down Payne Avenue in St. Paul, he passed a sporting goods store, where he stopped and bought a football for two dollars. He began practicing throwing and catching the ball with friends. The following fall he was an end on the varsity even though from that position he never threw a pass. He was hurt early in the season and was on crutches until after the holiday break.

Finally, all that practice throwing spirals paid off. Coaches shifted Shaughnessy to fullback, where he developed into what

Williams called "the finest forward passer Minnesota ever had, and, in my estimation, the best ever produced in the Midwest." Shaughnessy wound up playing fullback on offense, end on defense, and handled the forward passing and kicking.

After the 1912 season Shaughnessy was named an alternate on the Walter Camp All-American team, and in 1913 he was named on various All-Western and All-Conference teams as fullback, end, and tackle for his offensive and defensive skills.

Minnesota's 1914 yearbook recognized Shaughnessy's talent. The line under his Sigma Chi fraternity picture said simply, "Good old war horse . . . you'll sure succeed in this football stuff."

After graduation Shaughnessy stayed on as assistant. He said years later, "I'm not sure why I ever went into this business. You know, somebody comes along and offers you a job and you say: 'That looks interesting; I think I'll give it a try.'"

His coaching attracted the attention of three schools, including Tulane, which offered him a head coaching job at the age of twenty-three. For the yearly salary of $1,875, he also was athletic director and basketball and track coach. He had accepted the post because he liked New Orleans and building a football program intrigued him.

He was in for a shock when he arrived on the campus. He found the football field knee deep in grass and surrounded by a ramshackle wooden fence. The grandstands may have held two thousand fans. The football equipment was virtually useless and the athletic department bankrupt, so Shaughnessy signed a personal note to buy equipment to outfit the team. He discovered the Green Wave had only one game scheduled for the upcoming year. He then wrote letters to sixty schools around the country seeking games. The first was against Jefferson College in Louisiana, and the take for that day, collected by the team manager, was $160.

Shaughnessy began showing his coaching genius. Quarterback Edmund Faust remembered the complicated plays his new coach put in. "It meant mastering the most intricate signals," he said.

"I can recall plays that had two numbers, one with four numbers, and all sorts of variations." What was to be a harbinger of Shaughnessy's future success, Tulane stressed speed and deception, mainly because the players were small. They operated out of an unbalanced single wing, and backfield players often took direct snaps from the center.

From 1915 to 1926 Shaughnessy ran up a record of fifty-eight wins, twenty-seven losses, and six ties with an undefeated season in 1925. That team was offered an invitation to the Rose Bowl to play Washington, but school officials turned it down because they felt the players were too small. Instead, Alabama accepted the bid. Shaughnessy told friends that would probably be the only chance he would have to get to the Rose Bowl. How wrong he was.

Because of his success, Loyola lured Shaughnessy away in 1927 after a New Orleans millionaire offered him $175,000 to coach the team for ten years. (Replacing him at Tulane was Bernie Bierman, a former teammate at Minnesota who had joined Shaughnessy's staff two years earlier. Bierman went on to become one of the fabled football coaches in American, winning four national titles between 1932 and 1941 after he returned to coach his alma mater.)

Shaughnessy surprised his new players at Loyola by telling them they would be using from three hundred to four hundred plays, including single shift, fullback on a double shift, and tackle on a triple shift. "That's right," said end Peter Miller, "we shifted that often."

In 1928 Loyola traveled to South Bend, Indiana, to play legendary coach Knute Rockne's Fighting Irish. When Shaughnessy saw the 133-man squad on the field, he kept his players in the locker room until just before kickoff. The final score: 12–6 Notre Dame. Loyola had led at halftime 6–0. "Never get me another 'warm-up game' with a team coached by that guy," Rockne said after the game.

Job offers were pouring in for Shaughnessy, whose reputation

17

grew with each victory. The University of California offered him the head coach's job in 1931, followed by offers from Wisconsin and Louisiana State. Shaughnessy liked New Orleans, the city in which he met his wife. By the time Shaughnessy left in 1932 because of a snag in his ten-year contract, he had compiled thirty-eight wins, sixteen defeats, and six ties. When the University of Chicago came calling, Shaughnessy couldn't say no to coaching in the Big Ten. He apparently was unaware of an effort to deemphasize football at the school. Inducements to lure players to the school were all but eliminated. The best season he could put together was one in which he won half of his games.

When he was hired at Chicago, he gave a strong indication of his coaching philosophy. He told forty-one candidates who turned out for practice in 1933, "The regular quarterback on this team has got to be more than a mechanical man. He's got to have brains with ability. He's going to do about three-fourths of the work. . . . We've got to play an open game at Chicago with a wide assortment of plays instead of a set number. It looks like we are going to have a good, fast, heavy line, but a light backfield. Pass? Yes, we'll attempt to develop a fast passing game."

But he had little success at Chicago, running up a 17-34-4 record from 1933 to 1939, when the university abolished football.

Not long after he was out of a job at Chicago, Shaughnessy left for Los Angeles to attend the coaches convention. While at the Biltmore Hotel, he met with Walter Ames, chairman of the Stanford athletic board, and faculty representative William B. Owens. "You must be making a mistake, Mr. Ames. My record is hardly a pretty thing to look at," the coach said.

Stanford president Ray Lyman Wilbur had watched the Chicago Bears play in a 1939 NFL playoff game. The Bears' offense, which Shaughnessy had helped coach, impressed him. Athletic director (they were called "graduate managers" then) Al Masters had sought out the best football minds regarding who would fit

Stanford's need. Shaughnessy's name kept cropping up. They remembered the statement by Rockne that Clark Shaughnessy "was one of the two best coaches in America."

Jim Lawson, an assistant coach under Thornhill, talked with Shaughnessy at the Biltmore for an hour. "Boy," he said, "I thought I knew something about football but that guy knows football."

The next day Shaughnessy left Los Angeles by train for San Francisco. At Masters's direction, Don Liebendorfer, the athletic department's publicist, tracked down Shaughnessy on the train with a telegram asking to meet him when the train stopped in San Jose. Liebendorfer was then to report back to Masters about what he thought of the coach. Shaughnessy was suffering a horrific cold that day.

"So bad was his cold that I feared I might be talking to an incipient corpse," Liebendorfer said. He took Shaughnessy on a tour of the eighty-eight-hundred-acre campus, where they ran into several football players, including a senior fullback. Liebendorfer drove slowly around the Stanford campus, and he saw Norm Standlee. "See that fellow over there?" he said to Shaughnessy. "He's our fullback. Standlee. Weighs 217 pounds. Stands 6-1 and half. Is fast enough to run the ends." There was silence as Liebendorfer drove away. Then Shaughnessy looked at him and said in an almost incredulous voice, "Say it again, Don, will you? Say it again."

The last stop on the tour was at Stanford Stadium. Shaughnessy walked through the southern tunnel and into the ninety-thousand-seat stadium, took one look around, and sank into the nearest seat. The largest privately owned college football facility in the United States impressed Shaughnessy. It was built in 1921 at a cost of two hundred thousand dollars, and at the time it was one of the largest stadiums in the country.

Liebendorfer noted that Shaughnessy was quiet for several minutes and that when Liebendorfer said something to him, tears were streaming down the coach's face. "Then I knew we had him, if we wanted him, and for one, I did," Liebendorfer said.

"That got me," Shaughnessy said. "I could just visualize a team of mine down there—some of the big boys I'd seen. I thought to myself, before I die I want to coach some place where I have enough material to man a real football team. This may be it." But he also had some doubts. He looked up at the huge, empty stadium and "then I heard myself saying, 'Can I fill these stands? Can I win again?'"

He sought advice from Dr. Albert Boles, a Berkeley, California, physician who had been a close friend at Minnesota. "You are not as young as you think," Boles told Shaughnessy, "and you can't keep on taking punishment." He also told Shaughnessy he didn't believe football was as strong on the West Coast as in the rest of the country.

In addition, the climate at Stanford was unsettling at best. After such a dismal season, apathy toward football set in among the student body. Alumni were split, some lining up behind Thornhill, others backing Shaw, Oliver, DeGroot, and even Clipper Smith, a long-shot candidate from Villanova. That did not bother Shaughnessy; he had been through tougher times at Chicago.

The next day he returned to Stanford for an informal meeting with a group of university people, including Ames. His cold had worsened. As Shaughnessy recalled the meeting, he had practically no voice, "and the cold made me hate the world. The Stanford men patiently waited for me to state my qualifications. They asked a few questions to open the way, but the cold kept me close-mouthed. They looked at me. I looked at them. Nothing happened. After a few minutes I made a stumbling exit. I knew that any chance of an offer had gone glimmering, and I didn't care particularly.

"Later that evening, however, I told myself, 'I don't blame those Stanford men for not being interested in you. They think that all the spirit has been beaten out of you.' Mr. Ames was staying in the same hotel, so I left a note for him saying I would like to talk to him alone [the next morning]. He asked me to come to his room there. I gave him the works."

"The works" was Shaughnessy's plans for revitalizing Stanford football: the T formation. He dazzled Ames with his Xs and Os. Ames phoned two other members of the athletic board, Judge L. R. Weinmann and J. Wesley Howell, who came to Ames's room. From there, Shaughnessy left to meet with the Stanford athletic board, which quietly and unanimously offered Shaughnessy a contract.

Shaughnessy then paid a visit to President Wilbur. "My impression of [him]," Shaughnessy said, "intensified my desire to coach at Stanford." Wilbur offered him a five-year contract at slightly more than the nine thousand dollars a year Chicago paid him. The contract also called for a full professorship. Shaughnessy told Wilbur that he was still under contract with Chicago (even though it no longer fielded a team) and that would have to be settled.

Shaughnessy caught a plane back to Chicago, where "I did some thinking. I was old enough to know the value of security for my family. But, shucks, I wanted to stay alive, to prove that I could coach football." Shaughnessy decided to take the Stanford job and departed from Chicago after getting out of his contract and shaking hands with Hutchins. Although they exchanged pleasantries, deep in his heart Shaughnessy was extremely bitter toward Hutchins for destroying football at the university.

Shaughnessy knew that abolishing football was a mistake. "Instead of abolishing football here and there, we should have insisted on football . . . in the interests of national safety, of our very existence." After all, he said, the nation was on the brink of war.

Not long after Shaughnessy arrived on campus, he told the *Stanford Daily* that the "fine sense of balance between the mental, physical, and social activities" of Stanford's student body impressed him. "Football, its practice and its playing, has distinct educational value," he said. "Education means more to me than just the training of the intellect, and it is on that point that I differ with President Hutchins." This is one of the main reasons he decided to accept the Stanford job, he said.

In the *Daily* interview, he gave a hint of things to come: "The type of offensive maneuvering depends entirely on the material available and the defensive 'setups' of the opposition. You fit your system to the material. I personally like rhythm, movement, and deception in football."

When Stanford announced his appointment as director of football, you could almost hear the cry go up: "Who's Shaughnessy?" Al Masters noted that an unnamed Ivy League school and four Big Ten universities had tried to sign the coach while he was at the University of Chicago.

In 1977 *Sports Illustrated* writer Ron Fimrite wrote that Shaughnessy's hiring "struck most alumni, fans and critics at large as an act of folly comparable to employing an arsonist as fire chief." San Francisco's newspapers couldn't quite believe it. Said Prescott Sullivan, a sports columnist for the *San Francisco Examiner*, "We have heard it said that Shaughnessy has developed the knack of losing to the point where, with him, it is an exact science. In light of his record, we aren't at all surprised by this."

Not all the press was against Shaughnessy. *San Francisco Chronicle* sports editor Bill Leiser wrote, "They are bringing in new brains into [Pacific] Coast Conference football." After Thornhill's firing, rumors abounded that some players might not return. Said Leiser, "I predict here and now that no matter how many Stanford kids fail to return for football next fall (if any) that Clark Shaughnessy will surprise you with what he does with whatever there is to do it with. You'll see plenty of Norm Standlee and Frankie Albert operating together next season."

Shaughnessy almost immediately raised more doubts when he announced that "Stanford will use the T formation." One writer noted that howls went up from coast to coast. "The T? The old-fashioned T that had gone out before nose guards and moleskin pants came in? Some wags asked Shaughnessy if he was sure he hadn't meant tackles-back." Other protestors claimed that college players could not understand and execute complicated plays such as the Bears used. What was he doing?

"Our approach will be different," he said, perhaps trying to appease the naysayers. "We'll coil up the defense in as small an area as possible, then run around it or throw over it. It will make old offenses obsolete." One *Chronicle* headline called Shaughnessy a "Specialist in Trick Offense."

Even so, alumni were less than thrilled with Shaughnessy's selection. Some thought Stanford hired him to oversee the demise of football at the Farm as he had at Chicago. "If the school is really going to deflate football," one alumnus told the Board of Athletic Control, "then there is no need for assisting in any way the athletes in the fold."

The *Stanford Daily* noted that Shaughnessy would have his hands full. An editorial said the new coach might find it difficult to deal with meddling alumni who donated athletic scholarships and who "always feel that they have purchased the right to interfere with the coaching of the team." In addition, the editorial said, he "will have to deal with a group of football players who have had absolutely no respect for the authority of their coach [Thornhill] for the past three years, either on or off the field." Shaughnessy, the *Daily* said, would have the difficult task of trying to "capture the admiration and enthusiasm of one of the most indifferent student bodies on any campus."

Hampton Pool, who coached the Los Angeles Rams of the NFL from 1952 to 1954, was a graduating senior and a member of the Board of Athletic Control in 1940. "The board stopped at nothing to get the best man for Stanford," he said. "I am positive that Clark Shaughnessy is the man. I know that if every student knew as much as I do about the situation, he would feel the same way."

Albert said he didn't know much about Shaughnessy, "but I'm satisfied that he is a good choice." Said Standlee, "I'm glad it's settled, and I believe the fellows will work for him. Shaughnessy's appointment will mean new enthusiasm." Graduating senior half-back Jim Groves wasn't so sure: "I'm rather disappointed in the choice as it seems his record is poor."

"I thought, 'Here comes the undertaker,'" tackle Jack Warnecke said. "Shaughnessy killed off football at Chicago and now he's hired to kill the game at Stanford. Who in the world hired him, and why? What were they thinking?"

Even coaches from across the country chimed in with praise for Shaughnessy. Dutch Clark, coach of the Cleveland Rams, said Shaughnessy "knows football," and Tennessee coach Bob Neyland said, "Much as we like him personally, a lot of us were surely glad to see him leave our conference [at Tulane]. He was in our hair all the time." Chicago Bears guard George Musso said, "Shaughnessy sure knows a lot of football and he's a nut on it, too. He'll talk, work, and live it with you twenty-four hours a day if you'll let him."

Shaughnessy couldn't have cared less what anyone thought of him. He had a new formation, he liked the looks of some of the players he had met, and he brimmed with confidence. He couldn't wait for spring practice to begin.

3

Installing the T

Shaughnessy went to work right after signing his contract. He toured the state, meeting with alumni and fans in hopes of bringing renewed interest to Stanford football and quelling doubts about his abilities. He received warm greetings that were tempered with curiosity and a show-me attitude. By the time he was through, he had charmed them all.

For example, on March 7 Shaughnessy addressed fourteen hundred students in Memorial Hall in his first public appearance at the Farm and gave a hint at more of what was to come. "They say I'm Irish, hot-headed, and sentimental and perhaps they are right. I may say something sharp to you football players out there on the practice field, but it won't mean a thing—sometimes," he said with a smile.

He also told the assembly that football and academics go hand in hand. "I have a theory that the jails are filled with young men who refused to take the hard way to get ahead. It doesn't take courage to hit a man over the head. But it does take courage to face your problems, study them, and work out your own solution the honest way. I think a football field is one of the finest places for teaching a young man discipline, cooperation, and courage.

"I suppose you would all like to win some games," he said as the crowd roared. "Well, so would I."

After the assembly Shaughnessy left for San Francisco, where he was to address a Press Club luncheon at noon, and then at 6:15 he was to speak before a Block S Society alumni meeting at the Olympic Club. The next day he left for Southern California to make appearances before alumni in Bakersfield, Los Angeles, and Long Beach during a week's travel.

Back home he watched game films of the 1939 season over and over. "I watched only one man in every game straight through so you can figure how many times I had to go over each picture." He was impressed that Stanford's freshman team had won five and lost one, that one a defeat 13–12 at the hands of USC. Several players from that team would contribute to the Indians' success in the upcoming season. In fact, twelve of the twenty-two first- and second-team players in 1940 either moved up from the freshman squad or were transfers.

When Stanford football players returned from their winter break, they found not only a new coach but also three new assistants as well as two holdovers from Thornhill's staff. The size of Shaughnessy's staff was a far cry from the eleven or twelve coaches that teams have today.

Shaughnessy hired Marchmont "Marchie" Schwartz, a former Notre Dame All-American halfback who had spent one year under Shaughnessy at the University of Chicago and then five years as head coach at Creighton University in Nebraska. He would serve as backfield coach at Stanford. Shaughnessy named as line coach Phil Bengston, a former All-American tackle on Minnesota's 1934 national championship team coached by Shaughnessy's ex-teammate Bernie Bierman. Bengston later would follow Vince Lombardi as the Green Bay Packers' head coach. Shaughnessy then signed up former Chicago Bears quarterback Bernie Masterson just for the spring to teach Frankie Albert how to be a T-formation quarterback. Shaughnessy retained Jim Lawson, an All-American end at Stanford in 1924, and E. P. "Husky" Hunt, who had been chief scout for Thornhill. In addition, freshman coach Harry Shipkey remained.

Masterson, a Nebraska alumnus, admired Shaughnessy's work, saying he "is one of the outstanding coaches and unquestionably the greatest student of football in the country. . . . It's no exaggeration to say that Clark lives football 365 days a year and that he probably works on football theory on an average of fourteen hours a day. He's a human machine. It's football, football, football sometimes from before dawn, sometimes far into the night. Any success he achieves in the game he deserves."

Before he chose his assistants, he interviewed their wives, trying to determine whether they would be capable, cooperative, and understanding, because the assistants were going to be putting in long hours.

Shaughnessy wouldn't ask his coaches to do anything he wouldn't do. He rarely saw his wife, Mae; a daughter, Janice, a high school student; his mother-in-law; or his mother, who lived in a rented house in Palo Alto. A son, Clark Jr., was a javelin thrower at UCLA, and another daughter, Marcia, was studying drama at Stephens College in Columbia, Missouri.

Shaughnessy had not used the T at Chicago, but after watching game films of Stanford's 1939 season, he saw a talent being misused in the double wing that he thought would fit perfectly with the T. "I'd wanted to give this formation a test, and when I saw the personnel at Stanford I was convinced that this was the place," he said. Before Shaughnessy could teach players the T, he would have to teach it to his assistants in a big hurry. They put in countless hours after they signed on, going over Shaughnessy's complex T-formation plays.

If sportswriters, alumni, and fans were skeptical of Shaughnessy's hiring, they were almost incredulous when he announced the Indians would be using the T formation that fall. Leading the skepticism was the highly respected Pop Warner, the former Stanford coach, who planted huge doubts in the minds of the Indians' backers. "If Stanford ever wins a single game with that crazy formation, you can throw all the football I ever knew into the Pacific Ocean. What they're doing is ridiculous," he said.

Warner's reaction didn't surprise Shaughnessy. "You would expect the old school to react in that way to our type of game," he would say two years later. "The old-timers have always been exponents of the old power game of football." Sportswriters referred to the T as a "horse and buggy" formation because it dated back to 1890 and had gone out of style.

Shaughnessy often used military allusions when talking about football strategy. "The best and most satisfying thing I can find about the T-formation type of football lies in the fact that it just happens to be about the best type of offense to get into the psychology of the men, for the type of warfare imposed upon us by those lightning-quick types of war paraphernalia."

For the T formation to work effectively, a combination of psychology, confidence, deception, and talent had to be blended. "The other team may score on us with their power, but we'll score on them faster with our speed and finesse. There's much more room for individual initiative, originality and imagination in our system; it gives the players a chance to use their heads. Players who are successful in this type of play will have fast reactions and quick, keen perception." That described Albert to a, well, T. Shaughnessy noted that by giving players individual responsibility they gained confidence, and when that individual responsibility was spread out over the entire team, it gave the team confidence.

Certainly, any football player accepted into Stanford with its high academic standards had a good head on his shoulders. What the Wow Boys lacked in brawn, they made up in brains. Wrote Cyclone Covey: "It is possible that the all-time record that this backfield really holds is their combined IQ score, which may be unmatched by any other four players on a major college team of the past."

The psychology came into play by keeping the players contented. For example, unlike the single- or double-wings where one backfield player handled the ball and the others were blockers, in the T every back got a chance to carry the ball, and ends could receive passes instead of just blocking. "That's the sport; just as every ball player wants to bat [in baseball]. [Knute] Rockne went to a great a-do to build up publicity for the blockers. But [blocking] was sheer drudgery," Shaughnessy said.

T-formation linemen found they suffered less wear and tear with the brush blocking necessary for long gains to materialize. In previous offensive systems, linemen had to hold their blocks, an arduous job when they were not allowed to move their hands off their chests.

The offense was a game of psychological warfare because the opponents never knew the area of attack. The single- or double-wing football of "tell them where you are going and then go there" was straight ahead drives into the line. The T toyed with the opponents' heads by keeping them off balance with sweeps, quick darts into the line, short passes to the backs, and even bootlegs by the quarterback. The defense could not concentrate on one single point of attack.

Shaughnessy noted that a spread offense opened up wider territory to defend. "Instead of threatening a segment of ground scarcely wider than from end to end, we threaten continually the entire width of the playing field," he said.

Shaughnessy found that while his players seemed to be fast and quick, they lacked the size of some of the more prominent teams in the country, or even the Pacific Coast Conference. Fullback Norm Standlee at 217 pounds and 6 feet 1 inch tall was the biggest player on the team. Even that was a far cry from the size of today's behemoths who check in at 300 or more pounds and are 6 feet 6 to 8 inches tall. College quarterbacks today stand 6 feet 4 inches and weigh 220 pounds. Frankie Albert was 5 feet 9 inches and 170 pounds. Neither did 1940s players bulk up by lifting weights year-round as players do today. Their training was limited to agility and speed drills. Their strength was in their legs, rather than their upper body.

In Albert, Shaughnessy saw a quick, sure-footed ball handler with courage and a sense of bravado. During spring practice, for example, Albert tried a new pass play in which two defensive tackles were to be crossblocked as they rushed Albert. The offensive blockers failed to pick them up and the tackles drove into Albert, slamming him brutally to the ground. Although in pain, Albert got up and called the same play. "I knew I had a quarterback then," Shaughnessy said. "If a cannon were fired under him on the field, he would keep his head. He enjoys incredibly quick reactions. If you threw a football in this room with eleven players around and about, Frankie would get it."

Albert had played left halfback in the double wing, where he was misused. He moved between the first and second teams all year, alternating with Pete Kmetovic. "We weren't very good. Each of us would take turns fouling up the plays," Kmetovic said. Under the T, he noted, Albert had the "ability to come up with the unusual play at the right time, such as throwing in a situation where you wouldn't expect a pass."

Shaughnessy said Albert "couldn't run or block worth writing home about. He was too slight, almost delicate. He was, however, a superlative ball handler, a great kicker and passer and he could really call signals."

On another occasion he said, "Long before I went to Stanford I had heard of him. I knew he had exactly the requirements of the T formation. His talents were primarily as a faker; he could fool people. And by temperament he ate up that sort of assignment. His talents were more intellectual and psychological than physical. He was a poker player if there ever was one and the T formation gave him exactly the best opportunities to exploit those strengths of his to the utmost, at the same time covering up the shortcomings he had that would have put him at a great disadvantage in other styles of play."

Albert perfected the bootleg. He often failed to tell his teammates that a planned handoff was not going to take place. With the backs and blockers moving in one direction, Albert would fake a handoff and then keep the ball, heading the other way for big yardage. He found that the bootleg worked better if nobody knew, because they would carry out their fakes better.

Albert chose to wear the number 13 on his jersey despite the superstition that it brought bad luck. When coaches handed out freshman uniforms, Albert said, "Give me No. 13. I'll voodoo 'em with it." The real reason was that Albert admired USC scat back Cotton Warburton when he wore that number in previous seasons.

When Shaughnessy became coach, Albert was pleased to learn of Shaughnessy's attention to the books. "Any coach knows that it's not realistic to put football first and academics second. There's a place for each," Albert said. "Shaughnessy wanted us to contribute, to get good grades, and meet our other obligations."

Teammates were in awe of Albert's ability to quickly pick up the T. "Frank didn't have anyone to model—he was the first guy doing this," said second-string fullback Milt Vucinich. "We were all wondering, 'How in the hell is this going to work?' But he made it work. It was a formation made to order for Frank. Nobody could follow the ball after he got it from center, faking and then either throwing or handing off."

Albert was extremely adept at faking with the football, a now-you-see it, now-you-don't sleight of hand. He was an accurate passer who developed the jump pass for that quick throw over the line. He had to jump at times because of his short stature. Albert also had football smarts. His play calling was superlative and he often improvised plays, sometimes to Shaughnessy's distress. He also was an able defender and handled kicking and punting duties with great skill.

Albert showed extraordinary leadership ability and confidence that he could carry out Shaughnessy's plans. He kept players loose with a quip or a practical joke. During practice he would occasionally feign injury, lying prone on the ground, only to spring to his feet as the grim-faced Shaughnessy approached. "Shaughnessy was always so engrossed, thinking beyond what was happening in practice to the next game or the next opponent," Albert said. "You can work a lot of gags on a guy like that."

Shaughnessy noted that Albert also could play on defensive. "He was superb on defense, too," he said, "and that is the real test of an All-American. Goodness, it seems he always knows what to do in every situation." Albert meant every bit as much to Stanford football as Hank Luisetti did in basketball with the one-handed shot.

Fullback Norm Standlee of Long Beach, California, was fast for his size and a bruising runner. Under the T, he had to be more than a line plunger; he had to have the speed to go outside, to be the backfield workhorse. Shaughnessy called him his "bell cow," the cow that all the others followed. His nickname was "the Chief" because he worked for the campus fire department to help pay for room and board. "Everybody on the team just seemed to know that everything would be all right when 'The Chief' was around," Shaughnessy said.

Shaughnessy called Standlee "one of the greatest players I have ever known or seen" after the 1940 season, even though Standlee missed action because of injuries, and when he played injuries often slowed him down. In only two games was he completely healthy. Shaughnessy said Standlee was "a tremendous player, gifted by the gods with a terrific physique . . . [who] had remarkable speed for so large a man."

Despite his praise for Albert, Shaughnessy built Stanford's offense around Standlee. He was the prototype of the T-formation fullback. "He would have been a fine fullback in any system, but the type of ability he had was most effective in the T formation," Shaughnessy explained.

Said Albert, "He [Standlee] was as great a blocker as he was a runner. Having Norm behind me was like having an insurance policy. I never had to worry about that defensive end coming in from the blind side when Norm was there."

Halfback Pete Kmetovic of San Jose, California, couldn't pass, kick, or block, but he was a dangerous open field runner who was perfect for Shaughnessy's man in motion, especially when he caught a pass in the flat and had room to maneuver. Shaughnessy called him one of the greatest ball carriers who ever played. "In many systems he would have been useless," Shaughnessy said. That proved true in the double wing, where he was required to block and pass. He was too small at 5 feet 8 inches and 170 pounds. Shaughnessy said he couldn't pass for "sour owls." Vucinich said Kmetovic threw a pass like it was a punching bag wobbling through the air.

In the T his elusive change of pace left tacklers scattered all over the field. Nicknamed "the Jackrabbit" and "Perfect Pete" because of the way he ran his pass patterns, he could turn a 5-yard pass reception into a 50-yard gain with the swivel of his hips and a burst of his ten-flat, 100-yard speed. "He could spot a hole in a flash and dart for it, and then once in the clear, he was one of the finest open field runners I have ever seen," Shaughnessy said. "As a man in motion in the T formation, he was at his very best because of his speed, change of pace, and pass-catching ability."

The fourth player in the talented backfield was halfback Hugh "Duke" Gallarneau, a high school dropout from Chicago. He had quit school to help his family during the Depression. He worked in the stockyards but decided that he wanted something better and went back to school. His father wouldn't let him play football in high school. He studied hard enough to earn an academic scholarship to Stanford. He turned out for football, where he beat every back on the team, running the 100-yard dash in 9.6 seconds. He was faster even than Kmetovic, but he didn't start as fast.

He had been a blocking back in the Thornhill double wing but became a dependable ball carrier for Shaughnessy. The coach called him "my secret weapon" because other players like Albert and Standlee got more attention. Gallarneau would up the leading ground gainer in the conference, losing yardage only twice, each time for 1 yard. "He was a typical off-tackle runner, with an outstanding knack for starting from scratch and gathering speed in one stride," Shaughnessy said. "He was at his best running at the line straight ahead and by a slight deviation cutting into the hole without slackening pace. The T gave him such plays." The 6-foot Gallarneau, who weighed 190 pounds, also was an excellent blocker and a strong defensive player.

What made these players fit into the T so well, Shaughnessy said, was that they "were finished fakers by instinct and character. They liked to act. They were naturally fancy Dans, and that is important in making the fakes of our system real and convincing to the defense." After the season ended Shaughnessy called the four the best backfield combination in the history of football. That may hold true even today.

Chuck Taylor, another San Jose native, had been a freshman-team quarterback, where his primary job was as a blocker. Shaughnessy asked him to move to guard. Taylor embraced the idea; he was willing to do most anything to help the team succeed. He was a fierce competitor who charged off the ball with lightning speed at 5 feet 10 inches and 190 pounds. He was one of four first-year players on the varsity line. He became an All-American two years later.

Vic Lindskog was twenty-four years old and married when he joined the Indians as a transfer from Santa Ana (California) Junior College. He grew up in Cut Bank, Montana, where he followed his father in the mines. At Santa Ana he was a halfback in the double wing but had been tried a tight end, fullback, and tackle. Shaughnessy asked him to convert to center. When he balked, Shaughnessy asked him, "Which would you rather be, a mediocre halfback, or a great center?" "I want to play football," Lindskog answered.

Shaughnessy told Lindskog that he would be a key man in the offense because he was at the point of attack with his blocks. Lindskog could keep his head up while snapping the ball to the quarterback, thereby being ready to block. He became a solid performer who went on to play several years of professional football with the Philadelphia Eagles.

Other key players like Ed Stamm of Portland, Oregon, converted from an end to tackle. The 6-foot-2-inch, 215-pound sophomore helped anchor the inexperienced line.

Guard Bruno Banducci, a 5-foot-11-inch, 210-pound sophomore from Richmond, California, played savagely and looked savage with his nose guard, an early form of a face mask. He was a terrific blocker who had a long professional career with the San Francisco 49ers.

Tackle Dick Palmer of Oklahoma City, Oklahoma, was the defensive quarterback, a clairvoyant defensive signal caller. A tough, serious player, he may have been the team's most vicious blocker. He stood 6 feet 6 inches and weighed 205 pounds.

Shaughnessy even talked Clyde "Jiffy Jeff" Jeffrey, world record holder in the 100-yard dash with a time of 9.4 seconds, to come out for football that year. While he made the team, he didn't play much. Jeffrey, from Riverside, California, had served as a student representative on the Board of Athletic Control, which recommended hiring Shaughnessy.

Years later Albert said the line was the most important factor in the team's success, although it was lighter than opposing lines. "You needed horses to win ball games, and brother, we had the horses. But [Shaughnessy] found the right [positions] for each of us."

Shaughnessy brought more than a fancy-dancey, razzle-dazzle offense scheme to Stanford. He also brought discipline. Thornhill had been described as a "fun" coach, laid back and easygoing.

By contrast, Shaughnessy was all business. Unlike Tiny Thornhill, Shaughnessy was a self-disciplined, highly intelligent leader who, by his own example, convinced players and assistant coaches alike to follow his leadership willingly and gratefully.

California sportswriters had dubbed the Indians as "the Laughing Boys" because they would "rather crack jokes than crack a line and win games." Shaughnessy's stern demeanor quickly showed them football was no laughing matter. "Team morale," he told the players, "is a vital factor in a winning ball club. There'll be no loafing or horse play on the practice field."

He told a *Stanford Daily* sportswriter, "As to training, there is going to be no fooling around, no smoking, and no late hours if they want to make my team. Football is no joke. I expect every man, on his honor, to obey the rules." Gallarneau said, "It was like dying and going to heaven. Clark Shaughnessy was probably the smartest football man I met in my life."

Stanford publicist Don Liebendorfer recalled, "I've never seen anything like it. No reflection on Warner or Thornhill, you understand, but Shaughnessy conducts the most business-like practices I've ever seen. He has everything planned ahead and operates on schedule with each assistant keeping a group of boys occupied with instruction of some sort at all times. There is no lost motion, no delay."

Albert called Shaughnessy "the great craftsman. He could come up with the solution to every problem that might exist. His way instilled confidence in the players. He was a terrific organizer."

With his newly appointed staff, Shaughnessy worked virtually around the clock; 6 a.m. skull sessions were common. The coach often went to bed as early as 7 p.m. and was up no later than 4 a.m., ready for a full day's work. One nickname he picked up early on was "Four O'clock." Sometimes Shaughnessy would spend the night on a cot in the Encina gym and then summon his coaches in early the next day. During the season, after a Saturday game, Shaughnessy would get his coaches together at 6 a.m. on Sunday to prepare for the next game. Sometimes Albert would report at 6 a.m. for a couple of hours of skull sessions before classes began.

Bengston remembered early one morning looking down at his shoes to notice he was wearing different colored socks. "Shaughnessy called me down to discuss an idea," he explained. "I grabbed two socks out of the bureau in the dark."

After that initial meeting with Shaughnessy, the players were ready to go to work. Three days into practice he had his starting backfield picked out, and it would stay that way the entire season except if a player had to sit out because of an injury. The squad size would be pared down to about forty-five players, far less than teams today carry. Because players played both offense and defense, teams needed fewer players and fewer assistants to coach them.

Albert quickly became a believer. "In 1940 we were so hungry when Shaughnessy arrived we thought he was God. He was a genius."

Substitute halfback John Casey wrote to his uncle after several practices: "The new coach is really okay, as is the rest of his staff. . . . We are using . . . nothing but tricks. I can't even find the ball myself . . . lots of man-in-motion stuff. I am now a right half and not a fullback, which is all right. No more competition with a superman [Standlee]. We practice three times a week," Casey wrote, "and we have chalk talks . . . one gets no rest, always doing something, which is very unlike last year."

Shaughnessy told his players they had to be good actors as well as athletes to pull off the T formation. He explained years later that "if you can teach your players to be convincing when they're just making believe that they're carrying the ball, you can decoy the opposition out of position far more effectively than by blocking."

The players approached practices with a degree of skepticism. "A lesser man would have been afraid to try something as radical as the T," Albert said. "We ourselves were skeptical. But he sold us on it. Luck plays a part. We had talent we were wasting, but the coaching still had to teach it to us, and fast."

Shaughnessy had brought in Masterson, the Chicago Bears quarterback, just to teach Albert how to play the T. Masterson thought Albert to be the perfect type of player for the T—fast, a good passer, and a clear thinker. One problem Masterson had was that Albert was left handed while Masterson was right handed. "I had to work everything out sort of in reverse, you might say, but Frankie caught on in a hurry."

When Masterson first met Albert, he remarked to his new charge, "You're pretty light, aren't you?" Albert replied with his typical cockiness, "Yeah, but I'm strong as a bull and five times as smart." Once he told a reporter, "I love raw eggs. I eat raw meat. And I throw out my chest like this and then I'm plain dynamite."

Said Masterson, "I never saw anything like him," after the six-week training ended. "For two cents I'd bet his dad's name is Houdini."

Marchie Schwartz determined that one of the reasons for Albert's scattergun arm during the '39 season was that he'd been throwing off balance. By midseason Schwartz called Albert "one of the smartest passers I've ever seen. He may not be the best, but he throws with know-how. He's a better passer than his arm. He's cool under fire and is great at picking a receiver."

The team was slow at adapting to the T, however, and that disturbed Shaughnessy. He gave serious thought to abandoning it and returning to the single- or double-wing. After a particularly poor performance against freshman players who in those days were barred from playing on the varsity, Shaughnessy was depressed and shaken by what he had witnessed. Following a poor night's sleep, he went to Don Liebendorfer's office, where he told the Stanford publicist, "Do you know I'm very much tempted to forget the T after that sorry showing yesterday. I have a very good single-wing offense which I just might move in."

"Despite diligent teaching," tackle Jack Warnecke said, "this new strategy confused us. At practice Shaughnessy seemed super-natural, demanding the impossible. His scheme seemed beyond comprehension. We had no idea if it would work, or even what the moves would look like in an actual game. But we were desperate, listening with a mixture of amazement but mostly disbelief."

But Shaughnessy stuck with it. Repetition after repetition began to pay off. "He worked us and worked us," Gallarneau said. "And we started to understand how you could use deception."

Shaughnessy knew he had only a short time to put the T formation into effect. He worked the players hard. Practice equipment was rudimentary by today's standards. Shaughnessy kept them on the practice field running the same play over and over again to perfect timing.

Athletic director Al Masters complained to maintenance workers one night about "some idiot" leaving the lights on at the practice field. That "idiot" turned out to be Shaughnessy, who had kept his team on the field for extra practice. Shaughnessy practiced behind closed doors two of the three practices a week, not to hide from scouts from other schools, but so that the players wouldn't be distracted by spectators.

"I didn't tell anyone at that time but I was doing a lot of experimenting to see what plays fellows like Albert, Standlee, Kmetovic and Gallarneau could or couldn't handle," Shaughnessy said. "As a result of all this experimenting we looked pretty sad that spring. In fact, a number of alumni scratched their heads and referred to it as a 'goofy system.'"

In the final scrimmage of the spring, the varsity barely beat the freshmen 6–0. Then in the fall the freshmen won.

"We scrimmaged the freshmen before the season started [in the fall] and they beat us," Albert remembered. "They pushed us all over the field. They didn't have trouble finding the football and I'm sure the coaches felt the same way we did—very disappointed."

"They beat the hell out of us," Gallarneau said. "I thought, 'Oh my God. Here we go again.'"

However, Albert saw the T's potential. "I loved it from the start," he said. "I love fooling people anyway. I'd rather fool someone than overpower him. This formation gave me the opportunity to hide the football."

The *San Francisco Chronicle*'s sports editor, Bill Leiser, watched the last scrimmage of the spring. The team's talent impressed him. "But it wasn't the material," he wrote. "Others have more of it. What impressed at Stanford was the new method and purpose of the boys on The Farm. Their offense is different. It is calculated to keep a step in front of the defense at all times."

As time got closer to the season opener, the pieces began to fall in place. The team had learned sixty plays during the spring and fall practices. Second-string halfback Hoot Armstrong remembered "running, running, and running after those long 50-yard passes Frankie threw. I remember Shaughnessy hollering at us to 'run, run, run' adding, 'the strong live, the weak die.' Still he gave us the feeling that if we put ourselves in top physical condition and executed our plays well, we would win, and win we did." Jeffrey remembered running pass patterns, one after another. "I was fast but was not used to that football armor and I got completely winded and finally returned to the huddle wheezing and gasping to catch my breath. Everyone thought that was funny."

Shaughnessy was in his element. "I've had sixty big kids, tough, rugged fellows who love football, coming out every day for a month, coming from classes and laboratories on the run just to practice, then running back after practice to wait on tables and the like," he said. "There's tremendous football spirit at Stanford."

Three weeks before the season opener, Shaughnessy was in Los Angeles at the University Club, where he ran into *Los Angeles Times* sports columnist Paul Zimmerman. He told Zimmerman he was unfamiliar with West Coast teams, having only seen USC play once in a Rose Bowl game. "We are going to have an interesting team, I believe, but just how we stand with your other teams out here is something I can't say. . . . How do I like it out here?

Did you ever wake up from a dream and pinch yourself to see if it was true? Well, I'm still pinching myself. I can't believe it. We have some good boys. Maybe not enough. But I'm happy."

He was still holding practice behind closed doors. "If people want to see us play, why don't they come out on Saturdays?" he asked. "For the best interests of the team, we'll have to keep the doors of the practice field closed to the students and general public most of the time."

While the focus was on learning the T, players still had to practice their defensive system. In those days players played both offense and defense. Depending on the defensive alignment, most linemen stayed on the line. Lindskog would join Standlee as linebackers and Albert, Gallarneau, and Kmetovic would be defensive backs.

Sportswriters were starting to buy into Shaughnessy's scheme. Bill Leiser wrote that Stanford "might have the surprise team in the Pacific Coast Conference." It was difficult to tell how good Stanford would be, "but you can bank on it that the Indians under their new coach are going to be a most interesting team. . . . Stanford hardly will be a great team. It doesn't have the line material or the reserves for that. But it will have a fine first string backfield and of course the eleven can't help but be an improvement."

Columnist Dick Hyland of the *Los Angeles Times* wrote three weeks before the season opener that despite not winning a conference game in 1939, Shaughnessy's team might prove surprising. He noted that spirit had returned to Stanford football thanks to Shaughnessy. Hyland closely followed Stanford football; he was a three-year letterman for the Indians from 1925 to 1927. Hyland also noted that Stanford had not played up to its potential in 1939 and that the 1940 squad could make a two-touchdown difference against the same opponents. Using those figures against the 1939 scores, Stanford could win five games in 1940, Hyland wrote, certainly a respectable number after such a dismal year.

Eight days before the opening game of the season, Hyland wrote,

"Shaughnessy is quite a man, but no miracle worker; there IS a feeling of fire and spirit on the campus this year that has been lacking for many a yellow harvest moon; and last season's record was a most peculiar one capable upon analysis of generating hope for the present season." As for Shaughnessy, he said, "We've got a great crowd of boys. They are a pleasure to work with."

Stanford fans were being unrealistic to expect a trip to the Rose Bowl, Hyland wrote. "Miracles CAN happen here, but it will have to be a whopper to bring the Indians through with better than a .500 average for the season."

Shaughnessy was making no predictions of a whopper season. "It's impossible for the boys to begin to get a hold of what we were trying to do under five or six weeks—and that is early," Shaughnessy said. "They will not be really comfortable on the field until very late in the season or, perhaps, not until next season." Was that the way he really felt or just coach's talk to keep the expectations from being too high? Only Shaughnessy knew. A whopper season was indeed within reach.

4

"This stuff really works"

Packing lunches their mothers' had made, nine-year-old Bob Valli and a friend hopped a streetcar from North Beach to Kezar Stadium in San Francisco to see their first college football game on September 28, 1940. Little did they know as they entered the stadium in the city's Golden Gate Park that they would be seeing history in the making. They were going to watch the first big school football doubleheader in history. Coming of age as sports fans, the boys stayed until the final minute of the second game. Valli would become a lifelong sports fanatic, finishing his career as sports editor at the *Oakland Tribune* across San Francisco Bay.

It was a big weekend for college football in the Bay Area. Across the bay in Berkeley, the California Golden Bears were playing host to the Michigan Wolverines and their heralded running back Tom Harmon, who turned twenty-one years old that day. Harmon scored four touchdowns and passed for another in Michigan's 41–0 romp. He ran back the opening kickoff 94 yards for a touchdown and returned a punt 72 yards for another. His third touchdown was an 86-yard run from scrimmage. On that run a frustrated Cal fan along the sidelines, Harold J. "Bud" Brennan, tried to tackle Harmon but came up empty. A picture of the futile tackle dominated the newspapers the next day. Harmon ran for an 8-yard score and passed for another. He finished the day rushing for 110 yards on sixteen carries.

In the first game of the Kezar doubleheader, the Santa Clara Broncos, who would be Stanford's third opponent of the season, dropped Utah 34–13 before a crowd of thirty-five thousand. Radio broadcast the doubleheader, but not outside the San Francisco Bay Area. By season's end, millions would be listening to the Indians when they played in the Rose Bowl.

No television was available in those days, and most people either heard the game on the radio or read newspaper accounts the next day. Newspapers provided almost play-by-play rundowns of the game, much different from today's sportswriting, which recognizes that readers probably saw the game on TV and want to know behind-the-scenes material.

Harmon's presence and the past success of Buck Shaw's Broncos overshadowed Stanford's game against the University of San Francisco Dons on a long afternoon of college football. The game would be the start of a season for Stanford that would change the face of college football. Sixty-four years later, the Alameda Newspaper Group based across the bay from San Francisco ranked the remarkable games by Michigan and Stanford as No. 1 of 50 Forgotten Times. Bay Area fans were introduced to Michigan's superstar running back and Stanford's T formation, which would revolutionize football, both on the same day.

Going into the game, USF was a 10–7 favorite to defeat the Indians. That meant if you favored USF, you had to bet ten dollars to win seven. Conversely, if you were a Stanford fan, you had to bet only seven dollars to win ten. In four previous meetings between 1932 and 1935, Stanford had won every game. Those were the Vow Boys years, and that had no impact on what might happen this year.

In fact, no one expected much from the boys from the Farm, but fans were in for a surprise. Certainly coach George Malley's Dons had more experience, as 1939 had been their best season. They had tied Santa Clara's Sugar Bowl champion and beaten St. Mary's. Malley, however, was being low key. "We will have a stronger team this season than we had last," Malley said. "We then had some green boys who had never played football until they came out for our team. They are more experienced now and will be greatly improved. We have a nice ball club." The Dons were not fazed by the prospects of facing the T. They deemed it no more than an experiment by a desperate coach and a bad team.

No one knew what to expect from Stanford. Even some of Stanford's players were uncertain how the new T formation would work. The Indians had pregame jitters. End Stan Graff sat next to Gallarneau and Standlee on the bus ride from Palo Alto to Kezar, wondering whether the team would have another losing season. "Little did we know," Graff reminisced.

Not only that, but Stanford had one senior, two juniors (although one was a junior college transfer), and four sophomores on the line. Two—Chuck Taylor and Vic Lindskog—were playing new positions, after being shifted from the double-wing backfield. A harness prevented sophomore guard Bruno Banducci from raising his injured right arm above his head. He would play with the harness all season.

Assistant coach Marchie Schwartz wasn't worried. He told a news conference on the Thursday before the game that he was confident that "more than a majority of the boys who appear in our starting lineup Saturday would hold their own, and better, in Big Ten competition."

Shaughnessy wasn't so sure. When asked whether his young, inexperienced line would hold up in the tough Pacific Coast Conference, he replied, "That's the big question. Maybe they can't. Our only hope is to admit the other fellow will score and do our best to outscore him."

At a rally on campus the night before the game, Shaughnessy told students, "It will take a good team to beat [the Indians]. I'm counting on their ability as athletes, but more than that their spirit. They have spirit; you have spirit. So we'll have a great time this year." He then introduced his team. Both teams were ready, although Stanford had a scare the previous weekend when Albert spent time in the hospital suffering from a bad cold. He managed to practice most of the week.

On Friday the Dons went through a light workout Malley called a "calm down and get ready" practice. Not so in Palo Alto, where Shaughnessy sent his team through a moderate workout in full game uniforms, the new ones they would wear to open the season. As was his method, he paid attention to the slightest details. "If a shoe pinches, a shoulder pad is uncomfortable, if pants tend to bind a runner, we have time to correct the equipment Friday night, and have it to the player's liking by game time Saturday," Shaughnessy said.

The two players who were expected to stand out were the teams' two fullbacks: Stanford's Norm Standlee and USF's Cliff Fisk. "There is no better player in the Big Ten than Standlee," Marchie Schwartz said. That was high praise considering the extraordinary talent of Tom Harmon. Harmon would win the Heisman Trophy that year. USF's assistant coach Al Tassi thought the Dons had a better fullback. "Maybe there isn't a better fullback anywhere than Fisk," he said. If statistics are any measure, Standlee had it all over Fisk on that clear autumn day, rolling up 86 yards in eleven carries as compared with Fisk's 31 yards in ten carries.

While Standlee was getting the media attention, Stanford was pinning its hopes on a slight, left-handed quarterback, Frankie Albert, who was really the only bright spot for the 1939 squad. With Albert's deft play calling and sleight of hand, the Indians were hoping to baffle opponents with their new T formation. It should have come as no surprise, as sportswriters reported heavily—somewhat dubiously—about the formation's chances.

The *San Francisco Chronicle* sports editor, Bill Leiser, noted that while Notre Dame had used a T before shifting into its successful box formation, Stanford stopped with the T. What made Shaughnessy's T different than the T used in the past was that he employed a man in motion. "The man in motion may stop anywhere on the field," Leiser wrote. Albert, he said, "parks" himself right behind the center and takes the ball directly from the center on nearly all plays. "It's football unlike any previously played anywhere on the Coast," Leiser wrote. USF's disadvantage was that it was the first team to deal with the new formation without the benefit of scouting.

Stanford entered the game missing backup quarterback Thor Peterson, end Hank Norberg, and tackle Ed McCain because of injuries. Norberg may have been the best end on the team.

Shaughnessy wasn't much of a fiery locker room orator. He'd have signs with words like "quick" and "think" posted around the dressing room, but that was the extent of it. He did his best to prepare players for the game and then expected them to carry out the game plan. The closest he came to a rah-rah talk before the USF game was to tell them about Harmon's exploits. "Boys, I want you to know Tom Harmon just took the opening kickoff back for a touchdown at Cal," he said. "Now boys, let's go out and see if we can do something." Substitute fullback Milt Vucinich remembered the incident well. "It was something, Shaughnessy putting us in the same class with Harmon. He used [the reference] as a point of a pep talk."

When the Indians trotted onto the field, they were resplendent in their new uniforms—white pants, red jerseys, and white plastic helmets. It was rare for players to wear face masks then. The pants were made of airplane linen. Gallarneau called them the lightest material he had ever worn. Most team's uniforms were simple: dark leather helmets, gray pants, and a colored jersey. "I remember modeling different uniforms for Shaughnessy to choose from in the spring of 1940," Taylor said.

Vucinich said one of the reasons he picked Stanford was that he liked the team's colors, which were reversed in earlier years. He wasn't disappointed that day. "When we came running out, people went, 'Wow.' They couldn't believe the colorful uniforms."

Shaughnessy was always concerned with equipment. When he was Tulane's coach in 1924, he outfitted his team with lightweight balbriggan undershirts to wear instead of their usual green wool jerseys in a game against Vanderbilt on a particularly hot day. The grayish white shirts with buttons down the front were pulled over their shoulder pads. "There was a sudden shocked hush in the stands as the crowd saw the buttoned undershirts, the first time in the history of football that any team was garbed in such regalia," Shaughnessy said.

It's uncertain when the Indians picked up the nickname "the Wow Boys," but it probably came from their colorful uniforms and from a play on words of the three-time Rose Bowl team the Vow Boys. Its use gained more and more favor as the year went on, with even Shaughnessy referring to the Wow Boys, then and for years afterward.

The way Stanford started the game was unlikely to impress anyone. The Indians kicked off and the Dons began from their 17-yard line. USF moved the ball to its 49, but the Indians' defense held. Fisk then kicked a ball out of bounds on Stanford's 6-yard line. As often was the case in those days, Stanford punted on first down. In one of his rare lapses, Shaughnessy realized after it was too late that Lindskog had never centered the ball back in punt formation in a game and that Standlee had never punted in a game. The Chief got off a decent punt to midfield. Lindskog had only one bad snap from center all year, and that was against Washington when he injured his hand.

Stanford held again, but on its next series of downs the Indians lost 10 yards in penalties, had mix-ups in the backfield, and generally looked confused. It took six attempts to get off four plays. Standlee booted a 61-yard punt that set the Dons back deep in their territory. In a play rarely seen these days, the Dons quick-kicked, which is when the offense hopes to catch the defense looking for a run or pass, and the quarterback drops back quickly and punts the ball over the defense. The Dons' kick didn't travel far before Albert returned it 10 yards to the USF 41. That's when the Indians began to roll.

After a 5-yard penalty and a 2-yard run, Albert, who called all of the plays except on rare occasions when Shaughnessy would send in a play on a five-by-seven card, called for a pass to halfback Hugh Gallarneau. Albert crouched over center as Gallarneau went into motion. Albert took the snap from Lindskog and then froze the defense with a fake. Gallarneau was wide open when he turned downfield, as no defensive player followed him into the flat. This was college football's first look at the man-in-motion T formation. Albert hit Duke with a 17-yard pass to the Dons' 28.

On the next play the crowd saw how the modern T worked on running plays. Albert lined up to take a direct snap from Lindskog, his head bobbing as he called the signals. Gallarneau again ran in motion to the left. Albert took the snap, whirled around, and handed the ball to Standlee. By the time Standlee got the ball, the line had formed a V with Lindskog at the point. Then Standlee burst between Lindskog and guard Dick Palmer and bulled his way 20 yards up the middle to the 8. After Standlee's run, Albert burst out in the huddle, "Hey, this stuff really works."

Albert would find himself looking for indirect signals from Shaughnessy. If the coach looked comfortable, Albert knew he was calling the right plays; if Shaughnessy looked ill at ease, the quarterback revised his plays. Dressed in suit and tie and wearing a fedora, Shaughnessy stalked the sidelines with clipboard in hand, charting plays and thinking up new ones. "I'll almost swear that the little devil can read my mind," Shaughnessy said.

Shaughnessy noted that Albert sometimes called wrong plays. "Every good quarterback does. Oddly enough, many of the wrong plays he called were good for touchdowns. Luck? Possibly, but remember this: Wrong or right, Frankie gave the 1940 team such confidence that the boys made the plays work."

Albert often said that like a chess player, he tried to stay a play ahead of the one he was calling at the time. Albert also would say in the huddle, "Make the key block on this play and we'll go all the way. Here's the play—37 counter, 25—break." When the play worked, it gave the team confidence in Albert. "They then begin to think you know what you're calling and why when really I didn't," Albert said.

Two plays later, 5-foot-8-inch, 173-pound halfback Pete Kmetovic slipped through left guard for the game's first touchdown. The play baffled the Dons as Albert, Gallarneau, and Standlee began running left behind the line and Kmetovic countered back against the grain, catching the defense moving the wrong way. The counterplay was another T-formation innovation.

Sports Illustrated writer Ron Fimrite recounted years later, "It is entirely possible he was not even seen." Remarked Kmetovic, "You could tell by the holes we had that somebody was confused. We were running right by people who didn't know we had the ball." Albert, who later in the season would take over punting duties for the injured Standlee, kicked the extra point that gave the Indians a 7–0 lead.

As was the custom in those days, when sportsmanship was at a higher level than today's celebrations and trash talking, the Indians quietly ran up the field for the kickoff after the touchdown and conversion.

"I remember Stanford coming out and taking command as Albert faked handoffs, spun and gave the ball and the Indians ran wild," Valli recalled sixty-three years later. "Most of the time we didn't know who had the ball and neither did the Dons."

Albert would take the snap from Lindskog, turn his back to the line of scrimmage during the faking, and hand off the ball to the backs. The sleight of hand confused the defense with the quick handoffs, and the backs were through the line before the opposition could react. "They kept changing guards of me," Taylor said. "They couldn't handle the quick openers, didn't even seem to recognize them. Obviously, their linemen had instructions to get lower and lower. Eventually, they got so low, all I had to do was fall on my man."

Vucinich said Albert's ball handling was the key to the T formation's success. "Don't forget Frank did all this before anybody had done it," he said. "All that spinning, faking, and handing the ball off quickly. Kids learn that stuff today in grammar school. Frank learned it all in one spring and no one's ever been better at it. If we hadn't had an Albert, we probably wouldn't have used the T, and the game would be entirely different from what it is today."

"We put Kmetovic in motion and no one on the USF defense would move," Albert remembered years later. "I took the ball from center and we had a little quick pass that was almost a lateral to Kmetovic. He would take it over his shoulder and had quick speed so he faked to cut in and would go outside. With speed he'd make what today would be no gain or a loser into a first down or a 30- to 40-yard run on his ability. And Gallarneau the same way. It's hard to believe teams didn't defense better."

Said Leiser, "This type of football is different. Why, some of those Stanford kids running away from the play actually had defenders chasing them harder than other defenders were chasing the ball carrier."

Mac Speedie, who later became a star end for the Cleveland Browns, was in the shower after playing for Utah in its loss to Santa Clara when a teammate came rushing into the locker room to say, "Hey, get out here. There's the dangdest formation going on out there you've ever seen. You can't even follow the ball."

With 3 minutes left in the second quarter, Stanford substitutes scored the second touchdown as sophomore halfback Eric Armstrong raced 37 yards over left guard with halfback John Casey as an escort for the score. Substitute guard Ken Robesky kicked the extra point, and the Indians went into the locker room with a 14–0 lead.

Under rules then in place, coaches were allowed to substitute only once each quarter without a penalty, so Shaughnessy left his substitutes in.

The Indians scored again in the third quarter after Albert passed twice to end Stan "Bosco" Graff for gains of 24 and 13 yards, and Gallarneau broke loose for a 25-yard gain. With the ball on the Dons' 4, Standlee fumbled, but Graff recovered the ball. Then Standlee bulled his way behind blocks by Banducci and Lindskog into the end zone, knocking Fisk backward with a crushing blow to the chest.

The Indians weren't through yet. In the fourth quarter they stopped the Dons at the USF 11-yard line, forcing Fisk to punt. He got off a booming punt of nearly 50 yards, which Kmetovic gathered in. Behind blocks by guard Jack Francis and tackle Jack Warnecke, "Perfect Pete" darted 60 yards down the sidelines for a touchdown. Albert's extra point kick was good, ending the scoring for the day at 27–0. Punt returns like that earned Kmetovic the nickname "Twinkletoes," which led Pete to reply, "Twinkle-toes? Hell, I run like a duck."

Because of the relative ease of the game, Stanford used only eleven plays from its playbook, holding back on its myriad of offense schemes so as to not tip off scouts for upcoming games. The score would have been higher except that Shaughnessy chose to use all forty-two of his players. "I'm amazed," Shaughnessy said. "I never expected the boys to do so well with some of the stuff after so little work on it."

In a classic understatement, Shaughnessy said, "It's sure swell to win a ball game." After Shaughnessy's long streak of losses at Chicago, it probably was a good feeling.

Shaughnessy said the team astounded him at the way it played. "I had no idea they'd work like that, block so well, think so well. And so smoothly. Yes, today it was a great team. What it'll do next week nobody knows. They didn't have many plays with which to work, but used them all far beyond my expectation." After looking at game films, Shaughnessy wasn't so convinced, having spotted numerous "glaring faults in fundamentals."

Santa Clara coach Buck Shaw stayed around after his game to watch the Indians, whom the Broncos would play in two weeks. "This stuff [T formation] is different" was his only comment. Oregon coach Tex Oliver, Stanford's next opponent, was impressed. He said Albert did "everything but swallow the ball. . . . I saw so much that I can't go to sleep now. That stuff requires defense."

Overlooked because of the razzle-dazzle of the T formation was Stanford's defense. The players were surprised by their success as well. "The way our offense clicked . . . surprised the entire ball club," Albert said. Standlee could be heard shouting in the locker room, "It's fun playing that kind of football."

After the game the *Chronicle*'s Leiser said Malley looked like a man who had seen a ghost. "We were baffled, naturally," Malley said, "by that running around stuff in the backfield. Who wouldn't be when he hadn't seen such things before? They have everything—fast backs, power backs, oooh, that Standlee; a big, fast line, clean blocking, tackling."

Maybe the Dons weren't so good after all. The USF game turned out to be the easiest of the year for the Indians, and the Dons finished the season with one win, six losses, and a tie. Santa Clara beat the Dons by the identical score of 27–0 four weeks later.

Stanford outrushed the Dons 209 yards to 33 while USF gained 80 yards passing to the Indians' 63. Standlee was the leading ball carrier, picking up 86 yards in eleven rushes. Albert completed four of ten passes. College teams didn't pass often in those days, something the T formation changed in later years. The football's watermelon shape made it more difficult to pass than today's slim sphere. The rounder ball also may have led to longer punts, because the ball tended to roll forward more than take reverse bounces like today's streamlined model.

One other noteworthy score that weekend was Minnesota's 19–14 win over the Washington Huskies. The Golden Gophers would play a significant role in Stanford's recognition that year. While the Stanford–USF game attracted notice throughout the Bay Area, it received little attention in the rest of the country. Stanford had a national reputation, but USF was relatively unknown.

But the Indians and the T formation began to generate nation-wide headlines with their success at a time when college football already was the most popular sport in America. The excitement that the T brought that year and years after only heightened that popularity. Certainly, professional baseball had a huge following, but most of the major league teams were based in the Midwest or on the East Coast. Professional basketball virtually was nonexistent, while college basketball had a small following.

What made college football king was the built-in fan base of college students and alumni. Universities and colleges drew large crowds from their respective communities, whether in the Deep South, the Ivy League, the Midwest, or the Pacific Coast Conference. The pageantry of big-time football stretched almost the entire week during the fall season, due in part to day-to-day newspaper coverage.

Pregame festivities such as bonfires, pep rallies, homecoming parades with floats decorated by fraternities and sororities created excitement for the game. The hard-hitting action on the field and the spectacle of the cheerleaders, bands, and card stunts created a colorful afternoon that drew legions of fans. Postgame parties and dances continued the festivities surrounding the pageantry of college football.

Spectators were attracted to college football because it was a major event in small towns and cities across the nation where many colleges and universities were situated. University of Nebraska historian Benjamin G. Rader in his 1996 book, *American Sports: From the Age of Folk Games to the Age of Televised Sports*, wrote, "Citizens in states without a conspicuously significant history, great civic monuments, or remarkable physical scenery often formed strong emotional bonds to their state university football team."

Consider Nebraska. Nebraskans love their football, always have, always will. More than sixty-three thousand fans turned out for an intrasquad spring game in Lincoln in 2005. A 1951 article in the *Saturday Evening Post* noted that "football commands much more than the average amount of interest in Nebraska. In this prairie state of great open stretches and small communities, where the average town is only 375 people, the university's football team is one of the strongest bonds." Even the smallest high schools could field a football team, thanks to the invention of six-man football by a Hebron, Nebraska, high school teacher.

As author Michael Oriard pointed out, college football was deeply embedded in American life from the 1920s through the 1950s. Newspapers were the primary source of information about football, but magazines and radio drew huge audiences to feed their need for football news. "Fans were drawn to the game, in large part, by the sensationalized coverage in their daily newspapers," Oriard said. He wrote that out of 113 covers of major magazines such as *Colliers*, the *Saturday Evening Post*, and *Look*, 46 of them featured football. "Football was about all you could find on the radio on Saturday afternoons," Oriard said. Millions more learned about the game from newsreels at movie theaters, which accounted for about 25 percent of the newsreel footage. Moviegoers could have their choice of forty-eight full-length movies on football to choose from.

"Big-time college football reigned supreme in 1939 and saturated all the mass media; it was more difficult to remain oblivious to the sport than to encounter it somewhere," Oriard wrote.

Adding to the aura of college football that season was the excitement generated by Stanford's continuing success with the "newfangled" T formation. The USF–Stanford game did little to draw attention to West Coast football outside of the Pacific Coast Conference, but game by game the press began to take notice of that novel offense and the magician at quarterback. Stanford finally moved into the Associated Press poll after its fourth game, at No. 10. After that, it was a steady move upward as the victories mounted.

5

A Confidence Builder

University of Oregon coach Tex Oliver brought thirty-one play-ers to Palo Alto to play the Indians on October 5 in the second game of the year for both teams. While Stanford's skeptical fans and the press had taken notice of Shaughnessy's T formation in the first game against USF, little was known about the Ducks, who had beaten the San Diego Marines 12–2 in their first game. That game was nothing more than a scrimmage for Oregon, a game that didn't match the caliber of Pacific Coast Conference play. Against the Marines, the Ducks had played in the rain and used only five or six running plays, passing only once.

Oregon was given a chance to win the conference, so the Stanford game would be an opportunity to show what it could do. Stanford had something to prove, too, after the 10–0 debacle the previous year in Eugene, Oregon.

Oliver complained that his players practiced too little before the trip south because of typical rainy weather in Eugene. By contrast, the Indians had perfect weather and one night practiced under the lights—that "idiot" was at it again—until 6:30 p.m. The odds makers established the Indians as favorites to win the game.

"The odds of 2 to 1 on Stanford rather surprised my boys when they checked into Palo Alto," Oliver said. "I'm afraid a few made bets of a dollar or two with bellboys and 50 cents with coffee shop waitresses, although I try to discourage that sort of thing. I can't say that I blame them, though. The odds look tempting to me, too."

Oliver said he had no doubt the Ducks would score against the Indians. "In fact, I know we will. This is apt to be a high scoring game, 28–21, or something like that. I know Shaughnessy is strong on attack and we have a few maneuvers ourselves that shouldn't fall short of a touchdown or two. I'm not saying we'll win, only that each team should score more than once." He couldn't have been more wrong.

Coaches were becoming aware of Stanford's success, limited though it was. Occidental coach Gus Henderson had coached the Detroit Lions in 1939 when they beat the Chicago Bears, who were experimenting with the T formation. He thought he knew how to stop them:

"We went into a five-man line and shifted to a six just as the ball was snapped," Henderson said. "That crossed 'em up on their blocking assignments. You have to rush your tackles like guards. They screen the ball. My boys said they never saw the football all afternoon. The minute a team attempts to follow the ball it is sunk."

That was the strategy Stanford was using: deception, sleight of hand, trickery. And it would work once more.

Oliver planned to use a 6-2-2-1 defense against the Indians, often shifting into a 5-3-2-1 pattern.

As was typical of sportswriting of the time, the *San Francisco Chronicle*'s Will Connolly said that if Stanford won the game, he hoped they wouldn't be labeled Vow Boys II. "We always thought that term was melodramatic and although we use it for headline brevity now and then, 'Vow Boys' is a childish affectation not worthy of collegiate adults. As a matter of fact the 'Vow Boys' were lazy and shiftless skonks who never reached maximum efficiency."

It is not clear whether Connolly was being serious or facetious. It is difficult to imagine what he thought of the Wow Boys.

The Ducks were led by fullback Marsh "Bull" Stenstrom, the biggest first-string back in the Pacific Coast Conference—that was saying something considering Standlee's size—left half John Berry, who had scored both touchdowns against the Marines; tackle Jim Stuart, who would become second-team All-Coast that year; and Leonard Isberg, the triple-threat halfback and punter.

Kickoff was at 2:30 on a sunny autumn day before twenty thousand fans. Tickets were $1.25 ($18.08 in 2006 dollars) and "six bits" for end zone seats. Although the Indians drew a sparse crowd in the ninety-thousand-seat stadium, in future games that would change.

After Oregon kicked off, the Ducks' defense held and Standlee punted to the Oregon 44. Oregon ran the ball for two first downs, then after an incomplete pass, Berry picked up a third first down before fumbling on the 13. Albert and Gallarneau fell on the ball at the 10. Berry was kicked in the head on the play and left the game for the rest of the afternoon with a mild concussion.

The two teams exchanged punts again until Stanford put together a 72-yard touchdown drive. With the ball on the Indians' 28, Gallarneau picked up 6 yards on a quick opener over right guard. The play was vintage Shaughnessy. Albert called a fake reverse with the three backs behind Albert taking a step to the left before Albert gave the ball to Gallarneau. That play scored five touchdowns for the Indians that year. On the next play Oregon tackled Albert behind the line for a 6-yard loss.

Stanford lined up in punt formation on third down, but instead of kicking, Standlee passed to Albert 15 yards downfield. But Albert fumbled the ball into the air. The Indians' Jack Warnecke and Oregon fullback Bull Stenstrom collided going for the ball, with Stenstrom slapping it into the air as he went down. The ever-alert Albert grabbed the ball at his waist, picked up blockers, and raced to the Oregon 46 before the Ducks tackled him after a 26-yard gain.

Albert then passed to Standlee for 13 more yards. On the next play Albert rolled out to his left and with blocks from Standlee and guard Chuck Taylor picked up 15 yards to the 18. Three plays later Standlee swept around right end for 15 yards to the 3. Standlee gained a yard, then Kmetovic dived over from the 2 for the touchdown. Albert kicked the extra point as the first quarter came to a close.

Three plays later Oregon punted to the Stanford 34. On first down Kmetovic went into motion to the right, Albert faked to Standlee, who ran left, and handed to Gallarneau, who tore through a hole at right guard, cut across the field, and rambled 51 yards to the Oregon 15. The run was for naught, as two incomplete passes and a 15-yard penalty put the ball on the 30, where Albert tried a 37-yard field goal that barely missed.

Again Stanford held and Oregon punted to Kmetovic on his 15, and he returned the ball to the 29. Albert called on Gallarneau again. The speedy halfback dashed around right end for 25 yards across midfield to the Oregon 46. Standlee picked up 7 at right tackle with Gallarneau getting 3 more for a first down at the Ducks' 36. Then the Indians reverted to an old single-wing play wherein the center snapped the ball to Standlee, who lateraled to Albert. The quarterback skirted end for 15 yards to the 21. Seven plays and a 5-yard penalty later, Albert sneaked over from one foot out to score. Albert missed the extra point attempt, and the Indians left the field at halftime with a 13–0 lead.

Years later Stan Graff, the senior end from Oakland, California, recalled, "I was struck by the extremes in coaching methods that Shaughnessy and Thornhill used. Halftimes under Tiny were sort of disorganized rest periods. Shaughnessy's sessions were like a classroom, chair rows to sit in, and a blackboard on which he would describe, chapter and verse, as to what would or would not work and why."

A scoreless second half saw Shaughnessy play several reserves while Standlee's booming punts of 60, 55, and 50 yards pinned the Ducks deep in their own territory. Stanford threatened to score twice, but both times Oregon's Tommy Roblin intercepted Albert's passes.

Stanford started getting more attention after its second shutout in a row. The superlatives "razzle-dazzle," "flimflam," "hocus pocus," and "now you see it, now you don't" were cropping up regularly in news stories about the wizardry of Frankie Albert and the T-formation Indians. Coaches of future opponents noticed the Indians' formidable defense as well. Bengston was in charge of the defense. He later joined the Green Bay Packers' Vince Lombardi, who praised Bengston for his defensive coaching skills in the Packers' Super Bowl years.

The Indians had used fourteen plays in the game, three more than the USF game but far fewer than the sixty they had learned in practice. Stanford made fourteen first downs to Oregon's six and gained 199 yards rushing to Oregon's 128. Stanford passed for 72 yards while the Ducks failed to complete a pass in nine attempts, with one intercepted. They lost 19 yards in sacks.

"Until I see a better team, Stanford is the best on the coast," Oliver said.

Shaughnessy wasn't satisfied. He said the team had been ragged. Washington scouts, however, found Stanford "smoking hot." "Oregon showed plenty of power on the ground," scout Pest Welch said, "but was up against a truly inspired club."

Despite their triumph, the Indians were worried about Albert's charley horse. They knew they were in trouble without their field general.

Before the game Shaughnessy had been concerned his players might be looking past Oregon toward playing Santa Clara, which had beaten the Indians four years in a row. Sportswriters were saying that the game the following week against the Broncos would determine just how good Stanford was. Santa Clara, they said, was better than any Pacific Coast Conference team. The Broncos had beaten UCLA and the speedster Jackie Robinson that day 9–6. In another game that proved significant later in the year, Minnesota got by Nebraska 13–7.

The Indians won their first two games by shutouts and their confidence soared. They were ready to bring on the Broncos.

6

Shaughnessy the Man

Football obsessed Shaughnessy. He was so cerebral, so lost in his thoughts that sportswriters and friends often described him as dour, devoid of personality, humorless, even cold. His mind dwelled on little more than football's Xs and Os. Asked if he had any hobbies, Shaughnessy replied, "Hobbies? Why, football is my hobby."

One of his daughters remembered family meals when "we'd all be calmly eating. Suddenly Dad would leap from the table and leave the room" to write more symbols on paper. "A few minutes later he'd return. 'Good play,' he would say. And then resume eating."

Said Shaughnessy, "There's a lot of satisfaction in cooking up things and seeing them work, but it's no fun just copying things, or just doing what you're told to do. I love to try things. In fact, I always have a tendency to try too much. I usually throw out about three-quarters of everything worked out."

Shaughnessy seemed to be more preoccupied with football than with people. He wouldn't recognize friends on the street because he was so deep in thought. Stanford's Chuck Taylor, who became a second-team All-Coast guard in 1940, and later head football coach and athletic director at Stanford, said he wasn't sure Shaughnessy knew his name. "He knew my position and everything about it and he knew my jersey number but my name . . . I just don't know," Taylor said. Milt Vucinich, then a sophomore fullback, remembered Shaughnessy as having little sense of humor. "He wasn't a fun guy," he said. "He was all business."

Backup quarterback Ray Hammett agreed. "As a person, he didn't feel warm toward anyone," Hammett said. "He was not back patter. He was not a personality, or even tried to know the players' names." But "when he said something, we listened. It didn't take us long to realize he was a genius."

Shaughnessy was often so deep in thought about football that he paid too little attention to his driving. Los Angeles police pulled him over in 1949 when he was coach of the Los Angeles Rams because he was weaving back and forth on a busy street. He already had so many traffic tickets that once during a court appearance, he asked if he could "just keep $500 here on deposit." Once he even sketched Xs and Os on the windshield condensation while driving.

Assistant coach Marchie Schwartz remembered when someone asked the teetotaler Shaughnessy to have a drink with them. Sure, he said, "'Let's go drink a milk shake.' He disappointed a lot of newspapermen that way." Neither did Shaughnessy smoke.

Shaughnessy had a poor relationship with the press because he was overly sensitive to criticism. Once he ordered a columnist to leave a meeting of the Northern California Football Writers Association before he would speak. *Sports Illustrated* writer Ron Fimrite wrote that the meeting was abruptly adjourned. "At a time when coaches were as much public relations men as field bosses, Shaughnessy held himself apart; he was ascetic among hucksters," Fimrite wrote.

"The world lost the greatest undertaker when Clark Shaughnessy decided on football coaching," said coach Bob Zuppke of Illinois. Football historian Roger Treat said years later when Shaughnessy joined the Chicago Bears' staff that "I always looked upon Clark Shaughnessy as a Henry Wallace with brains—a conscientious idealist who might better have followed the trail of Father Flanagan of Boys Town. He may never be entirely happy in the jovial thuggery of pro football, where every man has a little assassin in him."

Nonetheless, his Stanford players loved him. "We'd cut off our right arms for the coach," Gallarneau said, pointing to the top of his arm, "clear up to here." "We all respected him," Albert said. "I'd never smoke in his presence. He had that kind of power over us." Kmetovic said that if it hadn't been for Shaughnessy and the T, he would have been a fourth-string tailback.

If Shaughnessy had a second passion, it was military strategy, which he found perfectly compatible with football. He wrote several articles and even had some written about his feelings that the military and football were important to the country's strength. He wrote in a 1942 *Esquire* article, "What sport is the most important in the military picture? I say football unqualifiedly, and that also happens to be the consensus of military men." He said football was the closest approach to war that there is in sports. "You mass men for a quick thrust here; you feint the enemy out of position. It's a quickness, precision, cooperation, determination. They all work together—in both football and war. With the machinery and equipment of modern warfare—tanks and planes—it's team, team, team, all the way through. It's not individual. Every individual has to know how to fit right into the organization. Football has the biggest place in the training program. It's the only game that can be twisted, turned and used to accomplish the objective."

"What is there about the game like football that makes it essential?" he asked in his book, *Football in War and Peace*. "The answer is—when American boys lose interest in vigorous competition in outdoor sport there will no longer be any American men fit to fight battles and win wars. We have awakened from a rosy dream to find, alas, that all our lives, that all we have done so far, was in preparation for battle.

"... The vital need for aggressive manhood is met and must be met by a national devotion to strenuous sports. . . . Football is a war game. There is no field sport that so closely simulates the strategy and tactics of battle. In the staff schools, football terms are used continually in putting across the idea of military tactics."

Shaughnessy quoted General Douglas MacArthur as saying, "The training of the athletic field which produces in a superlative degree the attributes of fortitude, self-control, resolution, courage, mental agility, and, of course physical development, is one completely fundamental to an efficient soldiery." Said Shaughnessy, "And let it be remembered that the man so physically and mentally conditioned is one who not only is fit to win in actual battle but is most likely to survive."

William Barry Furlong, a former sports columnist for the *Chicago Daily News*, wrote in a *Smithsonian* magazine article in 1986 that Shaughnessy regarded "the kind of football played in the 1920s and '30s as a strategic reprise of World War I. That is to say, the offense was slow, ponderous, mindless and usually ineffectual."

Shaughnessy found fault with a system like the single wing that saw the ball snapped 6 yards back and then moved 6 yards forward just to get back to the line of scrimmage. Shaughnessy said a team needed superior manpower for that type of offense. Instead, the T formation allowed the players of limited capabilities to take advantage of quick handoffs a yard behind the line and rush through an opening hole.

Shaughnessy told Furlong that the person who had the greatest impact in his field in his lifetime wasn't Notre Dame legend Knute Rockne or even the Bears' George Halas. It was Nazi general Heinz Guderian, who revolutionized land warfare with the panzer-led blitzkrieg that brought about the fall of France in the spring of 1940. Shaughnessy said nothing about Guderian until the '60s, probably because it was unwise to glorify a Nazi general before then. Shaughnessy said he had studied Guderian's military strategy during the 1930s and adapted it to his plans for the T formation. Football has often adopted war terminology, such as the line of scrimmage being "fighting in the trenches," the quarterback being the "field general," and the deep pass being called "throwing the bomb," Furlong pointed out.

Shaughnessy equated football as a "war game" in which two "armies" of eleven men each fought in a struggle in which the "front line" (the line of scrimmage) moved back and forth on the "battlefield" (gridiron) until one side or the other "planted a flag" (scored a touchdown) in the other side's "territory" (end zone.) Guderian's strategy, Furlong noted, was to act with surprise and speed.

The parallels between Shaughnessy's T and the Nazis' warfare are striking. The Germans eliminated foot soldiers because they slowed tank attacks. Shaughnessy did away with most backfield blocking because it slowed the explosive starts of his ball carriers. Guderian often sent his forces on the flank of the main lines to distract his opponents and then sent his tanks through the weakened defensive line. Shaughnessy's strategy sent a man in motion who would pull the defense away from the line, allowing runners to burst through openings created by brush-blocking linemen. Shaughnessy discovered that Guderian's tactics included sending twenty-nine divisions of soldiers, tanks, and artillery to the flanks of his attack to spread the defense. Shaughnessy did the same thing on the football field, sending a man in motion to the left or right toward the sideline to spread the opposing players.

This wasn't Shaughnessy's only allusion to military tactics. He noted that the strategies that the British viscount Montgomery used at El Alamein were very similar to those of the football T-formation play. "On a certain T-formation play, when run to the right as Montgomery did at El Alamein," Shaughnessy said, "the right half runs to the left to draw the defense that way. While the right half is in motion the fullback also makes a false start to the left. The left half simultaneously plunges into the center. The quarterback, pivoting, pretends to hand the ball to the left half but really hands it to the fullback, who turns back after his deceptive start and slices between the defensive left end and tackle, preceded by the guard to block out the defensive left half. At El Alamein," he continued, "the feint to the left by General Montgomery and his threat to the middle of the line prevented the Germans from shifting enough power to Montgomery's right to stop the onslaught of the British Tenth Corps. In football the play is called a fullback counter."

Shaughnessy wasn't alone in his linking of football and war. Boston College coach Frank Leahy said in 1939, "Football is the American substitute for war." In fact, it wouldn't be long before America's youths would be switching from football uniforms to military uniforms in service of their country. By 1943 former Stanford players serving in the military included, Army, Norm Standlee, Clem Tomerlin, Claude Purkitt; Navy, Frankie Albert, Bruno Banducci, Stan Graff, Pete Kmetovic, Ed Stamm, Chuck Taylor, Al Cole, Doug Stahle, Bob Crane, Ken Robesky; Air Corps, Dick Palmer, Fred Meyer, John Casey, Arnold Meiners; Marines, Hugh Gallarneau and Ed McCain. Casey died in action in the Pacific.

Shaughnessy had always felt that football was a good training ground for the military. "There are many reasons why football stands out [and one] is that it is a game that teaches men how to fight, prepares them physically for hard action, and more than anything else, being a compact team game, it fosters and stimulates team spirit and what we have all learned to understand as morale.

"Team morale in modern war is the one single most important thing that can be developed in soldiers, and in football, because of certain intangible, emotional and spiritual factors that are inherent in the game, develops team morale more successfully than any other known means.

"Morale, I may define, is the willingness to 'mix it' and keep on struggling until you win. Self-sacrifice for an ideal, and for an objective. That's what our boys have learned in their college games. . . . In football they learned how to play toward an ideal, the ideal of physical perfection, and mental and moral discipline; and they have to acquire those same ideals to be good soldiers. . . .

"Football is the closest approach to war that we have in sports."

Tackle Jack Warnecke reflected sixty-two years later that Shaughnessy had never mentioned his fascination with General Guderian. "The German Blitzkrieg was under way as we learned the T in the spring of 1940. But we never connected Hitler's feint toward Netherlands and Belgium with our man-in-motion, nor his tank breakthrough at Sedan with a Norm Standlee burst through a hole in the spread-out line. Shaughnessy quietly was teaching us the basic principles of [Guderian]."

7

The Scrappy Broncos

The Santa Clara Broncos had high hopes to gain a Sugar Bowl bid for the third time in five years when they opened the 1940 season. Although they didn't reach that goal, the Broncos were a formidable foe, ending the year losing only one game on a missed extra point and tying another they could have won had they not missed a field goal from the 6-yard line with 25 seconds left in the game.

Stanford expected a crowd of between fifty thousand and sixty thousand on October 12 at Stanford Stadium to see the only two remaining unbeaten and untied teams on the Pacific Coast. Stanford expected a larger than usual crowd because more fans wanted to see the Indians' new formation, and Santa Clara University was just down the road from Palo Alto, allowing thousands of its fans to make the short trip.

Santa Clara coach Lawrence "Buck" Shaw had never lost to Stanford, and Broncos fans didn't see it happening this year either.

Santa Clara was favored 10–7 to keep its streak alive. So far for the season, Santa Clara had beaten Utah in that doubleheader at Kezar Stadium and then eked out a 9–6 victory over UCLA.

The word on the Stanford campus was "Konko the Bronco" as student interest in the team's fortunes continued to climb. But Shaughnessy warned that Santa Clara "will be very hard to beat. We really haven't had enough time to work. And they're too far along for us." He was unhappy with the team's performance against the Ducks. "We didn't show improvement against Oregon," he said. "In fact, we went back a little. Sure, Oregon was unlucky in the first quarter and we were lucky." Shaughnessy also tried to dispel early talk of the Indians going to the Rose Bowl. "I don't even know the names of the hotels in Pasadena where the teams stop," he said. And he wasn't about to say anything bad about the Broncos. "I wish I knew what kind of defense Buck is going to use," Shaughnessy said. "From what I hear, this [halfback Jim] Johnson is a much better kicker than Standlee. We don't figure to win at all."

Shaw was into "coach-speak" as well. "I expect the toughest game I've had with Stanford in five years," he said. "I disagree with Mr. Shaughnessy that we have the edge because our entire team watched Stanford at Kezar. It isn't healthy for a team to see their opponents. They get the idea the opposition is either too good or too feeble and it's hard to talk them out of the extreme convictions."

Toward the end of the week before the game, Shaw held his first closed practice of the season. The public generally had been kept away from practices, but now even alumni and other hangers-on were barred from the field. He knew the value of this game.

Santa Clara was a scrappy team, its players about the same size as Stanford's but with less speed. The Broncos relied on power, running out of the single-wing offense that was the mode in that era. Santa Clara had no standout players but was talented across the board. And the Broncos proved to be a tough match for the

Indians. The Broncos' depth worried the Indians as well. They had solid first and second teams, both of which had played well in their win over UCLA the previous week. Assistant coach Marchie Schwartz said most of the Stanford players would have to play the full 60 minutes of the game.

Shaw had designed a defense he thought might stop the Indians. It was billed as the X defense, so the game came down to the T versus the X. The defense was the 5-2-2-1-1, with the right end playing about 5 yards behind the linebackers. The fact that it held Stanford's high-powered offense to a single touchdown showed Shaw's defensive genius.

Years later Albert, who played quarterback when Shaw coached the San Francisco 49ers, said, "Buck has a way with boys that is wonderful. He treats them as mature men—the kids respect him and seem to play harder for him than they might for someone else."

Stanford's injured ends, Hank Norberg, Fred Meyer, and Bill Willard, were available for the game, but the big relief was that Albert took to the practice field on Wednesday and showed no ill effects from his charley horse.

On game day Santa Clara took possession on its 20-yard line after the kickoff. The Broncos lost 5 yards on first down and then quick-kicked over the heads of the unsuspecting Indians. Kmetovic picked up the ball at the 10 and returned it to the 17.

On second down on the 22, a bad handoff from Albert to Kmetovic resulted in a fumble that the Broncos recovered. On first down halfback Ward Heiser started around end, but Bruno Banducci and Meyer trapped him. They chased him back to the 35, from where he threw the ball out of bounds, drawing a 15-yard penalty. Two downs later the Broncos punted into the end zone.

And so it went with neither team threatening to score as the first quarter ended 0–0.

In the second quarter Stanford took advantage of a poor kick, with Albert fielding the punt on the 50 and returning it to Santa Clara's 47. From there Stanford marched down the field for its only score. On second and seven from the 44, the speedy Kmetovic raced around right end down the sidelines, where linebacker Dick Clark tackled him at the 19. On the play Clark suffered a broken leg and was removed on a stretcher.

Three plays later the Indians faced a fourth and two at the 11. Gallarneau ran in motion to his left, raising his arms. Kmetovic ran toward left guard with his arms outstretched. Albert faked giving him the ball, stepped back, and handed to Standlee. The Chief drove toward right end, where tackle Frank Zmak had his eyes on Kmetovic. Zmak didn't realize Standlee had the ball. The fake to Kmetovic also drew two linebackers away from the play. Standlee bulled his way into the end zone, dragging a Bronco defender with him. Albert then kicked the extra point. The score remained 7–0 at halftime.

Santa Clara scored in the third quarter after Stanford's fourth fumble on a bad lateral that the Broncos recovered on the 42. On first down Standlee threw the ball carrier for a 3-yard loss, but on the next down Ken Casanega fired a long pass to Jim Thom, who caught it at the 6. Gallarneau caught him at the 2 but couldn't pull him down.

Jim Johnson, who had kicked the game-winning field goal the week before against UCLA, saw his kick go wide right under a furious charge from the Stanford defense, and the Indians still led 7–6. Santa Clara never mounted much offense the rest of the game. Shaw said after the game, "Johnson had a bad day, unusual for him, but I guess every boy deserves an off day. His best passing was inaccurate and his punting was not worthy of his best."

Stanford threatened to score three more times in the half but came up short. Once the Indians lost the ball on the Broncos' 3 on a fumble; the second time they moved the ball to the 10 when an interception stopped them; and finally they were on the Broncos' 9 when the game ended. On that last threat, Albert had intercepted a pass and the Indians took over on the Santa Clara 12. The Indians were content to run out the clock. After one running play gained no yards, Albert went back into the huddle and asked his players, "OK, who wants to lie down with it this time?" One last play and the game was over.

As the game ended, hundreds of Stanford students poured onto the field to mob the players. Line coach Phil Bengston said guard Dick Palmer was the best defensive signal caller he had ever seen. The usually unemotional Shaughnessy ran onto the field and hugged Palmer, who gave him the game ball.

Albert, Standlee, and Taylor played more than 50 minutes in the 60-minute game. Shaughnessy said he supposed someone would accuse him "of being an inhuman brute for keeping them in the game so long." But, he said, "The boys' willingness to play, despite the heat, inspired and stimulated me more than I can say. The fact is I was afraid to replace them. They knew it and carried on."

Statistically, Stanford and Santa Clara were almost even in rushing yards, with the Broncos holding the edge 52 to 50, while Santa Clara passed for more than twice as many yards as Stanford, 114 to 53. That last statistic was surprising because Stanford had worked on its passing offense almost exclusively in practice. Only four times did the Indians gain more than 7 yards from scrimmage. Santa Clara's longest gain was 12 yards. Stanford threw three interceptions, Santa Clara two. The Broncos punted thirteen times, the Indians eight.

Santa Clara also recovered five Stanford fumbles to one for the Indians. Santa Clara had the ball in Stanford territory only five times, four on fumble recoveries and once on a drive that bogged down at the Stanford 48.

A tie wouldn't have hurt Stanford, but the loss may have kept the Broncos out of another Sugar Bowl.

Shaughnessy praised Santa Clara for playing "a clean game for all its ferocity. I realize now how anxious the Stanford boys were to beat Santa Clara and how keyed up they were. I don't think Buck's boys were and maybe that's the difference."

After the game Shaw said, "I'm glad, as it was played, that Stanford won. Stanford deserved to win, and if we had tied the game, under the circumstances, there would have been a lot of discussion in the papers I would not like to read." Apparently he was referring to poor officiating in the game.

Shaw told sportswriters at the weekly San Francisco Press Club luncheon three days later, "The best team on the field that day won. It should have been a larger score against Santa Clara than only 7 to 6."

To celebrate the victory, Shaughnessy took his wife, Mae, out for chocolate nut sundaes. Later that night he was home preparing for the highly regarded Washington State Cougars on the road in Pullman, Washington.

8

The White Ghosts

T The Indians boarded a train for Pullman, Washington, on October 18 to take on the Cougars, who had beaten California and Montana and tied powerful Southern Cal. Twelve hundred cheering Stanford students saw them off at the train station. "We are in good shape and we're going to do everything to win," Shaughnessy told the students. Before they left the station, Albert told the fans, "We're not sleeping four nights on a train just to get our noses rubbed in dirt. I'm confident we're going to win."

The Indians made only two trips out of northern California during the nine-game regular season. Both times they took trains to play Washington State and UCLA. Their only other road games were at Kezar Stadium to play USF and in Berkeley against the Cal Bears. They were bused to both sites.

The California schools played so many home games because the Pacific Northwest schools drew smaller crowds. The gate receipts were much higher at the California schools than in the smaller stadiums as in Eugene and Corvallis, Oregon. Because they received more money from ticket sales at the California schools than at home, the Northwest schools didn't squawk much. Except for the Washington State game, Stanford played its games against the other three Pacific Northwest schools at home. Washington State was able to put twenty-four thousand people in the seats because it drew fans from nearby Spokane and Moscow, Idaho, as well as the team's home in Pullman.

Train was the main mode of transportation for most teams in the nation. Teams traveled by rail even when games were on the other side of the country, despite the several days it took. It might even have discouraged teams from intersectional games because of the time lost from school and practice. Stanford's trip to New York to play Dartmouth took three days and four nights.

Commercial air travel was relatively new. The Michigan Wolverines in 1940 flew on United Airlines from Ann Arbor, Michigan, to Oakland, California, a distance of twenty-four hundred miles. Players under the age of twenty-one were required to obtain permission to fly from their parents, and the airline sent along a company physician to monitor the effects of the trip. Several players became airsick flying in the DC–3 aircraft. The plane flew at a cruise speed of 207 mph at twenty-three thousand feet. Undoubtedly big football players found themselves crammed into tiny seats for the bumpy trip, which required a refueling stop along the way.

Train travel was more leisurely. Players could play cards, sleep, or study on the long trips, especially to the rolling hills of the Palouse in eastern Washington. The thirty-seven Indians traveled on the Southern Pacific Cascade from Palo Alto to Portland, Oregon, where they stopped over for eight hours for a workout at the University of Portland. From there they rolled on to Pullman, studying, sleeping, and playing bridge, the game of choice that replaced poker on previous trips. Perhaps that civilized game reflected more the style of Clark Shaughnessy than Tiny Thornhill. Several alumni went along, including Bones Hamilton, who helped Shaughnessy coach.

The long, boring ride from the Bay Area to Portland was broken up by a visit with the actor Pat O'Brien, the star of *Knute Rockne, All-American*, the movie then showing in theaters about the legendary Notre Dame coach. The film also starred Ronald Reagan as George Gipp. O'Brien was traveling with his wife, Heloise, and their two children on a vacation. They were housed in a compartment in the car in front of the Indians' car.

The O'Briens, who were on their way to watch the Washington–Oregon State game, spent the evening in the lounge car entertaining the Stanford players. O'Brien told the players he believed the team that won the Huskies-Beavers game would go to the Rose Bowl. O'Brien was a big fan of Huskies' coach Jimmy Phelan.

O'Brien doubted the Indians had what it took to make it to the Rose Bowl, and he didn't mind telling them so. He knew a little more about football than just playing a coach in a movie; he had been a third-string quarterback for Marquette twenty years earlier. It is safe to say that the ever-confident Indians disagreed with O'Brien's predictions.

While O'Brien held the players' attention, Shaughnessy as always was paying attention to details. He conferred with the train's dining car steward on the menu and the hours when the players would eat, coming and going. On the trip home, for example, he told the steward that the players were not to eat until 8 p.m. because they were too keyed up to digest their food properly.

While the Indians were traveling to Pullman, the T formation was attracting more and more attention—as well as controversy over who was responsible for its rebirth. Most sportswriters were giving much of the credit to the Chicago Bears, who had been using it extensively. But they lacked the flair and success the Indians were achieving. The Bears were still running a power rather than a finesse offense. Sportswriters were surprised to find that the Indians were able to make the offense work with only one power back, Norm Standlee.

Not Pop Warner. Standlee, he said, was one of the best football players he had ever seen. "I don't see that he has a weakness," Warner said. "He's big and powerful for line smashing. He's fast and once through a hole he's fairly shifty, quite so for a big man. He's a fine kicker, now leading the West in punting averages, and a terrific smasher on defense. And he can pass, although with Albert acting as the key thrower, Standlee has yet to prove this factor." Shaughnessy couldn't agree more. "They don't make 'em any better than Standlee," he said.

Shaughnessy told the press Stanford's success with the T pleased him. "After what I've been through [at the University of Chicago]," he said, "the Jayvee freshman team at Doakes' sanitarium for advanced cases of rickets would look like a juggernaut to me. These boys can handle the [Chicago] Bears' plays. Just give 'em time."

Bill Leiser, *San Francisco Chronicle* sports editor, came to Shaughnessy's defense. He asked the question, "Well, if it's the Bears' idea, why do they keep bringing Shaughnessy back to help them with their preliminary training each year?" Leiser gave at least three reasons that "the system is Shaughnessy's own, and belongs to no one else":

- He had three of the finest assistants in the country in Lawson, Schwartz, and Bengston.
- The players were in better shape than other teams, shown by the fact that several played the entire sixty minutes of their games.
- In college Shaughnessy must teach boys, who knew how, how to do what must be done to make plays work. The Chicago Bears must teach players who know all about how, WHAT to do. They don't have to teach "how." They hire boys who know how already.

"If anything, it's the Bears who are using Shaughnessy's ideas as to 'T formations' and 'men in motion,' as the Bears, including George Halas, will readily admit," Leiser concluded.

Another bit of news on October 18 also would be telling toward the end of the season. The University of Minnesota, the nation's seventh-ranked team at the time and coached by Bernie Bierman, Shaughnessy's former teammate, said if offered a trip to the Rose Bowl, it would turn it down.

The Indians were preparing themselves for a team that rarely lost at home. The Cougars had one of the best passers in the nation, twenty-four-year-old Billy Sewell, an ex-brewery worker. Sewell would end the season as the nation's leading passer. He fell eight pass completions short of Sammy Baugh's record of ninety-two. He also finished third in the nation in total yardage.

Stanford's assistant coach Jim Lawson scouted Washington State's games against USC and Cal. "Two fumbles on the 10 and 8 yard lines led to Trojan touchdowns," Lawson noted. "It was USC, not Washington State, that was lucky to get a tie. Usually the Cougars are short on manpower but this time [coach Olin "Babe"] Hollingbery has two good lines. The sub backs aren't so much. When Sewell and the first stringers go out the attack is definitely weakened. I haven't seen a team that could rush Sewell's passes. He gets them off too fast. He can duck and dodge if a rush does harass him. Hollingbery has the best pass attack I've watched this year, but of course, I haven't seen many games."

Other key players for the Cougars were fullback Dick Renfro, who scored the only touchdown in 1939 in WSC's 7–0 win over the Indians, and tackle Stanley Johnson, who would make third-string All-Coast at the end of the season.

The Cougars made Shaughnessy wary. "I'm really afraid of this one. I cannot afford to fire up the players every week, for after Washington State come in quick order the Trojans, the Bruins and the Huskies. There's no rest for the weary." Again, more coaches' talk. Shaughnessy wasn't much of a pep talker in the best of times. He prepared the men to play and they fired themselves up.

Shaughnessy also worried that being cooped up on the train without exercise would have an adverse effect on the Indians' chances. "We cannot possibly play our best game," he said. "I say this knowing our entire squad is in excellent physical shape for the three tough games we have been through. Our escaping [serious] injuries has been nothing short of miraculous." Except for left tackle Jack Warnecke, who had a pulled leg muscle, the team was physically fit for the WSC game.

Stanford had moved into tenth place in the AP poll. The Indians were 10–7 favorites to beat the Cougars in their annual homecoming game.

The Indians arrived in Pullman on Saturday, October 19, early enough for a short workout. Shaughnessy handled all of the coaching duties himself. Assistants Schwartz, Bengston, and Lawson were scouting other teams. He did get some assistance from Hamilton, now undoubtedly pleased with the Indians' improvement since he had lambasted them at halftime of the Dartmouth game the previous year.

At their three hundredth game, the Cougars were hoping to get some inspirational help from Cecil "Hippo" Wetsel, the WSC guard from the class of 1923. Wetsel earned his fame thwarting the kidnapping of a young boy in California, and he would be sitting on the Cougars' bench.

Stanford wore all-white uniforms with red stripes. Sportswriters said they looked like white ghosts, flourmill workers, or "gas station cadets." *San Francisco Chronicle* columnist Will Connolly said the uniforms were a "gaudy, if virginal, creation difficult to reconcile with [Shaughnessy's] nature."

With 4 minutes gone in the first quarter, Washington State scored first. The key play in the 68-yard drive came almost as a fluke. Sewell took the snap from center and rolled to his right and fired a wobbly pass 30 yards in the air to right half Felix Fletcher at the Stanford 42. When Gallarneau hit him, Fletcher fumbled the ball at the 22, then it went on one bounce to Johnny Rutherford, who ran it to the 17 before Vic Lindskog and Dick Palmer pushed him out of bounds.

With second and nine at the Stanford 16, Fletcher scored on a reverse. WSC was lucky to get the point after when the ball bounced to the holder before Stanley Johnson converted. It was the first time Stanford had trailed in its first four games.

Stanford got its chance to score after Albert made a leaping interception over his shoulder at the Indians' 38, where the Cougars immediately tackled him. On the first play Kmetovic took a handoff from Albert and burst through left tackle and toward the sideline. He got a block from end Fred Meyer at the Cougars' 30 and ran to the 10 before Walt Schloch tripped him up. On the next play Standlee swept around left end untouched to score. Albert's point-after kick tied the score at 7–7 with 3 minutes left in the first quarter.

Behind Sewell's passing, the Cougars threatened again, driving to the Stanford 22 before the Indians held. After stopping Stanford, Washington State marched again to the Stanford 36, but the defense forced the Cougars to punt to Kmetovic on the 5. Kmetovic returned it to the 17. Stanford got the ball to the 32 and went into punt formation on second down. Instead, Lindskog centered to Vucinich, who threw a 36-yard completion to Clem Tomerlin at the Cougars' 32. Three downs later Albert hooked up with 5-foot-7-inch halfback Hoot Armstrong for a 27-yard touchdown. Albert kicked the extra point to put the Indians up 14–7.

Early in the third quarter, Stanford scored again, going 74 yards in four plays. Standlee's 25-yard run put the ball on the Cougars' 33, where Albert passed to Meyer, who made a leaping catch at the goal line and tumbled in the end zone. A bad snap from center botched the extra-point try.

After the kickoff the Cougars' Frank Akins fumbled on a vicious hit by Lindskog, who recovered at the WSC 30. Three plays later, after two running plays, Albert sneaked over from the 1. Albert again missed the extra-point attempt. The Indians had scored two touchdowns in a 5-minute span, putting the game out of reach. The Cougars managed a meaningless touchdown late in the fourth quarter that made the final score 26–14.

The Cougars finished ahead of Stanford in virtually every statistical category except the final score. They made fifteen first downs to thirteen, outgained the Indians on the ground 230 yards to 146, and passing 149 yards to 120. The big statistical edge for Stanford was its four pass interceptions. Kmetovic had a 9.6-yard average on eleven carries to lead the Indians.

Stanford got out of the game without any serious injuries. Tomerlin, the junior end from Pasadena, California, had his sprained right hand put in a cast. He would play with the cast the rest of the year.

Shaughnessy called the game the best his team had played so far. He also said that some of the second-string players were improving. "We do have a better squad now than the 14 first stringers with whom we started the season," he said. "Every week we are adding a few new men on whom we can rely."

Hollingbery called Stanford "the best team we've met yet, particularly in the line." Considering the powerhouse backfield the Indians assembled, that came as quite a compliment. He said poor pass defense hurt the Cougars. "Stanford backs were just too fast," he conceded. Despite their good start to the season, the Cougars finished with four wins, four defeats, and two ties.

After the game Shaughnessy traveled with the players to Portland, then flew home at 6 a.m. to save time as he prepared for the Southern California game while the team traveled the rest of the way home by train.

People across the country were beginning to take notice of the Indians. They were moving up in the AP poll. The powerful Southern California Trojans, the team figured to top the Pacific Coast Conference that year, would be Stanford's first big test of the year.

9

Recruiting

Recruiting practices were far different in 1940 than they are today. That should come as no surprise. The financial stakes are far higher today. That doesn't mean competition for top athletes was any less intense or that little financial reward could be gained. Certainly the rules governing recruiting were far more lax in the 1930s.

Until 1940 alumni recruited most of the players at Pacific Coast Conference schools. For example, former Stanford great Jim Reynolds, who played in 1919, recruited Albert to the Farm. "He helped a lot of Southern California boys get up there," Albert said.

Coaches generally stayed out of recruiting. The core of Stanford's 1940 team had been recruited two years before the league put in new guidelines designed to quell worries that professionalism was creeping into the college football ranks.

USC also recruited Albert, even promising him meetings with movie stars. Albert replied somewhat jokingly, "Yeah, but they promised me I would shake hands with [Stanford alumnus] Herbert Hoover if I went to Stanford." Albert waited tables in a sorority house, mowed lawns, and washed cars to pay his way through school.

Milt Vucinich, a star tailback at San Francisco's Lowell High School, received an academic/athletic scholarship to Stanford. He said he had rooted for Stanford while listening to the Indians on the radio. A Stanford alumnus paid his tuition, he said, which "became illegal shortly [after he enrolled]." He also waited on tables in a dormitory and worked a summer job the school had arranged for him at thirty to forty dollars a month.

Ray Hammett, a backup quarterback, had planned to enroll at California after quarterbacking an unbeaten, untied team at Stockton High School in California's San Joaquin Valley. He said a Stockton doctor, a Stanford alumnus, provided him with a "special scholarship." He too "hashed" for his meals and worked on campus as an intramural director.

Bill Mannon, a tackle from Los Angeles, was recruited by a former Stanford shot-putter, Reg Coughy, who was a patent attorney. "He was an active guy getting guys to go to Stanford," Mannon said. He said he, running back Al Cole, and lineman Dick Palmer borrowed Coughy's car to visit Stanford. "We didn't meet a coach until the first day of practice," he said. Mannon also visited UCLA and USC, but "I just liked Stanford the best. Their [won-loss] record wasn't a factor." Mannon also hashed during his four years and was the house manager at his fraternity.

Woody Strode, one of the first black players to suit up in the Pacific Coast Conference when he played for UCLA with Jackie Robinson in 1939, gave an insight into recruiting in his 1990 autobiography. He noted that Robinson, who attended Pasadena Junior College, was the most sought-after athlete on the West Coast. Oregon recruited him, even thinking they had a lock on him because his brother Mack, a world-class long jumper, had gone there. "Some friends of the school came down and threw the keys to a brand-new Dodge on his porch," Strode wrote. He also said that an alumnus of Stanford offered to pay Robinson's way to any school back East just so he wouldn't play on a West Coast school where he might beat Stanford. Strode did not say why Stanford didn't recruit him. "UCLA ended up taking care of me and my whole family while I was in school," Strode wrote. "They gave me one hundred dollars a month and an eleven-dollar meal ticket. Every week they gave me twenty bucks under the table so I could pay the bills at home. They gave Kenny Washington [another black player] and me a car, all my books . . . and clothes free."

Strode said he had to earn his scholarship. "All the guys who were on scholarship did some kind of maintenance work for the school," he wrote. "A lot of great athletes were janitors; they scrubbed toilets. Kenny and I had good jobs; we used to walk around campus with a stick picking up papers, and we did a little gardening, too. That's how I earned my hundred bucks a month."

In late 1937, when Frankie Albert, Chuck Taylor, Pete Kmetovic, Milt Vucinich, and others were still in high school, select faculty members from the conferences' ten schools with little fanfare hired a former Federal Bureau of Investigation man—a "G-man," the newspapers called him—to survey "the general problem of sources of income of conference athletes. The survey is being conducted for the purpose of enabling the committee [of faculty members] to make further adjustments in the rules concerning what constitutes legitimate aid for athletes," said E. J. Miller, a dean at UCLA and the committee's chairman.

Apparently the Pacific Northwest members of the conference—Washington, Washington State, Oregon, Oregon State, Idaho, and Montana, known as "the Poor Relations"—blew the whistle on the four California schools because the Pacific Northwest schools were at a disadvantage in recruiting and finances.

The conference winner automatically went to the Rose Bowl and received a guaranteed $85,000 (about $1,229,464 in 2006 dollars) for playing in the game. That was soon to change, with all schools dividing 60 percent of the Rose Bowl guarantee. Of the twenty-three times the Rose Bowl was played with the PCC represented, the four California schools played in sixteen of them. They also had a larger fan base to draw on to fill their stadiums during the regular season. For example, Los Angeles had a population of almost 1.5 million while Eugene, Oregon, home of the Ducks, had almost 21,000. In 1939 UCLA had gross receipts of almost $550,000 while Washington State's were about $81,500.

The Pacific Northwest schools also told conference officials numerous stories of recruiting excesses by the California schools. "The Northwest colleges are jealous of our success," one Southern California official said. "They can't whip us on the athletic field, so they are trying to do it behind closed doors at conference meetings. It's just a gang-up deal."

Investigator Edwin N. Atherton officially went to work on January 1, 1938. The survey was expected to take a year, but almost exactly two years later, Atherton dropped into the committee's laps facts and figures that reportedly took two million words on six hundred thousand pages at a cost of $40,000 (about $578,570 in 2006 dollars).

After looking at the report, committee members—who must have been impressed, if not overwhelmed, by the detail—agreed to hire Atherton as the PCC's first commissioner, giving him a three-year contract. Atherton's main job was to enforce new guidelines the faculty representatives had adopted to clean up recruiting in the PCC. Perhaps the most far reaching was one that would eliminate the custom of alumni or friends of the colleges entertaining prospective athletes with the goal of persuading them to attend their institution. A violation of that rule would make the athlete ineligible to attend that school. "We intend to have the boy select the college, and stop the college selecting the boy," Atherton told a meeting of the Commonwealth Club in San Francisco on April 8.

Coaches were forbidden to make trips to recruit athletes, interview them, visit them or their family, or visit them at their school. Universities were prohibited from providing pleasure trips for athletes, travel expenses, complimentary tickets, or employment before their enrollment. The rules limited financial assistance in the form of employment to fifty cents an hour and fifty dollars a month.

One guideline that caused a problem for Stanford, and USC as well, permitted financial aid in the form of grants to the limit of each school's tuition. Stanford's fee was $345 a year ($4,996 in 2006 dollars) while USC's was $310, higher than other schools because they were private. Tuition at public schools, like California, was $62 ($890 in 2006 dollars); UCLA was $54. That meant those schools could pay for five athletes' tuition for every one of Stanford's.

In mid-July Atherton announced he was investigating violations of the new rules by PCC schools. He said he wanted to finish the probe before school began in the fall, so that any athletes who were declared ineligible at certain schools could enroll in other PCC schools if they wished. On September 4 Atherton ruled that three schools, California, UCLA, and Southern Cal, had violated the rules on ten occasions, including offering subsidies, free equipment, or entertainment to high school players. Those ten athletes would be ineligible to attend the schools that violated the rules, he said. Eventually, the total hit thirteen athletes.

One recruit, Johnny Petrovich, who was called one of the greatest triple-threat high school football players coming out of the Southland, was barred from playing at UCLA and USC for recruiting violations. Said his mother, Mary, "I think it is a crying shame that a boy can't do the things he wants to. My Johnny is a good boy and he has done nothing wrong. He likes to play football but foremost in his mind is getting an education."

Stanford, which did not lose any players because of violation, did gain one. Loren LaPrade of Phoenix, Arizona, a center, had been denied enrollment at USC, enrolled at the Farm, and turned out for the freshman team.

Apparently Atherton looked only at those three schools the first year. Another investigation the following summer omitted those three schools but shifted to Stanford, Washington, Washington State, Oregon, Oregon State, Idaho, and Montana. He declared thirty-five football players and other athletes who enrolled the previous year were ineligible to compete any longer. Eight of them were from Stanford, seven on the football team. In addition, thirteen other players from Texas and Oklahoma who had not yet enrolled at Stanford—or in fact may not have anyway—were barred from doing so. An unnamed person wrote them letters or made contracts making promises if they would attend Stanford. The seven football players were given tuition awards by alumni organizations with no official standing with the university, Atherton said. All of the enrolled students were allowed to transfer to other schools without having to sit out a year, which was standard for any other transfer.

Stanford accepted the decision; it really had no other choice. But it didn't have to like it. Shaughnessy was outraged, not because he lost seven players who would have been reserves on his 1941 team but because the players were punished; they were scapegoats for the misdeeds of others.

Atherton recognized the unfairness of the rule but said he was just enforcing the conference mandate. "Practically every one of these instances showed the boys themselves were not at fault," he said. "They were simply victims of the operations of alumni and other people. . . . Personally I think it is a shame they must suffer for the action of others."

In June the conference tightened rules more by banning free tuition for athletes and imposing fines of up to one thousand dollars for schools violating recruiting regulations. That was an effort to put the blame where it belonged—on the schools.

With World War II less than six months away, it didn't seem to matter much. Most young men were being recruited by another organization—the military. Stanford did no recruiting at all; it abandoned football for the war's duration.

The PCC wasn't the only organization concerned with college football losing its amateur standing. The National Collegiate Athletic Association was prompted to take some action to reform rules, interestingly enough following University of Chicago president Robert Hutchins's successful effort to abolish football at his school. Reformers saw Hutchins's action as a major landmark for bringing about that reform. Hutchins as much said football teams had to play honest football or not play at all, although there was no indication that anything dishonest was going on at his school.

It didn't take the NCAA long after Chicago abolished football for its board of trustees to adopt tougher rules regarding recruiting and subsidies to athletes. Simplified, the rules said scholarships should be based on need and that athletes could receive aid from their athletic departments only for legitimate jobs. Violators could be expelled from the NCAA by a two-thirds vote of the board of trustees. The NCAA's president was none other than Stanford professor William Owens. "The major problems which confront us today call for aggressive determined action," he said. "Isolated action by individual institutions or conferences will not adequately meet the problems."

The problem the NCAA faced was that it didn't have the financial resources to investigate schools that might be violating its new rules. But it didn't matter much—at least for the near future. The NCAA turned its attention toward its role in military preparedness and held the new rules in abeyance until after the war.

10

"Pop" Comes Around

Every game for Stanford was getting more challenging and expectations were getting higher. After four victories Stanford was favored against Southern California in their October 26 matchup. The previous year the Trojans dominated the Indians 33–0. The Indians, who were ranked ninth in the AP poll, were established as 10–8 favorites to beat the Trojans in this, the twenty-fourth meeting of the two schools. The Trojans had been tied twice already this season—Washington State 14–14 and Oregon State 0–0—and had beaten Oregon 13–0 and Illinois from the Big Ten 13–7.

Shaughnessy told his players that USC had been picked to win the conference championship. "But you did not go to USC. You enrolled at Stanford. You're smarter than they are," he said.

Bill Leiser, the incredibly accurate prognosticator for the *San Francisco Chronicle*—he picked every game correctly the week before—said Stanford would win. "It's getting to be a habit, which is as good a reason as any for picking any team," he wrote. Perhaps he was biased. Leiser was a Stanford graduate, had been editor of the *Stanford Daily*, and often spoke at football rallies on the campus. It was a clear conflict of interest, but ethics weren't what they are today.

The Indians attended a pep rally in the basketball pavilion on Friday night with Pop Warner, the former Stanford coach and early critic of the T formation, as the featured speaker. Warner was beginning to be a believer. "The Stanford team is being very capably handled and coached," he told the three thousand assembled students. "There never has been so much gotten out of this system as Shaughnessy gets now. I have confidence in the boys' ability to come through Saturday, and I want to see Stanford in the Rose Bowl."

Shaughnessy told the rally, "The boys on the team are all fighters and I like fighters. We're looking forward to one whale of a football game Saturday."

A crowd of more than sixty thousand was expected. And, oh yes, the price of tickets went up with the Indians' success. Reserved seats were now $2.50 ($36.16 in 2006 dollars) and end zone $1.50. Stanford's women wore red victory feathers in their hair, something they hadn't done since the last Rose Bowl. Men wore white shirts and rooters' caps while women wore white blouses and carried pompons. "All non-conformists will sit in the first three rows of the rooting section," the *Stanford Daily* wrote. Apparently those weren't good seats.

The Indians were facing the three hardest-hitting runners of the season in Bobby Robertson, Jack Banta, and Bob Peoples, who were averaging about 5 yards a carry. USC also expected Mickey Anderson, their best and fastest runner, back into action after an injury had kept him out all year. As it turned out, coaches held Anderson out of the game. The Trojans had averaged more than 200 rushing yards a game so far that year.

In preparing for the game, Shaughnessy studied scouting reports. "That is a very fine offense," he said. "I don't see how we can stop Robertson, Banta, and Peoples running those plays. Our only hope is to outscore them, and we can't do that unless we're lucky." The Trojans weren't nearly so good in the passing game. They had passed seventy times, completing twenty-seven for 245 yards. Clearly, USC based its offense on the running game.

Assistant coach Phil Bengston agreed. "We don't expect to hold them scoreless. The only way to beat them," he said, "is to score more points than they do and keep the ball as long as we can." Holding them scoreless would be even more difficult with the shoulder injury starting tackle Jack Warnecke suffered in practice that week. Ed "Truck" Stamm, a 215-pounder from Portland, Oregon, would replace him.

Shaughnessy played down the Indians' chances. "I have honestly been expecting us to be beaten every game since the San Francisco game," he said. "We are not a good football team. We've been lucky, that's all. Against the Trojans we are going to gamble," Shaughnessy said. "We think they are a better team than we are and have every reason to beat us. But if our gambles are lucky we can win."

Verne Landreth, who was going to referee the game, stopped by to watch the Indians practice. "I can't get over the machine-like manner in which Clark Shaughnessy and his assistant coaches run the Stanford practices," he said. "Each day's practice cores are planned in advance and the coaches run the players through the blocking, tackling, and other stunts on a schedule that conforms to time as strictly as a radio program," he said. "And I noticed that while the assistant coaches had the regulars and second-team players, Shaughnessy was away down at one end of the field working with the third- and fourth-string players on offense and defense."

Stanford had a potent running attack as well, although, with the exception of Standlee, the backs weren't power runners. USC coach Howard Jones recognized that "Kmetovic and Gallarneau are fast, and Albert is good. But the boys [USC players] said last year that Standlee was the hardest hitting fullback they'd played against so I guess he's the most consistent man they have." The Indians were averaging 225 yards a game on the ground. In passing, Stanford had attempted forty-eight and completed twenty for 296 yards. The statistical edge surely had to go to Stanford.

USC scout Bob McNeish said the Trojans particularly were concerned with stopping Stanford's passing game. "Here you have to hand it to Albert. He doesn't carry the ball much. Frankie just loves to sit in there back of center and figure out the best place to send the ball carrier. He's the brains of the whole setup and mixes up his attack exceptionally well. Of course, he is the best passer on the club and his handling of the ball back there also helps make the Shaughnessy system click."

The Trojans took the train from Los Angeles, stopping in Salinas, where they worked out on Friday before continuing to Palo Alto. "If hard work means anything," Jones said, "then we should have a chance."

When Saturday finally arrived, Stanford ran its first play from the 26 after the kickoff. Albert looked out over the Trojan defense and saw a 5-1-2-2-1 defense, the first of its kind this season. Two downs gained no yards and Standlee punted on third down to the USC 21. Stanford held, and on third down USC punted to Kmetovic at his 38. He was stopped at the 40.

Again the two teams traded punts. Shaughnessy sent in a pass play on a five-by-seven card to take advantage of the charging Banta. "Shaughnessy was like a fortune-teller," Albert said. "He'd tell us this or that would work and it always did. He'd invent plays in the middle of the game," Albert said, "and, heck, no one had more plays than we already had. . . . The guy was always thinking."

Albert said seeing the plays on those cards had a "very positive" effect on the team. "We had so much confidence in him, we just felt these impromptu plays would work. It's amazing how many of them did. By the end of the game, when I went to the locker room, I'd have maybe a half-dozen of those cards stuffed into my pants."

On second down from the Indians' 39, Gallarneau went left in motion then at the snap moved forward to block the defensive end, making the play look like a run. Standlee faked taking a handoff and ran left. Kmetovic meanwhile ran across the line of scrimmage. With the defense drawn in what looked like a run, Albert lofted a pass that Kmetovic caught on the USC 35, and without breaking stride he raced into the end zone with defensive back Floyd Phillips hanging on his back. Albert added the extra point.

"We won several games because [Shaughnessy] devised a new play which caught the defense flat-footed," Albert said. "That's what I call help from the bench."

Shaughnessy later sent in a running play with substitute guard Ken Robesky. "On it I drew the defense, indicated a nice hole to hit, and suggested that Frankie shoot a few at this hole," Shaughnessy said. "It was much easier than explaining. I carry pencils with me all the time." Robesky carried the card in his headgear and gave it to Albert.

Substitutes were prohibited from speaking in the huddle until after they had been in for one play. That rule was changed in 1941 as well as the one that prohibited a player who was taken out of the game from returning until the next quarter. The change led to two-platoon football.

Early in the second quarter, USC moved to the Stanford 23 before Robertson fumbled on fourth down and Gallarneau recovered the ball on the 26. The Trojans threatened again midway through the quarter. With the ball on the Stanford 28 and 8 yards to go on fourth down, substitute quarterback Ray Woods passed to right end Joe Davis at the goal line as Gallarneau defended. The pass fell incomplete, but field judge George Hicks ruled interference on Gallarneau, spotting the ball on the 1.

The crowd roared with disapproval. "I didn't think I touched him," Gallarneau said. "Maybe I did, but I don't think so. We both were playing the ball and if I brushed into him I did it accidentally." Said Shaughnessy, "Even had it ended in a 7–7 tie I wouldn't have complained [about the call]. It looked like Hugh had shoved the USC boy and that's a foul in any league." But the Los Angeles sportswriters agreed it was a bad call. Banta then dived over for the touchdown. The extra point tied the score at 7.

Quarterback Woods was leading the resurgent Trojans. The next time USC had the ball, he ran for 39 yards on three carries and USC moved the ball to the Indians' 15. Then the defense went to work. Standlee dropped Banta for a 3-yard loss. A clipping penalty made it second and twenty-eight, and then Tomerlin caught Woods before he could pass for 11 more yards lost. At fourth and thirty-nine, Banta punted. The Indians had the ball one more series of downs before the half but could only get to their own 31. Going into the locker room, USC seemed to have the momentum. Stanford looked tired on this warm Saturday afternoon, and the Trojans had far better depth than the Indians. Vic Lindskog, for example, lost 13 pounds that day, going from 196 to 183.

During halftime Stanford students put together a card stunt that didn't sit well with university officials. It showed a picture of a pregnant woman with the slogan reading "TROJANS ARE NO DAMN GOOD." Another one said, "NO THIRD TERM," which one sportswriter said had "cheap political significance," apparently referring to President Franklin Roosevelt's bid for a third term in office. But, students said, it was the third part of a three-part series of card stunts, the first two being "ROSE BOWL" and "FOR TROY." Who were they kidding?

Meanwhile, in the locker room the Indians made no defensive changes. Instead, the players talked among themselves about how to carry out their assignments. Shaughnessy moved around his linemen, linebackers, and backs on defense to close holes in both the line and the backfield. "They certainly had us scouted perfectly," said team center Ed Dempsey, USC's captain. "Stanford used three different defenses and they always seemed to come up with the right answer on everything we tried."

Shaughnessy also found the USC defense the sturdiest the Indians had encountered that season. He said the Trojans' five-man line did not attempt to break through the line of scrimmage but slid sideways in the direction of the play, standing up and holding back the Stanford men. "They used our men to block our own plays," he said. The Indians adjusted by passing more and running around the ends.

"USC's defense that year had a very big line that would hit and slide," Albert said years later. "They wouldn't come across and commit where you could trap them, and it made our passing a little easier because those big devils weren't back in our backfield. But it really cut off our quick openers, probably more effectively than any other team. The quarterback always was pretty well instructed with a game plan going into the game, but Coach Shaughnessy was pretty quick to spot weaknesses in a defense and he sent in a lot of help."

On the first drive of the second half, Stanford, except for one pass play, moved the ball on the ground to the 20. But Peoples intercepted Albert's pass on the goal line. Stanford held, and after a USC punt to midfield, Albert ran the ball back to the USC 40. Standlee ran 8 yards to the 32, but on the next play Banta intercepted Albert's pass on the 15.

At one point in the second half, Albert took over the punting chores from Standlee, who was nursing a charley horse, an injury that would hamper him the rest of the year. Stanford didn't lose much with Albert's punting, however.

At the beginning of the fourth quarter, Stanford got the ball at the USC 49 after a punt. Then the Indians tried a trick play. Albert lateraled back to Hoot Armstrong, who was subbing for Gallarneau. Armstrong unleashed a pass 40 to 45 yards in the air, but Peoples again intercepted, on the 15.

The Indians mounted another drive, getting to the USC 11 before bogging down. Albert then missed a field goal wide right. Albert was having trouble. Stanford had three passes intercepted to cut short their drives in the second half.

Clark Shaughnessy changed the face of college football when he introduced the modern T formation as head coach at Stanford. Photo courtesy of Tournament of Roses Archives.

PETER KMETOVIC, Stanford University
Rose Bowl Player of Game, 1941

Halfback Pete Kmetovic was a dangerous, shifty runner who often turned short gains into long touchdowns. Photo courtesy of Tournament of Roses Archives.

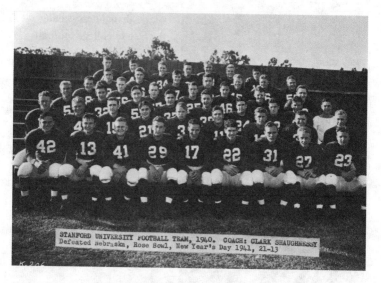

STANFORD UNIVERSITY FOOTBALL TEAM, 1940. COACH: CLARK SHAUGHNESSY
Defeated Nebraska, Rose Bowl, New Year's Day 1941, 21-13

The 1940 undefeated Stanford Indians football team. Among those in the front row are Frankie Albert (13), Hugh Gallarneau (29), Pete Kmetovic (17), and Norm Standlee (22). Photo courtesy of Tournament of Roses Archives.

Quarterback Frankie Albert was a superb punter and place kicker as well as a magician with the ball. Photo courtesy of Tournament of Roses Archives.

The Wow Boys coaching staff: from left to right, Assistant Coach E. P. (Husky) Hunt, Backfield Coach Marchie Schwartz (third from left unknown), Head Coach Clark Shaughnessy, Freshman Coach Harry Shipley, Line Coach Phil Bengston, and End Coach Jim Lawson. Photo courtesy of College Football Hall of Fame.

Halfback Hugh Gallarneau was Coach Clark Shaughnessy's "secret weapon." Photo courtesy of College Football Hall of Fame.

Offensive guard Chuck Taylor may have been the only player to have represented the same school in three different Rose Bowls, as a player (1941), coach (1952), and athletic director (1971, 1972). Photo courtesy of College Football Hall of Fame.

Ten of the starting Stanford eleven line up. On the line from the left are right end Fred Meyer, right tackle Bruno Banducci, right guard Dick Palmer, center Vic Lindskog, left guard Chuck Taylor, and left tackle Ed Stamm. In the backfield from the left are Hugh Gallarneau, Norm Standlee, Frankie Albert, and Pete Kmetovic. Missing from the photo is left end Stan Graff. Photo courtesy of College Football Hall of Fame.

With 4:30 to go, Stanford had the ball on its 20-yard line. Two runs got the ball to the 33. The time was down to 4 minutes. Albert took the ball from center and followed his three backs as if to circle end. Two Trojan linemen broke through, causing Albert to fumble. Stanford's Robesky recovered for a 7-yard loss.

Assistant coach Jim Lawson nearly jumped out of his seat and phoned down from the press box: "Gee whiz, Clark, tell 'em to hang on to that ball. We don't want to lose the game now."

"Tell 'em nothing," Shaughnessy replied. "We're going to win this one."

The ball was now on the 17. Albert walked into the huddle and said, "If any of you guys are tired, you'd better yell now for substitutions 'cause we're going for a long walk—eighty yards. Hey, midget [Al Cole, the 5-foot-8-inch, 160-pound halfback just a shade smaller than Albert], I'm pitching to you right at the expense of old Antelope Krueger [a USC end] and midget, don't miss it." Albert then uncorked a high wobbly pass to Cole, who leaped over Robertson to make the catch at midfield. The crowd was on its feet and would stay that way the rest of the game.

A play later Albert connected with Clem Tomerlin for 25 yards. With the ball on the 25, Albert passed to the tightly covered Meyer and the pass fell incomplete. Cries of pass interference rained down from the Stanford fans, but it wasn't called. In the huddle the ever-confident Albert said, "The same play, same place; and, Meyer, you are going to catch this one."

With Peoples draped over his shoulder, Meyer grabbed a pass from Albert at the 4. From there Standlee crashed over, putting the Indians ahead 14–7 after Albert's conversion. Just as Albert had predicted, the Indians went 80 yards in eight plays.

After the kickoff USC had the ball on its 12 with time running out. Woods attempted a pass to fullback Mel Bleeker. Albert stepped in front of the pass at the 13, picked up a block from Gallarneau, and ran the ball into the end zone. Albert's extra point made the score 21–7.

Shaughnessy substituted for Albert, and as he came off the field, the coach lifted him off his feet with a big hug and kissed him on the forehead. When the game ended thousands of Stanford fans poured on the field in celebration.

"Oh, me," Shaughnessy said. "How those kids battle, how they battle. The tighter the ball game gets, the madder they get and the harder they battle. I've never seen anything like it before. Whew, I'm dead tired."

When a friend told USC coach Howard Jones on the train ride home that USC should have had a tie, he remarked, "No, we never deserved a tie against that ball club. The score tells the true story; a tie would have lied." Jones called Stanford more versatile than the "Vowing Sophomores" and just as effective as either Duke or Tennessee, the two teams the Trojans had beaten in the Rose Bowl the previous two years. "They deserved to win, played the better game," Jones said.

"That's about as smartly a coached team as you'll see this year," Jones said. "And Stanford will do as a Rose Bowl candidate until a better team comes along. I don't think any team in the country can keep Stanford from scoring."

Peoples said that several conference teams had better players than Stanford, but the key to Stanford's success was spirit. He also noted that Meyer was a teammate with him at Classen High School in Oklahoma City. "I can think of at least four passes I threw to him over the goal line in prep school and the son-of-a-gun dropped all of them. Would he drop one Saturday in our game? Oh, no. Not Freddie. And he was my man to cover on that deep throw which led to the second Stanford touchdown. I have a right to be sore."

Statistically, Stanford ran for 144 yards to USC's 113 and completed ten out of twenty-four passes for an additional 208 yards. The Trojans failed to complete a pass in ten attempts. The Trojans did not have possession of the ball in Stanford territory the entire second half. Each team had three interceptions.

Shaughnessy celebrated the win over the Trojans by taking his wife down Palo Alto's main street about 10 p.m. for waffles. Stanford students danced away the night in the women's gym to the music of Charlie Travis and his ten-piece band.

Five days after the victory, Pop Warner finally came around to crediting the T formation with Stanford's remarkable season. "Shaughnessy is entitled to the fullest credit for the phenomenal way he is making use of the T formation," he said. "The methods by which Shaughnessy gets so much deception from the formation is a tribute to his coaching strategy. He has given football out this way a tremendous lift. It is something new and a tonic for the game."

In another significant game that day, Washington edged Cal 7–6, helping the Huskies keep pace with the Indians. Later in the week Stanford moved up to No. 6 in the AP poll. The UCLA Bruins and the fleet Jackie Robinson were up next, this one at the Los Angeles Coliseum.

11

Meeting Jackie Robinson

As Stanford prepared for its game against UCLA, the *Stanford Daily* ran a cartoon with the headline "Dynamite Won't Stop This Injun." It showed a Stanford Indian waving a tomahawk while traveling in a race car headed on a road to do battle with the Bruins. On a hill above the race car, a Bruin is pushing over a boulder while saying, "O.K. Jackie Boy. Let Him Have It!" On the road in front of the car stands an African American man, clearly a reference to Jackie Robinson, getting set to push a plunger down on TNT. The stereotypical caricature, with the addition of a tail, replies to the Bruin, "Yas suh boss."

Earlier, on September 20, 1940, when an Associated Press story carried a typographical error, the *Stanford Daily* ran the story with the error that said former UCLA star Kenny Washington, while playing as a pro, broke away for a "330-yard run." The headline over the story said, "Kenny Washington Sho' Do Travel."

This wasn't just the work of immature college students. Sportswriters on newspapers across the country called the handful of blacks playing college football Negroes or colored boys. Washington and Robinson often were described as "the flashy Negro back" and "the sensational Negro back." That's how readers could tell how many, or how few, African Americans suited up on a Saturday afternoon.

Los Angeles Times headlines often referred to Washington as "Kingfish." The *Times* referred to Sam McDonald as "the old Negro groundskeeper" at Stanford Stadium. African American football players often were targeted with excessive violence on the field, although no evidence of that existed in PCC football in 1940.

Michael Oriard points out in *King Football* that *Collier's* magazine wrote about a "gorilla-chested old East Texas Negro," who was the unofficial mascot and trainer for an orphanage team. Oriard noted that *Los Angeles Times*' Dick Hyland "set up a 'miracle eye' camera to discover the secret of Jackie Robinson's elusiveness as a running back—merely human sight was inadequate—the elaborate procedure created a distinct sense that Robinson's body and instincts defied human limits. No one set up a miracle eye camera to demystify Tom Harmon's open-field running, or performed psychological tests on Sammy Baugh. Perhaps . . . Robinson [was] simply more wondrous to those who saw [him]. But perhaps the wonder [he] invoked derived from [his] race."

In an era in which few African Americans played college football, the University of California at Los Angeles was the exception. No other school had black players in the Pacific Coast Conference besides UCLA, which was one of the few to recruit African Americans. In 1939, in addition to the Bruins' Washington and Robinson, two other African Americans played prominent roles on the team: Woody Strode and Ray Bartlett. All but Barlett were starters. Of the three, Washington, a running back, was the best. Washington went on to play pro football, Strode became a Hollywood actor after a brief professional career, and Robinson became the most famous of all when he broke the "color line" in Major League Baseball.

Before them, African American players in college football were few and far between. Fritz Pollard earned All-American honors at Colgate in 1915 and was inducted into the Pro Football Hall of Fame in 2005, Paul Robeson starred as end for Rutgers in 1917, Duke Slater played tackle for Iowa from 1919 through 1921, and Brud Holland was an All-American end at Cornell in 1939. For one school to have four black players was unprecedented.

"UCLA was a friendly place for the black student, and the gifted black athlete was welcome," Arnold Rampersad wrote in his biography of Robinson. "Eager for fame, the university placed a premium on athletics . . . also because the young university was on the whole more democratic, UCLA reached out to black athletes when other universities turned their backs on them."

Said Bartlett, "I would say that UCLA was ahead of its time, and the coaches were too. I don't think any of those coaches showed any racial prejudice."

In his autobiography, Strode wrote that UCLA's athletic director wanted to make UCLA a national name, and the color of a player's skin did not matter. "As far as [he] was concerned we were all Christian, all went to church on Sundays, and took our baths on Saturday," Strode wrote.

Not until World War II began did the integration of college football teams begin to quicken because of the need to replace players who were serving in the military.

After playing a rugged game against USC, the Indians were grateful for taking on UCLA, a team that hadn't won a game so far that year. The Indians were favored 2.5 to 1 to beat UCLA in the Bruins' homecoming game on Nov. 2.

The Bruins started the year 0-5, scoring 19 points while giving up 41. They had never lost a game by more than 7 points and never allowed any team more than 9 points. Going into the Stanford game, they had lost 9–6 to Santa Clara, 9–6 to Southern Methodist, 7–0 to Oregon State, 9–7 to California, and 7–0 to Texas

A&M. They ended the year winning one game out of ten. Nonetheless, with elusive Jackie Robinson, the Bruins were dangerous. In addition, the game was being played at the Los Angeles Coliseum, where UCLA drew the second-largest crowds of any college team in the country. In four home games the Bruins attracted 248,000 fans, runner-up to Michigan's 252,552. The Stanford game would draw 55,000.

Robinson was an extraordinary athlete. He was the first four-sport letterman in UCLA history. In 1940 he led the PCC in scoring in basketball with a 12.4 average in twelve league games, won the NCAA title in the long jump (24 feet, 10¼ inches), and played baseball, although he hit only .097. He did everything but play in the band at halftime. Some called him "the Jim Thorpe of his race," referring to the Native American athlete who won five letters in five sports at Carlisle at the beginning of the 1900s.

Robinson almost beat Stanford by himself in 1939, and the following year he almost single-handedly kept the Bruins in the Stanford game. In '39 he scored both touchdowns in the 14–14 tie, one on a 52-yard run from scrimmage and the other on a 51-yard interception return. Tiny Thornhill had called him the greatest backfield runner he had seen in his twenty-five years of coaching. Others called him the second-greatest back in the country behind Michigan's Tom Harmon in 1940.

Robinson returned nineteen punts for 399 yards in 1940, a 21-yard average, then a national record. His career average of 18.8 yards ranks fourth in NCAA history. He finished second in the PCC that year in total offense with 383 yards rushing and 444 passing, all behind a weak offensive line. In his two-year career, Robinson averaged 5.9 yards a carry. In their opening game, the Bruins' loss to Southern Methodist, Robinson scored the only touchdown on an 87-yard broken field punt return.

The Bruins' coach Babe Horrell held secret practices but made no secret of the fact he planned to pass the ball more against the Indians. He also shuffled his lineup to move Robinson back to right half, where he had proved so effective in 1939. "We'll open up," Horrell said. "All of our former cripples are now in good shape. If we lose, no alibis."

That didn't surprise Shaughnessy. "That's just what we expected," he said, and about Robinson, "we know he'll be dangerous."

Shaughnessy as usual played down the Indians' chances of winning the game, but Horrell was optimistic. "We haven't conceded anything to Stanford," he said. "We shouldn't be surprised if we should happen to win one this week." Shaughnessy worried his players were looking ahead to next week's game against Washington. He spent the week building up the Bruins. Shaughnessy also noted that his players were tired. "You know we're outweighed 10 to 20 pounds in each game we play," he said. "It takes something out of our boys."

The coaches expected guard Chuck Taylor to play, but he didn't; Ken Robesky started in his spot. Jack Warnecke also was going to play but not start. Ed Stamm replaced him.

With each game Albert was getting better. A reporter asked Shaughnessy what would happen if Albert were injured. "I'd fall off the bench," he replied. Shaughnessy knew he would be in trouble if anything happened to Albert and tried to protect him in scrimmages. Shaughnessy trailed along behind Albert and blew his whistle whenever his star player was about to be tackled hard. Just before the UCLA game during a scrimmage, Albert went down hard after a vicious tackle and Shaughnessy screamed, "Get a stretcher." When Shaughnessy reached the moaning Albert, the quarterback leaped to his feet and said, "I just wanted to see if you'd miss me, coach."

Hundreds of Stanford fans rode Southern Pacific trains to the game. The men and women students slept in sleeping cars separated by three lounge cars in which they ate sandwiches and cookies and drank beer, coffee, and soda. They left Friday night and returned Monday morning. In Los Angeles they stayed at the Arcardy Hotel for two dollars a night single or the Chapman Park for three dollars. They also visited Coconut Grove, Earl Carroll's, and the new Palladium to listen to Tommy Dorsey and his orchestra. The next day they saw a particularly rough game.

After UCLA punted following the kickoff, Stanford moved downfield from the Bruins' 44 to the 18, where Kmetovic fumbled. The Indians got the ball right back and began their first touchdown march. Kmetovic made the big play of the 66-yard drive, sweeping around right end behind blocks by Banducci, Meyer, and Palmer, and was headed for the goal line until Robinson knocked him out of bounds at the 5. Gallarneau then scored over right guard behind blocks by Banducci and Palmer. Albert's extra-point kick made it 7–0.

The Indians and Bruins exchanged punts, the last one by Standlee traveling nearly 60 yards in the air. Robinson electrified the crowd when he gathered in the punt over his shoulder at the 25 and turned upfield toward the left sideline. Bartlett put a ferocious block on Palmer at the 35 to free Robinson to midfield. Kmetovic had a shot at tackling Robinson, but center Ted Jones shoved him out of bounds. Lindskog finally pulled him down at the Stanford 35 for a runback of 40 yards.

The Bruins moved the ball to the 13-yard line before bogging down. From there the Indians went on a long drive. Kmetovic picked up 5 yards over right tackle. Then Standlee took a handoff from Albert and faked a pass before bursting off right tackle. Bartlett hit Standlee but bounced off as the hard-running back stumbled forward. He regained his balance just as Warnecke leveled Robinson. Standlee leaped over Robinson and rambled to the 38 before being tackled. The 44-yard run was Standlee's longest of the season.

Gallarneau picked up 14 yards, but two penalties threatened to stall the drive. Stanford had the ball on the 16 on third down and 14 yards to go for a first down. Albert took the snap, raced to his left, and, with a Bruin hanging from his right foot, jumped and threw to Tomerlin in the end zone. Tomerlin leaped over Robinson and Bartlett to make the catch. Albert again kicked the extra point, making the score 14–0.

In the third quarter Robinson again showed athleticism and daring when Standlee punted from the 45. The ball bounced loose at the 16 with three Stanford players waiting to touch it down. Robinson suddenly burst between the startled Indians, picked up the ball, and started downfield. At about the UCLA 45, Standlee managed to grab Robinson by the leg. The elusive runner freed himself, looping back across the field to his 35 before heading toward the goal again. Palmer finally got a hand on him before Gallarneau piled on to drop him at the Stanford 43 for a 43-yard punt return that may have taken 100 yards to complete.

The Bruins were able to gain only 7 more yards before being forced to punt. With the ball on the Bruins' 43, the Indians moved the ball to the UCLA 23. Albert fumbled when hit while trying to pass, and the Bruins recovered on the 33.

UCLA moved the ball to Stanford's 36, where, on third and eight, left halfback Leo Cantor fired a 20-yard pass to Don Macpherson at the 16 over Hoot Armstrong and rolled into the end zone. Shaughnessy said after the game, "We gave UCLA that first touchdown, just a little mistake on defense, but the boys are entitled to a mistake now and then." Robinson (who else?) kicked the extra point.

Early in the fourth quarter, Stanford saw another drive fall short. The Indians had a first down from the 50-yard line, but they turned it over on downs at the 2. The Bruins immediately punted from their end zone to Kmetovic, who fielded it at the 50 and got down to the 42.

Three downs later the Indians had moved the ball only 8 yards. It was now fourth down and 2 yards for a first down. Shaughnessy often would use the next play to describe how Albert used his intellect with successful results: "The question was whether to do the ordinary thing and kick with chances about 20 to 1 that the ball would go into the end zone and UCLA would bring it out to the 20, making a move of only 10 yards on the exchange of the ball," Shaughnessy said. "Albert figured the chances were too much against his hitting the coffin corner."

Albert had been watching the situation, much like a chess player, for several previous plays and felt certain he knew a pass that would work. Albert crossed up the Bruins by passing to Kmetovic, who caught the ball at the 18 near the sideline and was pushed out at the 11 for a first down. "Nobody in the stands, nobody, agreed with his judgment," Shaughnessy said. "To them it was unsound football."

When Albert later came off the field, Shaughnessy said to him, "That was quite a play. What was your reason? Why didn't you kick it?" The coach said he wasn't questioning the call; he only wanted to know how Albert arrived at his decision. Albert told Shaughnessy, "Coach, if I'd kicked, the chances were I'd gone over the goal. I decided to gamble the ten yards against a first down; besides I felt positive I had that spot open."

On the next play Gallarneau ran over right guard for 7 yards to the 4. He then followed that up with a touchdown over center. Albert missed the extra-point attempt, leaving the score 20–7.

Stanford started another drive at its 14 and reached the Bruins' 27 with a first down. On third down Albert kept the ball, running left. While stiff-arming a Bruin, Albert tripped and fumbled. He picked up the ball, reversed to his right, and threw a pass. Robinson picked it off at his 20, returning it to the 33.

On the first play Robinson dropped back to his 20 to pass but instead took off running to the Stanford 38 before being run out of bounds. He faded back to pass again, but again ran, taking the ball to the Stanford 22. At the 19 Robinson dropped back again, faked a run, then passed to end Milt Smith, who tumbled into the end zone with 1 minute remaining. Robinson added the extra point to make it 20–14. Stanford then ran out the clock.

For the game Stanford gained 410 yards to the Bruins' 169. The Indians ground out 372 rushing yards, led by Standlee with 136 in eighteen carries and Gallarneau with 114 in twenty rushes. Kmetovic picked up 81 yards in eleven rushes. Robinson led UCLA with 70 yards on ten carries. Albert completed two of ten passes for 38 yards and one interception, but there was no need to pass with the ground game in high gear. UCLA had the ball fifteen times, giving it up eleven times on punts.

About Robinson, Shaughnessy said, "Once a year is too much for me with that boy on the other side. A very dangerous back. One of the best I have ever seen. We saw two of the best backs on the Coast out there today. Robinson and Standlee. But the rest of my boys were good, too."

He said his players were tired. "This was a hard, bruising game. It took more out of us than any game so far. . . . This team has gone farther than I have had any right to expect. . . . These boys are great fighters. That's why we have won so far. . . . Did you see how they went out there and got that third touchdown after UCLA scored? That's the way they have been going all year."

Shaughnessy compared the Indians to his 1925 Tulane team that went undefeated. "The same type of boys; small but hard fighters. We had to depend on opening up the defense on quick plays just like this year. The other fellows made the most yards; we made more touchdowns."

The Washington Huskies were up next for the game that would decide which team went to the Rose Bowl. Huskies' scout Pest Welch noted that the Indians played more conservatively against the Bruins than they did versus USC. Stanford's "speed and spirit" impressed Welch, who called the Indians the "fastest team I have seen."

12

Closing In

The team many picked for first in the Pacific Coast Conference traveled to Palo Alto to play the team many said would finish last. The Huskies had lost only one game, that to the Minnesota Golden Gophers 19–14 in the first game of the year. After the Minnesota game, which saw the Gophers convert Huskies' fumbles into two touchdowns and a safety, Washington had allowed only 6 points in five games.

The Gophers were now ranked No. 2 in the Associated Press poll, with Stanford in sixth place.

As many as sixty-five thousand fans were expected to file into Stanford Stadium on November 9, paying $1.50 for reserved seats and $1.10 for end zone seats, with the Rose Bowl on the line. Stanford was a 10–7 favorite. Despite rain earlier in the week, the weather and the field were ideal for the 2 p.m. football game.

"Never mind the Rose Bowl," snapped the Huskies' coach Jimmy Phelan. "We're playing Saturday in the Stanford Stadium and nowhere else." Phelan wasn't buying that last-place stuff about Stanford. He was well aware of Shaughnessy's talents as a coach. When he heard whom Stanford had picked as its new coach, he told his assistants, "From here on those Stanford kids are going to be tough." He predicted that Stanford would finish first in the conference.

Washington had three All-American candidates: center Rudy Mucha, guard Ray Frankowski, and halfback Dean McAdams, who was the team leader. During the 1939 season he ranked sixteenth in the nation with his .461 percent in pass completions, third on the basis of average net gain per attempt. He even caught ten passes. Frankowski made the All-Coast team in 1939. Mucha was the Huskies' best lineman. He was a solid blocker on offense and a terror as a linebacker.

The Huskies were far more experienced than the Indians. Washington returned nine starters from the 1939 squad. The Huskies also were rested after having two weeks off between games. In addition, the Huskies had an advantage over earlier Stanford opponents because they had scouted more of Stanford's games.

Phelan liked the role of the underdog to the Indians. He was going to beat the T formation by outscoring the Indians. "Nuts on a defense for Clark Shaughnessy's T formation," Phelan said. "We're going to try to score early and often and let the defense take care of itself. We're not going down there to stop Stanford. Stanford will have to stop us. If my team has the ball and has enough offense to keep the ball most of the game, how is the other club going to run up a score on us?"

After viewing films of Stanford games, Phelan decided to employ a 6-2-2-1 defense and occasionally shift to a 5-3-2-1 system. On offense the Huskies used the single wing. With an average weight of 190 pounds, far heavier than Stanford's defense, Washington hoped to grind down the Indians with powerful runs up the middle.

Worn out from their hard-fought game against UCLA and the train ride home on Saturday night, the players had Monday off to rest. "Don't even want you on the field," Shaughnessy said.

"Stay away. What you fellows need is rest." Teams usually stayed in Los Angeles overnight and left the next day, but Shaughnessy ordered them home. "They didn't like it much at first," he told football writers at the San Francisco Press Club, "but when the tired bunch of youngsters actually got on the train and realized how fagged out they were, they told me they were glad we were on the way home."

Shaughnessy downplayed the success of his remarkable team. "We've been lucky," he said. "We've had to gamble and we've won gambling, but we've been lucky."

He also talked the typical coach's talk about his opponent. "When I think of what Washington has," he said, "I don't see how we can stop them. We must simply outscore them. And then I think of the way our boys have surprised me every Saturday and I don't know. Frankly, I don't know what they can do or will do, but our first team is beginning to be a good football team. They improve every week."

Shaughnessy might have had something up his sleeve for the game. He introduced several new plays during practice that week. He was banking on the team's speed overcoming the Huskies' size. On defense the Indians would use a six-man line with three line-backers and two defensive backs. They lined up with five men on the line, then Dick Palmer shifted into the line in an effort to stop the run. Sometimes Stanford would move a defensive back into a linebacker's position, leaving Albert alone to defend against the deep pass. That showed the confidence Shaughnessy had in Albert's pass protection talents.

The Indians might be playing without four starters: Warnecke, Taylor (ankle), Lindskog (hand), and Standlee (charley horse). In addition, backup halfback Al Cole turned his ankle in a volleyball game the night before the game, and coaches doubted he would play.

The night before the important game, the assistant coaches addressed two thousand students on campus. They told the crowd they liked the Indians' chances. Shaughnessy said he wasn't sure why they were so optimistic. "I guess it's that Frankie Albert. Stay around that fellow long enough and you'll believe you can do anything. He's got the team believing 30 seconds is too long to take to score a touchdown once they get under way."

The next day Stanford took the opening kickoff but was able to move the ball only to the 34, where Albert kicked on fourth down. A 28-yard run by Gallarneau had been wiped out by a backfield-in-motion penalty. Albert had to make a leaping catch of a bad snap from center Lindskog, who may have been bothered by his bandaged hand. Albert still managed to get off a 62-yard punt that the Huskies' captain Bill "Bomber" Gleason gathered at the 3, dipped back to the 1, and then moved up to the 14.

Stanford held and McAdams's punt from the 10 rolled dead on the Stanford 39. Primarily on the ground, the Indians moved the ball to the Huskies' 7-yard line, but the drive stalled. Albert then missed a field goal.

The Huskies took over on their 20-yard line and pushed the ball to their 39, when the first break of the game came. A vicious crossblock injured Standlee's ankle. Sophomore Milt Vucinich replaced him. "When Standlee came off the field our No. 1 offensive threat was gone," Shaughnessy said. "He took with him our bread-and-butter plays. But the boys got their heads together and Albert and Gallarneau decided that Gallarneau would carry all of Standlee's plays from his regular right half position. . . . That shows Gallarneau's natural versatility and adaptability." Standlee was a cinch to make Grantland Rice's All-American team as a fullback—pictures already had been taken—when the injury slowed down his season.

The Huskies pushed the ball to their 49, but the Stanford defense stiffened. McAdams's punt rolled into the end zone for a touchback. On first down from the 20, Albert punted to Gleason at the Huskies' 32. He returned the ball 10 yards. On first down Palmer knocked the ball loose from Gleason and Albert recovered the fumble at the Stanford 45 as the first quarter came to an end.

Again the Indians moved the ball, driving to the Huskies' 23 before Clem Tomerlin dropped a fourth-down pass while being hit. On first down from the 23, Bruno Banducci pulled down Gleason 7 yards behind the line at the 16. McAdams punted on second down and the ball bounced to the 32. Kmetovic grabbed the ball, but the Huskies forced him out of bounds at the 33. Stanford failed to pick up much yardage, and Tomerlin knocked Albert's punt out of bounds at the 9.

On the next play tailback Jack Stackpool broke a tackle attempt by Taylor behind the line and raced 55 yards before Kmetovic ran him down at the Stanford 36. The Indians held the Huskies to no gain on the next two plays before McAdams hooked up with Earl Younglove on a 36-yard TD pass over Albert. Younglove caught the ball at the 15 and crossed the goal line untouched. John Mizen's kick put Washington up 7–0.

Albert didn't seem particularly worried. When Standlee's replacement Vucinich joined the huddle after Kmetovic returned the kickoff from the 10 to the 39, Albert said, "Look who's here, the slashing Slav from Lowell [High School in San Francisco]." Said Vucinich later, "That helped to take the pressure off."

The Indians drove into Husky territory when at the 22, Albert threw to Kmetovic at the 5, but McAdams stepped in front of him for the interception. Just after he caught the ball, Vucinich slammed into him, causing the ball to pop out. Kmetovic and Steele reached for the ball, and Steele came away with it before Palmer dropped him at the 6. It was the third lost scoring opportunity.

Steele fumbled on the next play, and Fred Meyer recovered for Stanford at the 12. Four plays saw the Indians lose 7 yards, with a fourth-down pass from Albert to Kmetovic falling incomplete. Another scoring chance passed for Stanford.

The Indians held again, forcing the Huskies to punt from their 28-yard line. McAdams punted 45 yards to Kmetovic, who ran behind an Albert block 20 yards to Stanford's 47 as the half ended. It was the first time Stanford had been behind at the half.

Reserve guard John Kerman remembered saying to himself that Shaughnessy was going to "read us the riot act. We got into the dressing room and he told everyone to be quiet and pay attention. He then pulled out those charts with plays on them. He told us to memorize our assignments and when the time was right he would send them in to Frank and that was all. No tirade, no threats, just relax and get ready for the second half."

Gallarneau ran the second-half kickoff back from the 7 to the 36-yard line, but after three plays Albert went into punt formation at his 28-yard line. Lindskog, who was playing with a bandaged hand—Shaughnessy said it was the worst cleat cut he'd ever seen—centered the ball over Albert's head. Albert recovered the ball at the Stanford 19. Washington ran the ball six times to the Stanford 9. A McAdams pass fell incomplete. John Mizen then kicked a field goal from the 16 to give Washington a 10–0 lead.

All of a sudden Stanford's game had gone flat. Starting at their 26, the Indians managed only to get to the 42 before Albert went into punt formation. His kick traveled 22 yards. With the ball in good field position, McAdams passed again to Younglove, who ran to the Stanford 39 before Albert knocked him out of bounds. Stackpool then carried on the same play that led to the Huskies' touchdown and gained 9 yards before being tackled by Vucinich. The struggling Indians took a time-out.

With 5:30 remaining in the third quarter, Washington had the ball on the Stanford 30 with 1 yard to go for a first down. It didn't look good for the Indians. Then came the turning point of the game. Moments after the Stanford cheering section let out a "Give 'em the ax," Chuck Taylor went to work. On three straight plays the rugged guard stopped Husky runners short of the first down, each time blowing by the All-American candidate Mucha to tackle the runner. For the remaining six possessions of the game, Washington was able to gain a total of only 9 yards.

Taylor had suffered an ankle injury in the game against UCLA. He sat out most of that game. The injury limited his speed and mobility. "I had a pretty well wrapped ankle which kept me from doing much except for playing my position and protecting a territory of five or six yards. By virtue of being semi-crippled and confined to a small area that particular day, I got pretty lucky because I couldn't chase myself and make a lot of mistakes and run out of there." Taylor said he was able to make the stops because he couldn't move much out of his position. "I don't think it was the turning point, but at least it stimulated the team and from then on Frank and the other guys did a helluva job." A revived Stanford team then rolled into high gear against the exhausted Huskies.

On first down Gallarneau gained 5 yards up the middle and on the next play broke several tackles to pick up 10 yards to the Stanford 44. When Albert came back into the huddle, he told his teammates, "I've got good news, gang. The play is forty-four. Pete don't miss this one 'cause it's going to hit you right in the belly."

When they broke from the huddle, Kmetovic went into motion followed by defensive end Bill Sloan, who was no match for Perfect Pete's speed. Albert hit Kmetovic with a pass just across midfield, and the speedy halfback raced untouched into the end zone. Albert kicked the point after with 3 minutes remaining in the third quarter.

"[Kmetovic's touchdown] was a go-stop pass. We dug it out of the bag between halves," Shaughnessy said. The Huskies' defensive back backpedaled to keep himself between the goal and Kmetovic, so Pete slammed on the brakes, turned to catch the ball, and then sprinted 47 yards for a touchdown.

After the Huskies ran the kickoff back to their 30 and were stopped on two runs, McAdams tried a Statue of Liberty play, one rarely seen these days in football. That's when the passer fades back with his arm raised and a halfback comes behind him to take the ball. The ball carrier then either runs around end or looks to pass. Gleason decided to pass. Bad choice. From the 20 he threw to Younglove, but Albert wasn't fooled, intercepting the ball at the Washington 46 and returning it to the 42. Albert had to rub it in a bit with some rare trash talk. "Now you went and done it. Look at Phelan over there. What do you suppose he thinks of that skull you just pulled?"

A 13-yard pass from Albert to Meyer took the ball to the 29. Vucinich ran up the middle for just short of 10 yards as the quarter ended. Albert sneaked for the first down on the next play to the 16. Gallarneau gained 2 yards, then Al Cole, playing despite a sprained ankle, took a lateral from Albert but tripped and fell for a 5-yard loss. From the 19 Albert hit Tomerlin with an 11-yard pass between two defenders. Gallarneau picked up 4 yards to the 4 behind a crushing block by Vucinich. Gallarneau carried again to the 1. He was then dropped for a yard loss. On third and two Gallarneau bulled over against the eight-man line for the go-ahead touchdown. Albert kicked the point after to make the score 14–10.

Phelan would say later that he thought the Indians played better without Standlee. "Not that Standlee isn't good, but when he was removed, the Stanford team just seemed to say, 'Well, The Chief is out, now we've got to play twice as well to make up for it.' And that guy Vucinich, who took Standlee's place, wasn't a statue. He almost pulverized my ends a couple of times."

Stanford's defense held again, and the Huskies punted. The Indians took the ball at their own 26 before gaining a first down at their 40. Albert then ran a bootleg—he faked to a halfback then tucked the ball behind his leg and ran the opposite direction—to the Washington 46. Actually, the bootleg was an improvised play by Albert. Vucinich beat the count and went by Albert, who still had the ball. When the quarterback had no one to hand the ball to, he tucked it behind his leg and picked up 14 yards in the other direction. "From that time on, including the following year, I was never sure when I was going to keep the ball. So that there was a good fake, Frank would never tell me," Vucinich said. On the next play Kmetovic fumbled and the Huskies recovered on their 44.

Stanford's defense held, but then so did Washington's. The Huskies had the ball on their 33-yard line when McAdams dropped back to his 21 and looked to pass to Younglove. Kmetovic made up for an earlier fumble by stepping in front of Younglove to intercept the ball at the 43, bobbling it until he reached the 40. Kmetovic streaked down the sidelines to score, putting the game out of reach. The Huskies blocked Albert's point-after attempt. Neither team mounted much offense after that, and the game ended with Stanford on top 20–10.

Gallarneau was the unsung hero of the game. "When Standlee was hurt, Gallarneau took over the Big Chief's heavy duties—the smashes and the slashes," Shaughnessy said. "How many times did he carry the ball this afternoon? I should say nearly 30 times [actually 24]. A really great back. They never trapped him. Terrific pickup. Fast. No man on the team could run with him." Shaughnessy told a reporter he kept quiet about Gallarneau's skills because, "Do you advertise your ace in the hole?"

After the game a reporter asked Albert what had impressed him most about the game. "Shaughnessy's chin when we were behind," he said. "It was trembling like a kite in a hurricane."

Despite trailing most of the game, the Indians dominated the Huskies, statistics showed. They had the ball for seventy-six plays compared with Washington's forty-five. They ran up 297 total yards to 188 for the Huskies. The big difference was in passing, with Stanford throwing for 135 yards to Washington's 60. Gallarneau rushed for 100 yards on twenty-four carries while Kmetovic carried fifteen times for 56 yards. Albert completed eight passes in eighteen attempts for one touchdown.

After the game George Dunscomb of the *Saturday Evening Post* asked Shaughnessy how he felt. "How do you think I feel after Chicago? I guess they're not feeling sorry for me back in the Big Ten now," he said with a smile. Then he remarked, "That Taylor. That Taylor. He's all fire and combustion."

Vucinich told *San Francisco Chronicle* reporter Bob Stevens after the game, "You know, Bob, we weren't bothered very much at all. Sure it was close, but somehow all of us felt we'd win. Say, it's better than beating Polytechnic." Vucinich was referring to his Lowell High School team in San Francisco beating its rival.

The boys were in high spirits. Kmetovic exclaimed, "Say, it's sensational. I can walk around San Jose with head high, prance around the campus with a smile, and even the professors are playing ball. Why last year, while we were losing, all the profs did was ask you if you played football and then flunked you."

Years later Kmetovic said, "After that game I think that all of us knew that we could beat anyone in the country. We knew that Clark Shaughnessy could pull anything out of the hat that we needed to win, and he did, too."

Asked to compare the Indians to Minnesota, Phelan answered, "There's nothing to choose. Minnesota has backs that may scamper all the way to a touchdown. So has Stanford. Minnesota has power. So has Stanford. You can't beat Stanford down with power. We lost to the best team on the coast today, that's all." He told a reporter from the *Stanford Daily*, "I wouldn't pick any team over Stanford. The Indians beat us today. Minnesota was lucky to beat us," Phelan said, without committing himself as to which team was better.

Shaughnessy said Stanford played its best game of the year. On November 12 the AP moved Stanford from sixth place to fourth with Minnesota No. 1.

As Stanford prepared for Oregon State, Pop Warner continued to sing Shaughnessy's praises. "Give him credit," Warner said. "Shaughnessy has taken that T formation we used when I played at Cornell in 1892 and made it work as it has never worked before. This is because he has added his own ideas. There is no mystery about Shaughnessy's success at Stanford as I see it. The only mystery is where the ball is on some of those tricky plays of his."

13

Life on Campus

In 1940 football didn't dominate an athlete's life as it does on today's campuses, where players spend most of their time outside the classroom on the practice field. The Wow Boys belonged to fraternities, held jobs on and off campus to make ends meet, attended campus functions, and ran for student body office. Football was only one part of being a student.

Students strolled the eucalyptus-studded campus, studied in the Hoover Library, and played touch football on the grass of the eighty-eight-hundred-acre campus. Men wore slacks and V-neck sweaters over white shirts. As for the women, "The 'thirties also brought a trend toward naturalness and comfort with the establishment of the sweater and [knee-length] skirt as the campus uniform," the *Stanford Daily* noted. Red, or cardinal if you'd prefer, was the most worn color. And what did the *Stanford Daily* think of the women on campus? "No more does that noxious old maxim apply: 'Four out of five women are good-looking—and the fifth goes to Stanford.'. . . Those days are gone forever. All Stanford women are queens now. . . . But do they have the requisites to be good housewives? Anyone knows that 99 percent of local womanhood is looking for a mate," the *Daily* noted in an editorial.

Students also didn't miss out on the latest in entertainment. They saw the movies at neighboring Palo Alto theaters, including James Cagney and Ann Sheridan in *City for Conquest*, and *The Sea Hawk* with Errol Flynn. They also took in campus concerts by famed musicians such as Isaac Stern and Yehudi Menuhin.

One student who was seen walking to and from classrooms where he was auditing classes in the business school was John F. Kennedy, the future president of the United States. "I picked Stanford principally because of your ex–Student Body President and Student Manager Tom Killefer," he said. "He was my brother's roommate at Harvard, and [his brother] sneered so at the Florida climate when he was staying with us there that I had to find out if it really was the climate or just Killefer," he said, with a grin. "So far he's right, but wait till I see that first cloud." As for the Stanford football team, Kennedy remarked, "You have no idea how it feels to yell for a winning team." He graduated from Harvard, which was not known for its football prowess.

Like college students of any era, Stanford students were concerned with rising tuition and the cost of living. They were heartened by a *Stanford Daily* story that found their tuition $112 a year lower than the average charged by seven eastern and midwestern universities of equal scholastic caliber. Stanford's 4,577 students—men outnumbered women 2.5 to 1—each paid $412 a year in tuition. That was during a time when a loaf of bread cost 8 cents and gasoline 18 cents a gallon, the average yearly income was $1,906, a new home cost $3,925, and the national debt was $43 billion. Americans also were told their life expectancy was 62.9 years.

The *Daily* also kept students informed of the armed forces draft and conducted polls on the likelihood of war. Forty-four percent of Stanford's students thought it unlikely the United States would become involved in war, and 32 percent gave it a fifty-fifty chance of remaining neutral. The student newspaper noted as the 1939–40 school year came to a close, "And to the whispered echo of marching feet and gunfire across the Atlantic, Stanford is still eating its dinners at 6:15." That was to say, life goes on, especially on a college campus.

Five months later seventeen million men across the nation waited anxiously for the draft lottery to classify them for a year of military service. Twenty-four students and two professors from Stanford were among those whose names were drawn. Nationwide, the eighteenth number drawn in Washington DC belonged to John F. Kennedy, who later distinguished himself in the navy. He never returned to Stanford. Within two years Kennedy and hundreds of those current and former Stanford students would be serving in World War II in the Pacific and Europe.

As the presidential election approached on November 5 between President Roosevelt and Wendell Willkie, Stanford students cast their voices in a straw poll. By a ratio of three to one, they expressed their preference for Willkie.

From the 1920s through the 1950s, fraternities and sororities dominated the nation's system of higher education. About a quarter or a third of all U.S. college students belonged to a Greek organization. At Stanford almost eleven hundred students out of four thousand joined one of the twenty-four fraternities and nine sororities. Virtually all of the campus leaders and athletes were members, and their grade point averages were just about the same as those of the nonaffiliated students. University-wide, the average grade point was 2.57 on a 4.0 scale, a far cry from the grade inflation seen today on college campuses.

Frankie Albert joined wholeheartedly in campus life. He was active in his fraternity, Delta Kappa Epsilon, and was a traditional prankster. He wasn't beyond putting cracker crumbs on a fraternity brother's sheets, a pan of cold water by his bed, or a turtle in a teammate's uniform. When Milt Vucinich, his fraternity brother, was sunbathing, the fun-loving Albert threw a bucket of water on him. Vucinich vowed to get even. A few days later he got a bucket of water in a room above an entrance and talked one of his fraternity brothers into coaxing Albert outside so he could drop the water on him. When Albert walked out, Vucinich dropped the water only to find out Albert had been wearing one of Vucinich's new suits.

To help with living expenses, Albert worked his way through Stanford waiting on tables at the Pi Beta Phi sorority, mowing lawns, and washing cars. One day he showed up at the Pi Phi sorority house wearing a tuxedo. Why? the women asked. "I thought you girls needed a change of pace," Albert replied with a Cheshire cat grin.

In 1941 he lost a race for student body president. His teammate Ed Stamm was elected student body president in 1942.

Duke Gallarneau was a heavyweight boxer who was a Pacific Coast Conference and campus champion. He also found time to play rugby along with Pete Kmetovic. Norm Standlee was a counselor in a dormitory.

Academics placed a demand on the players' time as well. The strain of balancing football was reflected in their collective grade point average, which was the lowest of the varsity sports at 2.33.

One interesting sidelight of the preseason practices was that Bill Kreutzmann, a freshman fullback that year, later married one of Shaughnessy's daughters. The Kreutzmanns became the father of Bill Kreutzmann Jr., drummer for the Grateful Dead. The football-playing Kreutzmann broke an ankle and missed six weeks of the season. He never figured prominently in the Indians' plans.

No college campus was without drinking, and Stanford's football players were not immune. Not long after Shaughnessy came on campus, Standlee pleaded guilty to drunken driving and was sentenced to spend one hundred hours of labor at the Palo Alto city woodpile. He was arrested after his car missed a turn, plowed through a fence, and stopped in a field.

There was little doubt, though, that the main attraction outside of the classroom at Stanford was the success of its football team. In the fall virtually all of Stanford's social activities related in one form or another to supporting or appreciating its undefeated team. The players really were the BMOC—Big Men on Campus.

14

Another Tough Matchup

It sounds like a familiar refrain, but Stanford was wary of its next opponent. Oregon State had lost only one game—to Washington 19–0—and tied USC. The Beavers had the makings of a team that would go to the Rose Bowl the next year. The Indians were bruised and battered after three tough games in a row. Except for the USF game, none had been a walkover for Stanford.

Some sportswriters were predicting that the Indians were due for a letdown despite the 2-to-1 odds favoring them. They would be without one of their best players, Norm Standlee, who was on crutches after an ankle injury on top of that nagging charley horse. Milt Vucinich was a formidable backup, and the Indians would get some surprise play out of a fourth-string fullback.

Pete Kmetovic had a pulled thigh muscle and returned to practice only on the Thursday before the game. His play against the Beavers seemed to indicate no long-term problem.

Assistant coach Phil Bengston told the weekly sportswriters' luncheon that Oregon State should be favored. "No, I'm not kidding. Sure, we feared them all, but this is one game that has Mr. Shaughnessy and all of us worried."

Oregon State wasn't buying it. osc publicist Bud Forrester said that Bengston's story was a well-rehearsed plot, nothing more. He said that as he was riding the train from Corvallis, where Bengston had scouted the Beavers, Bengston kept telling him how good Oregon State was. "Honestly, I think he was just practicing on me to make a swell speech before the Press Club Monday noon," Forrester said. "His rehearsal on the train was well spent, even if I did have to listen to it over every clatter of the tracks and every whistle of the engine."

Forrester's only concession was that his Beavers were the best team on the coast behind Stanford. He and the Beavers' coach Lou Stiner thought the game was a toss-up.

Oregon State had a big bruising team that had stopped Washington State's prolific passer Bill Sewell. The Beavers were hoping that with a four-man line and three linebackers, they could stop quick-opening plays from developing into long gainers. osc was banking on John Leovich at left end to stop Kmetovic from sweeps, while calling on right guard Bob Rambo to thwart Albert's flat passes.

Stiner worked up the plan based on his knowledge of the T. In 1935 he had brought in a backfield coach from the Chicago Bears to install the formation at Oregon State. He didn't have the fast backs or the ball-handling wizardry of a Frankie Albert to make it work, so he shifted back to the single wing.

The Beavers were blessed with three excellent passers in their single-wing power offense. Their system used the quarterback as a blocker. QB George "Little Abner" Peters was second-string All Coast behind Albert, although their assignments were far different. Stiner called Peters the best player he had ever coached. The backfield may have been the fastest in the league behind Stanford.

osc's best player was Jim Kisselburgh, a 195-pound fullback out of Hollywood, California's Fairfax High School. He finished second to Standlee for All-Coast honors and was a third-team All American. Shaughnessy called him the best fullback on the coast behind Standlee and praised the entire backfield. "For the first time this year, I'll have to do some coaching," he predicted.

On the line the Beavers had two All-Coast players, Vic Sears at left tackle and Leonard Younce at right guard. Left end John Leovich was third-team All Coast and considered the team's best athlete by some. He also played baseball and hockey. The Beavers also had depth, with their second team virtually equal to the starters. Stiner substituted a new team each quarter, keeping both units fresh.

Stiner believed this was the greatest team he had yet coached. (The next year he led the Beavers to the Rose Bowl and a victory over Duke 20–16.) "We have the best team on the coast outside of Stanford," Stiner said. "We'll score. They may outscore us, but so help me, we'll score."

Up to two days before the game, Shaughnessy thought the Indians would lose to Oregon State. Then, he said, team morale and sharpness began to pick up. Rod Parker, a fourth-string fullback, caught Shaughnessy's eye. He would be Vucinich's backup. Things began to look up.

Albert continued to astonish Shaughnessy. At the weekly meeting of the Northern California Sportswriters Association, Bengston said that Shaughnessy told him in a private conversation that Albert was making him a winning coach. "Albert called plays in the second half [of the Washington game] that Mr. Shaughnessy did not think were possible. It is true too much has been written about the Stanford coaches and not enough about the boys."

On game day attendance was down to about thirty-three thousand for the game, despite it being the Indians' last home game of the year. Oregon State wasn't a big draw, and fans were looking ahead to the Big Game against Cal in two weeks.

The Beavers kicked off to Gallarneau at the 15 and he returned it to the 29. Oregon State employed a four-man line and dropped back players to stop the quick-opening plays. It was a no-brainer to figure Stanford would pass more with Standlee out, but that was not the case. The Indians ran right at the Beavers, driving the length of the field in 4½ minutes to score. Kmetovic ran for 29 yards and 13 yards. With the ball on the 1, Vucinich powered over the left tackle, lost the ball, and while in a sitting position retrieved the ball in the air for the touchdown. Albert kicked the point after.

"In one respect, [Stiner's] plan was successful," Albert said. "We had no long gainers, but our backs did reel off four or five yards a crack."

Late in the first quarter, Albert, who took over Standlee's punting duties, got off a 55-yard punt. The Beavers mounted a drive from their 41. Halfback Dan Durdan ran for 20 yards before Albert grabbed Durdan's straight arm and pulled him down at the Stanford 35. At the 30 Durdan started to run around right end, then stopped to toss a pass over Kmetovic's head to Norm Peters at the 10. He ran in untouched to tie the score.

Stanford stalled on the next drive, and Albert unleashed an 89-yard punt that stopped on the 1, but Clem Tomerlin fell on the ball and his momentum carried him into the end zone. The touchback put the ball on the 20. Albert's kicking got the Indians out of trouble all day. Despite one punt of only 14 yards, Albert still averaged 52.6 yards a punt on eight kicks. On the 14-yard kick, Albert had tried for the coffin corner. After the game Shaughnessy said Albert wouldn't be trying that kick any more. "He likes to get everything he can into that ball, remarkable for a small man, and we may have to find someone else for the coffin corner department."

The game turned into a defensive struggle in the second quarter until Kmetovic slashed off left tackle at the Stanford 40 and veered right toward the Stanford sideline. An Oregon State player knocked field judge Lee Eisen into the pole vault pit. Eisen bounced up to notice that Kmetovic had stepped out of bounds by inches at the 50, nullifying Perfect Pete's touchdown. That was the last threat of the half, and the teams went into the locker room dead-locked at 7.

Stanford held after the second-half kickoff, then took over at midfield after Kisselburgh's 28-yard punt. Three running plays netted 9 yards, and on fourth and one at the 41, Albert gambled. He handed off to Gallarneau, who picked up the first down. On the next play Kmetovic appeared trapped 10 yards behind the line after taking a lateral from Albert, but Kmetovic slipped away after a crushing block by Taylor. Thirteen yards past the line of scrimmage, Kmetovic put on a move that froze defensive halfback Bob Dethman at the 26. Kmetovic completed the 39-yard TD run untouched. Albert converted to make the score 14–7.

Ninety seconds later the Indians scored again. On the OSC 23, Durdan took a reverse and was 10 yards downfield when Fred Meyer hit him, causing a fumble that Kmetovic fell on at the 33. Two plays and a penalty later, OSC pushed Stanford back to its 39. Then Albert threw one of his few passes of the day, hitting Gallarneau at the 1. Before crossing the goal, Gallarneau stumbled, fumbled, and fell into the end zone. The officials ruled he had possession to complete the 39-yard touchdown. Just as Albert had delivered the ball to Gallarneau, a Beaver hit the quarterback with a crushing blow. Lying on his side, he appeared to be injured. When the team physician ran out to him, he asked where it hurt. Albert looked up with a smile and said, "I was just admiring that catch. It sure looked pretty." Albert then kicked the extra point for a score of 21–7.

Three minutes later the Indians put the game out of reach. Trailing by two touchdowns late in the third quarter, the Beavers tried to play catch-up by passing more. At the Oregon State 36, Dethman threw a deep pass that Kmetovic intercepted at his 30 and ran back to his 39. Runs by Gallarneau and Albert put the ball on the Beavers' 40. Vucinich's backup Rod Parker rambled around right end for 12 more yards. Al Cole picked up 10 on a shovel pass. With the ball on the 18, Cole dropped a bullet pass from Albert, and on the next play Albert overthrew Meyer at the goal line by inches. Again Albert called on Parker, who headed left, cut back to his right through center, and, leaving a trail of would-be tacklers, boomed into the end zone. Albert put the finishing touches on Stanford's scoring with his fourth extra point.

Parker, a senior, said years later that he approached Shaughnessy with a question before the game. After sitting on the bench for most of three years, could he get in the game that day? "He said, 'Parker, I have a winning combination.' I turned away. Then he said 'but I will try to use you.' . . . After the game he came up to me and said 'Parker, if I had you four years ago you would be an All American. You are the fastest man on the team.'"

Shaughnessy put in his substitutes, which led to the Beavers' second touchdown. They recovered a muffed lateral at the 19. Two plays later Dethman hooked up with Leovich for an 11-yard touchdown pass to lessen the gap to 28–14. That was as close as it got. With the ball on the Stanford 46 late in the game, Dethman threw a pass that Albert picked off at the 21, and the Indians ran out the clock. The victory gave Stanford the PCC title. The following week Stanford moved up to third in the AP poll, with Minnesota No. 1 and Texas A&M second.

In all, Albert threw only four passes. Shaughnessy told his players to keep running the ball. "We hit for four and five yards a pop against the Oregon State four-man line as that is the weakness of it," Albert said. "The line spacing is such that it is quite easy to pick up short yardage," but "the four-man line does hold the long gaining plays to a minimum."

Bill Leiser, the *San Francisco Chronicle* sports editor, sang Albert's praises. "Gosh the kid can put the ball in one hand and make a fake with it, to one man, and with the other hand, in which there is no football, he can fake to another man, and make defending players who are looking chase both men while he still has the leather close to his jersey. There's an expertness in that that few men can ever approach."

Stiner had nothing but praise for Albert's punting. "Our safety men must have sore necks by running backwards and grabbing those things out of the air," he said.

Albert credited assistant coach Marchie Schwartz for developing his punting. "I was holding the ball fairly low and pointing the tip upwards," Albert said. "This gave me pretty good height but the distance wasn't so good. All last week Marchie worked with me on a plan of keeping the ball high, almost level with my head, and pointing the tip downward. I was surprised to find the ball spiraling way out there, with that tail end hook that gives it a nice forward bounce if the safety man didn't catch it."

Shaughnessy said Oregon State was the best team the Indians had played. "I was worried about their offense and we devoted the entire week to defensive drill. The determined northerners were terrifically hard to stop once they had the ball.

"Until last Thursday," he continued, "I wouldn't have given a dime for our chances to win against Oregon State. On Thursday the team morale and sharpness began to pick up, and Parker began to show important ability, along with Vucinich, at fullback, and it began to look as if we'd be able to play a fair game."

Stiner countered: "Stanford is the greatest attack team I've ever seen. . . . Before game time Saturday I was never so sure we'd win a football contest in my life. I really thought we had them."

In total yardage Stanford outgained Oregon State 337 yards to 268. Kmetovic carried for 85 yards and Gallarneau for 67 yards. Albert completed one of only four passes, that the touchdown to Gallarneau. Stanford also intercepted five passes.

Except for Gallarneau, who was badly bruised and sat out practice until the following weekend, the Indians escaped virtually unscathed. Standlee's ankle injury still slowed him. They had two weeks to recoup before the Big Game.

Now that Stanford had all but earned the trip to the Rose Bowl, the next step was deciding whom the Indians would invite to Pasadena as their opponent. Among the teams mentioned were Cornell, Minnesota, Texas A&M, Notre Dame, Tennessee, Boston College, and Georgetown. One name that didn't pop up in the speculation was Nebraska.

Albert was hoping to play A&M, Gallarneau either Cornell or Minnesota, and Stan Graff wanted Cornell because "I'd like to prick that Cornell bubble." Shaughnessy was having none of this talk. "We've still got to beat California a week from Saturday," he said.

15

Big Game Fever

There is the "big game," and then there is the Big Game. Stanford had played several big games (i.e., important games), but what set the Big Game apart from the others was its pageantry and rivalry, not to mention significance. The matchup between the California Bears and the Indians has been played since 1892. Today the Big Game ranks as the tenth-longest rivalry in college football.

The Indians needed to win this final regular season game to ensure their trip to the Rose Bowl.

Over the years won-loss records didn't matter when California and Stanford met on the gridiron. Upsets were common, and the Golden Bears would have liked nothing better than to spoil their rival's perfect record.

Each school had two weeks to get worked up over the November 30 game. So intense was the school spirit that the game was often an afterthought to the students—but not the alumni, fans, and the press. Because the pregame festivities tended to get out of hand, Cal student body president John McPherson and his Stanford counterpart, Bruce Jessup, signed an agreement that neither college would invade the other's campus to carry out pranks or mischievous acts. It was the eighth year the two schools had entered such an agreement. Every year it had been broken. It didn't take long for that pact to be broken again. The relatively short distance between the two campuses, Palo Alto on the peninsula about thirty-three miles from San Francisco, and Berkeley across San Francisco Bay, made it easy for students to carry out their high jinks.

Stanford students painted a large red *S* on one of the streets running through the Cal campus. Police also arrested a Stanford student for a traffic violation. The student said he was heading to Grizzly Peak to paint the big *C* overlooking Memorial Stadium red. Cal students burned *C*s into the lawn at the Stanford Quad.

On the day before the game, in Berkeley fraternities and sororities held open houses, a parade marched down streets, a bonfire and rally took place at the Greek Theater, and a dance was held in the men's gym. At Stanford the students put on a parade consisting of "a motley crew of floats and students [who] will assemble at the Fiji House dressed to represent anything from the Hoover Libe [Library] to a blind date with the curves of a broom handle," the *Stanford Daily* said.

After the parade five thousand students and fans headed to a bonfire at Lagunita Lake. The bonfire consisted of wood—mostly from ten thousand beer boxes—stacked sixty feet high and sprayed with five hundred gallons of oil donated by a local Shell dealer. Once the fire roared into the sky, students threw an effigy of the Cal Golden Bear into the blaze to thunderous cheers as it burst into flames.

Coach Stub Allison's Bears had bounced back to become a respectable team after their 41–0 shellacking at the hands of Tom Harmon and his Michigan Wolverines in their first game. They picked up a win over St. Mary's 9–6; lost by 3 points to Washington State; beat UCLA 9–7; lost to Washington 7–6; lost to Oregon

State 19–13; and then beat USC 20–7, 1 point less than the score of Stanford's victory over USC, and Oregon 14–6 compared with Stanford's 13–0 score. Comparable scores often are misleading. In fact, odds on the game favored Stanford 3 to 1.

Harry Shipkey, Stanford's freshman football coach, saw two Cal games: Michigan and Oregon. "I noted an unbelievable improvement, especially in the line. Cal's line charge, both on defense and offense, is second to none on the Coast. The danger to Stanford is that Cal is not a team on the downgrade, but one that is only now realizing its full capabilities."

Key players for California were guard Bob Reinhard, who was named an All American at season's end; halfback Orville Hatcher; and fullback Jack McQuary. Hatcher had a 53-yard touchdown run against USC, while McQuary was one of the league's top rushers.

The schools had agreed to two weeks instead of the usual one between games so that the Big Game would not fall on Thanksgiving weekend. Shaughnessy welcomed the extra time. "These boys need rest. They need a chance at their books. [How many times today do you hear that from a coach?] They've had too much pressure and strain. They need a chance to relax." Neither team practiced during the first two days of the two-week period.

Stanford's appearance in the Rose Bowl was all but guaranteed, although the vote by the league's schools would have to wait until after the Big Game. Some doubt about whether Stanford would get the bid if it lost to Cal cropped up three days before the game. If the Indians lost and the Huskies dominated Washington State, the two teams would be tied with records of 6-1. Because the Indians beat the Huskies they seemed likely to get the bowl bid. There was one hitch. Faculty representatives from the ten PCC schools—Montana and Idaho also belonged, although they didn't play in the league round robin—would vote on which team to send to Pasadena. Six of those representatives were from Northwest schools and could vote for the Huskies, making the vote six to four. If the reps were to vote provincially, the best team might not go to the Rose Bowl.

The Northwest schools were still sore about the clear dominance of the California schools in recruiting and the resultant revenues that winning teams brought in. Playing in the Rose Bowl would give Washington an eighty-five-thousand-dollar payday. Stanford could ensure it would get the bowl bid only by beating the Bears.

The extra week gave more time for Standlee's aches and pains to go away. Shaughnessy was confident he would play. "He won't have much practice, but he's a football player, and you can count on him to go whether he's had any practice or not. Surely, our plans include Standlee, and he'll be in there, too." But Shaughnessy later backed off. He doubted that Standlee would even suit up for the game. It would be like that for the entire two weeks before the game: No, Standlee's not playing. Yes, Standlee's playing.

In fact, team physician Fritz Roth had cleared Standlee to play. He would begin practicing the Thursday of the week before the game and begin scrimmaging the following Monday. Then his ankle flared up over the weekend, making his availability again in doubt. By Thursday before the game, he was ready to play again.

A sportswriter asked Shaughnessy if Gallarneau, the leading ground gainer in the Pacific Coast Conference, was Stanford's most dangerous backfield man. Ever diplomatic, Shaughnessy, not wanting to slight Kmetovic or Standlee, replied that no one was more dangerous. Gallarneau had gained 474 yards for an average of 5.7 yards a carry. "When you're the leading ground gainer in the Pacific Coast Conference, you're a real ball player," Shaughnessy said. Gallarneau's father, who had prohibited his son from playing football in high school, was at practice the Saturday before the game to lend moral support.

Going into the Big Game, Stanford led the PCC in offense and was second in rushing defense. The Indians rolled up 1,417 yards rushing to lead the league and were second in passing offense, despite completing only thirty-seven of ninety-four passes for 671 yards. The Indians yielded just 117.6 yards against the rush.

On the Friday of the first week, Shaughnessy said his team went through its worst workout of the season. "But it doesn't mean much. I rather expected them to look sloppy and they did," he said. The three days of rest also made the players rusty, he said. "But it's natural to expect a letdown. . . . I worked them hard for almost four hours polishing timing and spent a good deal of time with the seconds and thirds [strings]. I'm afraid we're going to need reserves."

Allison, who held practices behind locked gates, said stopping Stanford's offense would be difficult at best. "You can't gamble in planning a defense in this game. . . . Against them you have to defend against everything. You can't overlook anything. Records show that Stanford has been stopped in this department, and in that. But the Indians have always gone into some other department to score. You've got to cover the field when you defend against them, and it's a tough job." But, he said, "We see no reason at all why we can't be at tops and go in and win the game."

Allison was worried about the T. He said he was more impressed with the T than any other formation he had seen. All week the team worked on a 4-3-1-1-1 defensive alignment. More often than not in this alignment, linebackers would shift and it would become a 7-2-1-1 defense.

Shaughnessy stuck to a five-man line, and the Bears would test it repeatedly. They attempted only five passes in the game.

Assistant coach Marchie Schwartz said the Cal game would be Stanford's toughest of the year. "I mean that. The Bears have improved vastly in their last three games. Aside from the psychological lift of The Big Game, California has a great line and more backfield reserves that Stanford can offer."

No Big Game could go by without some controversy. Shaughnessy complained about Cal's use of the "rocker shift," which initially brought protests from Washington's Jimmy Phelan after its game. It's somewhat of a misnomer to call it a shift because no players change positions. The rocker part has the linemen change from a low crouch to a high crouch, with no two men moving at the same time. Official rules said that any movement designed to draw the defense offside was illegal.

Marchie Schwartz termed it a throwback to "old-time football that has been outlawed for years." "Mind you, I have yet to see California play," Shaughnessy said. "I'm new on this coast. But from movies I've seen of California games I would say the rocker is not in keeping with the letter or intent of the national rules." Shaughnessy said he had no plans to formally protest the move, leaving it to game officials to police it. A national rules committee was looking at the films, but no decision had been made by game time. After the season was over, the shift was ruled illegal.

Stanford was accused of a little skullduggery of its own. Questions were raised about whether Albert sometimes handed the ball forward instead of backward or laterally, which would be an illegal forward pass. Neither of the two complaints would be a factor in the game.

On game day Shaughnessy was up at 7 a.m. at the Rancho Hacienda, the team's overnight stay in Pleasanton, about 25 miles south of Berkeley. The players arose in time to hustle downstairs for a chalk talk by Shaughnessy and then head for breakfast. Later in the morning some listened to the Army-Navy game in Philadelphia, others played ping-pong, and others talked among themselves. Shaughnessy took Albert off by himself for a half hour to discuss game strategy.

During the Army-Navy halftime, Shaughnessy was hooked up nationwide on the radio to talk about Stanford's remarkable season. Shortly thereafter the team boarded a bus for Memorial Stadium for the 2 p.m. kickoff. The good-natured ribbing the players earlier had been giving each other ended, and they put on their game faces. Gallarneau was so intense that he put his shoulder pads on outside his jersey. After putting on their uniforms, they listened to one of Shaughnessy's rare pep talks. He told his players that "football is like life—dog eat dog." "Let's get the first bite," whooped the Indians as they ran out onto the field.

On the Bears' side of the field, their All-American tackle Bob Reinhard, who played with Albert at Glendale High School during their championship year, came down with the flu on Friday night and spent game day in Cowell Hospital. Some Stanford players were feeling ill as well. Shaughnessy didn't say anything about it for fear it might sound like an alibi if the Indians lost, but half the Stanford team had sore throats a couple of days before the game. Kmetovic spent one night in the hospital. The players tired easily, especially Taylor, who left the game several times because of exhaustion.

Memorial Stadium was filled almost to its eighty-thousand-seat capacity. The fans had begun arriving early at the compact campus, where parking was at a premium. Several hundred fans were perched on the hillside in Strawberry Canyon above the stadium for a free view of the game. They also had a spectacular view of the San Francisco skyline across the bay.

The winner of the game would receive the Stanford ax. The origin of the ax is disputed. One story has the ax with a fifteen-inch blade being purchased in 1899 by Stanford for $3.50 in a San Francisco store. Another says workmen found it while digging a trench in the 1880s on the Stanford campus. It then disappeared until the first ax rally on April 14, 1899.

Whatever the truth, Billy Erb first used the ax to decapitate a stuffed bear to rally students at a baseball game. A mob of Bear fans wrested it away. A student ran into a butcher shop and cut off the long handle to make it easier to conceal. Cal kept the ax in a vault for the next thirty-one years, taking it out only for baseball and football rallies. Stanford students stole it back in 1930, when they posed as Cal students on a photo assignment. They used fake cameras and tear gas to pull off the theft. In 1933 the two schools agreed to make the ax the trophy of the Big Game.

The Cal rooting section of ten thousand was the largest in the country. With only forty-five hundred students, Stanford couldn't match them in size or noise. About twenty-two hundred students made up the card section, with women allowed for the first time this year, to perform the twelve stunts. In card stunts, stacks of cards are placed on seats in the student section on the 50-yard line. On a signal, each student in the section would hold up a specific card. The thousand or so cards created a picture that could be seen across the field. Stanford originated card stunts in 1904 at the Big Game when a graduate student, Thomas Jewell, came up with forming a block *S* by having students hold pieces of white muslin and raising them above their shoulders.

Even that is in contention, as California tradition has it that Cal invented card stunts in 1910. Over the years as the stunts swept the nation, they became more elaborate. Before the game Cal students formed a card stunt that showed a gold *C* on a blue background while both sides taunted each other.

When Stanford ran out onto the field, Shaughnessy commented sarcastically, "It must have rained here last night." The Bears apparently had watered the grass heavily to slow down the Indians' speed burners.

After Stanford kicked off, one of Cal's best players, halfback Jim Jurkovich, left the game for the rest of the day with a severe cleat wound to the head. Cal had started at its 25, but two offside penalties and Taylor's tackle of Jurkovich's replacement, Carlton Hoberg, for a 5-yard loss pushed them back to the 10. On second down Hoberg punted to Kmetovic on the Stanford 47. He returned the ball 4 yards.

The Indians seemed in good field position at the Cal 49. After Kmetovic and Standlee each gained a yard, Albert went into punt formation on third down. Instead, he tried a long pass to Kmetovic that went incomplete at the 5. Albert then punted out of bounds at the 15.

The battle on the field was rough. Stanford center Vic Lindskog was knocked woozy trying to tackle Hatcher, who also suffered a gash over his right eye. He played the rest of the game with a bandage around his head. Standlee limped out in the second quarter, and Taylor was wearing himself out battering the Bears' center, Harland Gough. Taylor's work paid off when Gough centered the ball over Hatcher's head just before a charging Taylor hit him. The Indians tackled Hatcher for a 16-yard loss.

With the ball on the 33, Hoberg punted 33 yards to the Stanford 34, where Kmetovic fielded the ball and returned it to the 42. Gallarneau on his first carry of the day ran 22 yards behind blocks by Taylor and Standlee. But the Bears dropped Kmetovic for a 4-yard loss on the Stanford 40. Albert passed 12 yards to Tomerlin, and then Gallarneau ripped off 7 yards for a first down.

Kmetovic picked up 20 yards to the 1 with a little razzle-dazzle, shifty running, and great blocking by Stamm, Taylor, and Tomerlin. Hatcher grabbed Kmetovic at the 5, and the 160-pound halfback dragged him to the 1 as the quarter ended.

Kmetovic then took a handoff and dived over the left side of the line for the touchdown. Albert converted and Stanford led 7–0.

The Bears started at their own 24. On second down, at the 25 Hatcher burst off right tackle and bolted to the 48 before Kmetovic dragged him down. The next play Gough centered the ball under McQuary's legs, and end Stan Graff recovered at the Bears' 44.

Albert hit Gallarneau with a pass at the 35, which he carried to the 30. A penalty, two short runs, and two incomplete passes put the ball on the 32 with fourth down and 11 yards for a first down. Albert then missed a field goal.

The Bears moved the ball from their 20 to Stanford's 41, when Gough again centered the ball poorly. It bounced back wide and low and rolled 24 yards until kicker Stan Cox recovered at the Bears' 35. It was the third bad snap by Gough under Taylor's relentless pressure. Gough had to keep his head down when centering the ball, but because of Taylor's aggressiveness, he may have been looking up too soon while snapping the ball and thereby losing concentration.

On first down Albert took the snap, spun counterclockwise, and handed the ball to Gallarneau, who ran for 11 yards before Gough tackled him. Standlee then took a direct pass from center and threw a pass to Graff good for 9 yards. Two plays later Standlee limped off the field to be replaced by Vucinich.

On the next play Albert took the snap under center and spun to hand the ball to Vucinich but kept the ball instead and took off. The play certainly confused the Bears. They tried to tackle Vucinich, while Albert rolled to the 3 for a 12-yard pickup. On the next play Vucinich did get the ball, plunging ahead for a yard. On second down Kmetovic and Vucinich faked to the right at the snap, while Gallarneau took a counterclockwise handoff and plowed off right tackle. He ran into a handful of defenders but managed to squeeze into the end zone. Albert missed the attempted conversion, leaving the score at 13–0.

At halftime a California card stunt depicted a bear chopping down a Stanford tree with an ax and then setting fire to it. A Stanford stunt had a bear cub with its mouth opened while an eight ball moved across the section and into the bear's mouth. Stanford also set up a red Indian with hand upraised and then waved at the Bears' rooting section. Cal responded by having a bear shake hands with an Indian.

Stanford's rooting section early and often yelled out its ax cheer:

Give 'em the ax, the ax, the ax
Give 'em the ax, the ax, the ax
Give 'em the ax, give 'em the ax, give 'em the ax where?
Right in the neck, the neck, the neck
Right in the neck, the neck, the neck
Right in the neck, right in the neck, right in the neck there.

The third quarter turned into a defensive battle as the teams exchanged punts.

Then came a crucial play that saw Albert become a goat in one moment and a hero the next. On the Bears' 49 Albert, on third and fourteen, went into punt formation. Instead of punting Albert stepped forward to pass. Tackle Cox grabbed Albert by the right leg at the 43. As he tried to get away, Ray Dunn lunged at Albert, who threw the pass intended for Al Cole. Hoberg at full gallop stepped in front of Cole and started downfield with four blockers in front of him. Albert cut across the field, leaped over one potential blocker, shook off a block by another, sidestepped a third, and caught Hoberg by the right arm at the 10. That slowed Hoberg enough for Jack Francis to catch him at the 5. Albert and Francis finally pulled him down at the 1 as the third quarter ended.

It appeared that with four downs from the 1 that Cal would edge to within a touchdown of the Indians. On first down fullback McQuary lost a yard, and on second down McQuary got the yard back. McQuary got the call again, but Palmer anticipated the play and dropped McQuary two feet short of the goal. Now it was Hatcher's turn. He tried going around right end, but Tomerlin, Albert, Kmetovic, and Stahle met him for no gain. Stanford took over on downs at the 1.

Albert kicked on first down, punting the yards to Hatcher, who fielded it on the Stanford 48 and ran it back 15 yards. The Bears were within striking distance again. Cal moved the ball to the 22, where, on fourth down, Hatcher unleashed a pass to Dunn in the end zone. He had both hands on the ball when Albert, three inches shorter than Dunn, leaped and knocked the ball away.

Stanford's offense had been stymied most of the second half. The Indians moved the ball to the Cal 48. Then Gallarneau fumbled after a 5-yard gain, and Hatcher recovered. Cal clearly had the Indians back on their heels. The Bears drove the ball to the Stanford 41, when Hatcher tried to pass to McQuary. Stahle intercepted and ran the ball back 7 yards to the Indians' 43. Stanford drove to the Cal 32, where the exhausted Indians turned the ball over on downs with 3:30 left to play.

That was enough time for Cal to score a touchdown, but not enough for two. The Bears moved to the Stanford 30 after Hatcher's 35-yard gallop. Cal got to the 10, when McQuary burst over left guard and bulled his way into the end zone. McQuary converted to lessen the gap to 13–7.

Football rules didn't allow for onside kicks in those years. With 16 seconds left on the clock, Vucinich took the ball back to the 15, when the clock ran out. Hundreds of Stanford fans poured on the field to congratulate their heroes.

Two players played the entire 60 minutes, quarterbacks Frankie Albert and Bill Elmore. Later that night Kmetovic and Rod Parker spent the night in the Stanford Hospital with the flu. Parker played in the game during the last 5 minutes despite a doctor's recommendation.

After the game Cal student body president McPherson turned the ax over to Stanford. It was the first time since 1935 that Stanford had the ax in its possession. Cal students chanted, "We'll get it back next year," which they did, and Stanford students retorted, "The hell you will." And then, "The hell we won't." On and on. To everyone's dismay, Stanford students tore down the steel goal posts, a task thought impossible because they were imbedded in concrete. The rumor was that two Stanford students had sneaked into the stadium on Friday night and cut the posts halfway through to weaken them.

Shaughnessy was just happy to escape with a victory. "We played one of our poorest games of the season," he said. "We had only two running backs, without the real Standlee in there. He did well, but not like the Standlee I've seen. I'll tell you our boys don't scrimmage, and they just can't be expected to stand up under sturdy, fierce 60-minute football. Sure they weakened in the second half.

"You know we might have staved off that California touchdown if I had put fresh men into the line, but I knew we'd take a five-yard penalty, so I let it go. We played a five-man line defense against a power-attacking team, on the assumption we could concede them small yardage but hold down the long gainers. If it hadn't been for that little Hatcher, we might have succeeded better. Hatcher and McQuary are two fine backs."

Shaughnessy praised guard Dick Palmer, whom he described as "amazing, simply amazing." He particularly was referring to the goal line stand on the Indians' 1.

Allison, of course, was disappointed in the outcome. "We wanted this ball game. We were up against a very, very good ball club. They had a good offense, a good defensive line, they had kicking, passing, and speed in the backfield. We made mistakes and Stanford capitalized on them like any good team would. When we had the opportunity, we failed."

About his Bears, Allison said, "I'm proud as hell of them. Under adverse conditions they didn't quit and fall apart. They were determined to score and finally did. It's been a pleasure to work with these boys, especially the seniors."

In total yards the teams were very close. Stanford gained 233 yards to the Bears' 224. Cal completed only one pass in five, Stanford three out of ten. Each team punted seven times, attesting to the defensive struggle. Hatcher carried the ball twenty-nine times for 126 yards and McQuary sixteen times for 74 yards. Gallarneau led the Indians with 92 yards on twelve rushes, followed by Kmetovic with 68 yards on twelve carries.

In the locker room after the game, assistant coach Marchie Schwartz dispelled rumors that he would replace Babe Horrell as UCLA coach. "Listen," Schwartz said, "I've never been happier in any football setup than I am right now. Shaughnessy's been like a father to me."

In its seven PCC games, Stanford had scored 141 points and allowed 66. Second-place Washington scored 134 and allowed 35, 20 of those to Stanford in their lone defeat.

The night after the game, hundreds of students descended on the San Francisco Golf and Country Club from 10 p.m. to 2 a.m. for the second annual Big Game Dance to the music of 1936 Stanford alumnus Freddy Nagel and his orchestra.

Stanford capped the end of the regular season by finishing second in the AP poll behind Minnesota. The Golden Gophers received sixty-five first-place votes to Stanford's forty-four.

On December 6 the All-Pacific Coast team included four Stanford players: Meyer, Albert, Standlee, and Kmetovic. Banducci, Taylor, Lindskog, and Gallarneau were named to the second team.

The next day, when the AP All-America team was announced, only one Stanford player was picked—Albert. Surprisingly, no other Indian made the second or third teams. Injuries may have kept Standlee off the team, but he received honorable mention. When he was told he was named All American, Albert said, "Just a lucky break for me when Standlee cracked his knee."

Later Shaughnessy was selected as football's Coach of the Year.

16

Bring on Nebraska

The night after the Big Game, it became official: Stanford was to represent the PCC in the twenty-sixth Rose Bowl. It would be Stanford's seventh appearance in the game. (The Indians had lost three, won two, and tied one.) The selection prompted a letter from Whitey Fuller, Dartmouth's publicity director, to Stanford publicist Don Liebendorfer that brought up the Indians' win over Dartmouth on that rainy day in 1939. He congratulated Stanford on going "from the Mud Bowl to the Rose Bowl."

The next morning a streamlined edition of the Board of Athletic Control held a special meeting. The three-member board made up of athletic director Al Masters; professor William B. Owens, president of the National Collegiate Athletic Association and a Stanford faculty member; and Norm Standlee agreed to ask Nebraska to play in the New Year's Day game.

Their choice had been narrowed because Texas A&M had lost, Tennessee and Boston had agreed to play in the Sugar Bowl, Cornell and Penn refused to come west, and Michigan and Minnesota were prohibited from playing in postseason games. Seventh-ranked Nebraska was the best team available. The Huskers had lost only one game—to Minnesota 13–7 in their first game of the year. Nebraska beat Indiana 13–7, Kansas 53–2, Missouri 20–7, Oklahoma 13–0, Iowa 14–6, Pittsburgh 9–7, Iowa State 21–12, and Kansas State 20–0.

Nebraska had to poll Big Six members on whether they would waive a league ban against postseason play. On Sunday morning Masters announced that the Cornhuskers would be Stanford's opponent in Pasadena. It would be the first bowl game in what would be the long, storied Cornhusker football history. And it came on the fiftieth anniversary of collegiate football at Nebraska.

Nebraskans hadn't had such big news in a long time. Gregg McBride, the veteran sportswriter for the *Omaha World-Herald*, said of the selection, "It's the greatest thing that has happened to Nebraska since William Jennings Bryan ran for the presidency." The student newspaper, the *Daily Nebraskan*, blared in huge type, "BOWL ENTHUSIASTS DISRUPT CAMPUS" with a subhead, "Pep-fired rooters paint town red." The story reported that "horns have been tooting, drums beating, mobs running, classes dismissing and lungs bellowing the cheer and enthusiasm that celebrate the acceptance of the bid to play."

The celebration lasted twenty-four hours. The university canceled classes and three thousand students stormed the state capitol, demanding the governor lead the singing of the school song, "There Is No Place Like Nebraska." Backs Herman Rohrig and Vike Francis addressed the crowd. "This is an honor of a lifetime," Rohrig shouted, while Francis told the crowd, "We won't let any Husker fans down on New Year's Day."

"We were like a kid who got his first bicycle," Rohrig said about being picked to play in the Rose Bowl. "You wish for something and you think you're never going to get it. Then it happened. Everybody was so overjoyed they began running around the campus."

Said Wayne Blue years later, "It was something out of this world, getting asked to play in a game halfway across the country like that. We'd never imagined it, not in our wildest dream. A lot of us were naïve farm boys. Not very many of us would have set foot outside the state if not for football. I just couldn't visualize it. . . . I also didn't figure we were that good."

Ed Schwartzkopf, a guard on the Huskers' squad, said, "I remember my professor got us all into his classroom, then jumped up on the desk and dismissed class. Everyone went crazy. It was quite a scene."

Nebraska coach Lawrence McCeney "Biff" Jones knew his work was just beginning. He said the defensive assignments the Huskers had learned over the year would have to be thrown out and new strategies put in to stop the T. "Our hardest task will be between now and New Year's Day. If we don't, then we are likely to be caught short."

The demand for Rose Bowl tickets was tremendous. Ticket requests inundated Masters. "There will be special blocks [of tickets] for the alumni of the two schools, of course. Lincoln [home of the University of Nebraska] reports an amazing demand. I guess the whole state's figuring on coming out. And there will be tickets available to the public, too. . . . Right now, it looks like a quick sellout."

The first day tickets went on sale at the Rose Bowl, thousands stood in line under a cold, gray dawn. Hundreds brought cots, blankets, pillows, thermos jugs with coffee, and caps with earmuffs to spend the night in line. Two hours after the box office opened, 15,000 tickets were sold. That's all that were available. Stanford alumni bought up 44,000 and Nebraska received 9,800. Some 13,745 went to Tournament of Roses people.

Tickets that sold from $3.50 ($50.63 in 2006 dollars) to $5.50 ($79.55 in 2006 dollars) were hard to come by. Dozens of Nebraskans who had no tickets when they left home were forced to dole out $25 to scalpers if they wanted to get into the Rose Bowl.

Newspapers were full of stories saying that never before had the bowl game attracted so much attention from out-of-state visitors. Masters said he could have sold 250,000 tickets to the game.

In 1940 the Rose Bowl really was the "Granddaddy of All Bowl Games." The Bowl Championship Series to determine the national championship was years away. Although it was the biggest game of only a handful of year-end games, sportswriters chose Minnesota No. 1 long before the bowl games were played.

The game brought the T formation to the forefront of college football. Stanford's games had been played in the relative obscurity of West Coast football. Now the entire country was learning what the hoopla was all about. The game matched Stanford's deception against Nebraska's brawn.

Shaughnessy gave his team two weeks off to rest up and study for quarterly exams while he traveled to Chicago to help the Bears prepare for their championship game against the Redskins. He told sportswriters he was in Chicago to visit his brothers. The Bears' owner and coach, George Halas, who had only two assistants, asked Shaughnessy to help him. The two men stayed up all night reviewing game films. "We chose about twenty plays. We selected other plays to fit every conceivable pertinent defense Washington might adopt," Halas said. One plan was to send halfback George McAfee in motion in one direction but to have the ball go in the other direction—a counterplay, they called it.

In studying the films, Shaughnessy noticed that Washington stayed in a 5-3-3 defense that had the linebackers moving with the man in motion. "He pinpointed every facet of the Redskins' defense, and his observations were incorporated in our explosive T-formation attack," Halas said. That's when he saw the value of the counterplay, where the ball carrier moved against the grain of the shifting players.

Shaughnessy addressed the Bears before practice one day, an act uncommon for consultants. Shaughnessy's eyes had a gleam to them as he took a piece of chalk to the blackboard. He sketched out the counterplay and then said to the players, reminiscent of his first locker room speech to the Stanford players, "Men, I promise you this one will go for a touchdown and if it doesn't work, I've got another coming up that will." The counterplay used the first modern pro set with two ends split.

Nebraska coach Biff Jones flew to Washington DC to watch the Bears, with their T-formation offense, battle the Redskins for the pro football championship on December 8 before thirty-five thousand fans, the largest crowd to watch a pro football game at the time. If Jones hoped to see a defense that might stop the T, he wasn't going to view it in that game. Halas said, "He [Jones] believed those uninformed persons who claimed that Washington had conceived a strategy which could demolish our T."

Jones said after watching the game that the players, not the formation, made the offense: "Stanford has some good men, but I don't think they can handle the tricky maneuvers the Bears used quite as nifty as Chicago did against Washington."

It's not clear whether Jones knew that Shaughnessy had been helping the Bears, because Shaughnessy had returned home to prepare his Indians for the Rose Bowl. Shaughnessy didn't return empty handed. He brought with him Halas's longtime assistant Luke Johnsos, who would play an important role in the Rose Bowl game. He sat in the press box mapping out plays that he relayed to Shaughnessy on the field based on Nebraska's defense.

The Redskins beat the Bears 7–3 during the regular season, but Washington was no match for Chicago in the championship game. With Shaughnessy's help in preparing them, the Bears rolled over the Redskins 73–0. The Bears gained 273 yards rushing and held Washington to 3. On the first of three plays Shaughnessy called at the beginning of the game, the Bears rushed for a 7-yard gain. On the second the Bears called the counterplay with halfback Bill Osmanski feinting right, then taking a handoff from quarterback Sid Luckman and streaking across the grain to the sideline, where he scored on a 68-yard run.

A dropped pass early in the game lent itself to one of the great quotes of early professional football. The Redskins' sure-fingered Charley Malone let a pass slip through his hands that would have been a sure touchdown. Quarterback Sammy Baugh, when asked after the game if that play might have made a difference, remarked, "Hell, yes, the score would have been 73–6."

One hundred and fifty sportswriters attended the game and fed the word to millions of readers about the wonders of the T formation.

As they were preparing for the Rose Bowl, the Indians learned that the AP had picked Stanford as the third most outstanding team performance of the year behind the Cincinnati Reds, who won the World Series, and the Minnesota football team. To show how much college football dominated in interest over the pros in those days, three of the top four teams in that honor were from colleges, while the NFL Bears finished seventh.

Shaughnessy also received some vindication for his coaching abilities while at the University of Chicago, when the school newspaper, the *Maroon*, editorialized December 3 that his performance at Stanford "had disproved charges occasionally leveled against him that he failed to inspire confidence . . . and lacked the ability to make his men fight." The editorial called him a "superb tactician," noting, "Not only did the Indians outthink their nine rivals, they outfought them in every game and it was Shaughnessy who inspired that fight." Shaughnessy, the editorial said, "was a master strategist and an excellent coach . . . a friendly, cooperative sort of man who made the most of the skimpy material that an unsubsidized team provided him with, and who never complained of the competition he was forced to face under the conditions."

On the train carrying the Nebraska band to Pasadena, band director Don Lentz found out that no copyrighted songs could be played near radio microphones at the Rose Parade because permission could not be obtained from the American Society of Composers, Authors, and Publishers, which was on strike. Lentz and others from the band decided to put new words to "Song of the Vaga-bonds," from the operetta *The Vagabond King*. The song was in the public domain, so it could be played without permission. So the music "The Band Song" was written and continues today to be sung by band members before every home game as they march to Memorial Stadium.

Stanford's band won third place in the education category of the annual Rose Parade in Pasadena. Fifty-three floats and thirty-five hundred participants thrilled the 1.5 million spectators along the parade route.

In an interesting sidelight, two days before the Rose Parade, Sally Stanton, queen of the Tournament of Roses, and Governor Culbert Olson cut the ribbon for the start of construction for the Arroyo Seco Parkway near Pasadena, the first freeway in the West. "Autoists are going to discover the thrills and time-saving advantages of driving over the stopless motorways planned for Los Angeles' future when a long stretch of the Arroyo Seco Parkway is opened to travel [in January]," the *Los Angeles Times* gushed. The six-mile stretch cost four million dollars.

About eight thousand Nebraskans made the eighteen-hundred-mile trip to Pasadena, many of them on ten to twelve special Southern Pacific trains. A train ticket, hotel room, and ticket to the game cost $58.95. Nebraska fans stayed at the Rosslyn, Biltmore, and Ambassador hotels, where the refrains of the school song could be heard in the hallways:

> There is no place like Nebraska
> Dear old Nebraska U
> Where the girls are the fairest,
> The boys are the squarest
> Of any old school that I know.

Earlier in December speculation arose that Nebraska coach Biff Jones, who was in his fourth season, might take the head coaching job at West Point. He was, after all, an army major. He put an end to the speculation by saying the school song "goes for me 100 percent."

The Nebraska University Alumni Association of Southern California held a banquet at the Ambassador, featuring comedian Bob Hope as master of ceremonies and Nebraska chancellor C. S. Boucher as the principal speaker. Nebraska governor Dwight Griswold didn't attend because he was taking the oath of office in Lincoln on New Year's Day.

Nebraska had six players selected to the All–Big 6 first team, and two of them, guard Warren Alfson and tackle Forrest Behm, became All Americans. Four were named to the All–Big 6 second team.

Halfback Allen Zikmund, a farm boy from Ord, Nebraska, had agreed to come to Nebraska if the school could provide some financial assistance. Jones found him a job spreading fresh horse manure around the campus lawns and flower beds. Zikmund remembered walking into the Rose Bowl on game day. "It was a fantastic experience," he said. "I was just an eighteen-year-old sophomore, so my eyes were pretty wide. When you walk into a place with ninety-two thousand people, you feel rather insignificant." His first trip out of Nebraska was when the team traveled to play Minnesota. All but one of the Cornhuskers' forty-four players were from Nebraska, and that one was from neighboring Kansas. Thirteen were from Lincoln. When the players walked into the Rose Bowl in Pasadena, Zikmund said one teammate standing next to him remarked, "'Boy, this place would really hold a lot of hay.'"

Knute Rockne, the legendary Notre Dame coach, once noted that Nebraska's system "is to raise big, strong, fast boys and then just keep 'em."

Virtually from the day Nebraska boys could walk and talk, their elders preached to them that they might want to star for Nebraska football. Once in a while out-of-state schools would lure away players, but it was rare. Nebraska had more former players in pro football than any other school. It was a former Husker, Bernie Masterson, quarterback for the Bears, who taught Albert how to handle the ball in the T. When Masterson was asked whom he liked in the Rose Bowl, he replied, "I'm strictly neutral in this Rose Bowl business. I want 'em both to win, so I guess the only 'out' for me is a tie game. And that outcome wouldn't surprise me either."

Before leaving for Pasadena, the Huskers practiced in thirty-five-degree weather with fourth-string players operating out of the T to give the defense some idea of what to expect. Flu may have laid up some players, but at least two missed practice to catch up on schoolwork, an excuse that isn't heard often in today's football. The Cornhuskers watched films of Stanford's game against Washington, but Zikmund said, "It was far different when we saw it firsthand."

Heavy snow in Nebraska forced the Huskers inside for practice. So Jones decided to take the Huskers to warmer climes—Arizona. On December 19 ten thousand fans turned out in freezing weather to give the Huskers a rousing sendoff from the Rock Island depot. The Huskers were headed for Phoenix, where they were greeted by hundreds of winter visitors, the mayor, and cowboys with blazing six-shooters.

In Phoenix the Cornhuskers held twice-a-day practices behind locked gates at North Phoenix High School. Coach Steve Owens of the New York Giants stopped by to meet with Jones. They discussed methods of stopping the T, which the Bears had used against the Giants. "Sure that T formation can be stopped," Owens said. "The main thing in setting up the right kind of defense is to have the personnel to start with. Those Nebraska boys look good to me."

Link Lyman, the Huskers' line coach, had played for the Chicago Bears in the early 1930s when they started using the T formation. Lyman said the man in motion is "thrown out there as bait, and it isn't hard for a linebacker to over shift in his anxiety to cover his potential pass receiver."

Former Nebraska lineman Ray Richards, a line coach for UCLA, watched the Huskers practice. "This ball game has me stumped. . . . I believe you'll find that not only does Nebraska have a great line but a better set of backs than some people think. But this Stanford team seems to have a way of 'getting to' another team sooner or later. They keep battering away, and suddenly they've won the ball game. They're like dynamite. You don't know how hard they hit until they explode, and then it's too late."

While in Phoenix the players talked Jones into letting them attend a rodeo in Wickenburg, a dude ranch city, fifty miles northwest of Phoenix after practice on December 21. The players enjoyed two-pound steaks and biscuits served by an Arizona cowboy.

Lyman, who owned a cattle ranch in western Nebraska, wanted to get in on an exhibition of bronc busting, bulldogging, and other rodeo events, but Jones wouldn't allow it. "You'll have plenty of Wild West on your hands when those Stanford Indians start tearing big holes in your line," he joked with some degree of prophecy. Back at their hotel, the Camelback Inn, the team and coaches had a Christmas party the next day, exchanging gifts around a tree.

Fifteen to twenty Indians came down with the flu in the two weeks before the game, drastically cutting into practice time. On December 21 they practiced in the rain, but they were ready for any kind of weather on game day. "The wet ball didn't bother us a bit," Albert said. Shaughnessy told his team that rain "doesn't mean a thing; it's all in the mind." He also said, "If the weather doesn't get better and the flu doesn't let us alone, it'll be a sorry game for us on New Year's Day."

Nebraska players also came down with the flu, including two of their best players, halfbacks Harry Hopp and Rohrig. And the rains came down in Phoenix on Christmas Eve, but the Huskers practiced anyway. Al Wolf, a *Los Angeles Times* reporter, revealed why he thought the Huskers had such "terrific power." He said he noticed that while the players were wearing shorts, "each and every kid, it seems is equipped with a set of legs that look like spare parts of a piano—big, solid, muscular, rock-hard. No wonder they drive like a herd of buffaloes, to use a simile in keeping with these surroundings." One more thing: Wolf graduated from Nebraska.

On Christmas day the Huskers enjoyed a turkey dinner with Chancellor Boucher and his wife, and then took a tour of the Salt River Valley. Shaughnessy, too, gave his players the day off. Some went home to be with their families.

On the first day in Southern California, the Huskers visited the Rose Bowl and then the Pacific Ocean. Both teams attended the game between the Chicago Bears and the National League All-Stars in Los Angeles won by the Bears and their T formation 28–14. Jones's team got its look at the T that day, and it soon would see more than enough of it before leaving California. Nebraska got in a light workout at Occidental College while Stanford worked out at Brookside Park near the Rose Bowl.

Stanford was an 11 to 5 favorite. Jones dodged questions about the odds. "I don't believe in odds," he said. "A college football team is a college football team."

The *Times*' Wolf waxed poetic over Nebraska's chances:

> If the Cornhusker warriors win in their first visit to Arroyo Seco [where the Rose Bowl was situated], it'll be New Year's Eve in Nebraska for weeks and weeks. They'll name babies (boy and girl), dogs, breakfast foods and parks after Coach Biff Jones.
>
> If those Huskers take a trouncing, Nebraska will go into virtual mourning for weeks and weeks—cows will give skim milk, the curl will go out of piggies' tails, traveling salesmen will throw stones at farmers' daughters and the Biffer will commit hari kari.

Stanford released statistics that showed Albert's value to the team. He had played 467 minutes in nine games, by far the most of any player on the team. And he played the entire Rose Bowl game. Gallarneau logged 427 minutes and Kmetovic 397. Other Indians who played considerably were Taylor with 455, Palmer with 444, Banducci with 440, Meyer with 413, and Lindskog with 363.

Stanford averaged 4.45 yards a carry during the season while the Huskers averaged 3.62. In passing Stanford threw for 764 yards to Nebraska's 602. The Indians threw 111 passes and completed 44, while Nebraska completed 44 in 81 attempts. Stanford ran up 2,578 total yards to 2,403 for the Huskers. Stanford also scored 175 points to Nebraska's 170.

"I've taught the boys all the football I know," Shaughnessy said. "Now my job is to have them mentally fit for the task ahead." He noted that his players never responded well to practices but that they were all "Saturday players," meaning game-day players.

"We are expecting an extra tough brand of opposition," Shaughnessy said. "If anything happens to our starting regulars, we may be in something of a fix. We are short of capable reserves, whereas I have every reason to believe that Nebraska will have the edge in that particular department. Right now, I feel that we have no better than a 50–50 chance."

Nebraska had a potent offense that concerned Shaughnessy. The Huskers scored nineteen times out of twenty-eight chances during the season inside the 20-yard line. Three times they failed was when the third string was playing. Against Kansas, the Huskers got inside the 20 seven times and scored each time.

If Stanford had players with an interesting background, so did Nebraska. George Abel was a millionaire. His late father was one of Lincoln's leading contractors and builders. Substitute quarterback Theos Thompson was a member of Phi Beta Kappa, the nation's most prestigious academic honorary. Vike Francis's real first name was Viscount. Substitute end Willard Bunker was Lincoln's checker champion. Harry Hopp's brother Johnny was an outfielder with the St. Louis Cardinals. Five team members were married. Substitute quarterback George Knight once held the state high school javelin record. Behm was badly burned on his legs when he was five years old, and doctors said one of his legs should be amputated. His father refused and helped his son rehabilitate the leg. Behm had regained full use of his legs by his senior year in high school, when he played football. He walked on at Nebraska, but the team could not afford to buy him shoes for his size fifteen feet, so he bought them himself.

There was no doubt the Huskers were pumped for the game. The players wrote their own fighting words to the tune of "California Here I Come":

> California here we come—to put those Stanfords on the run,
>> We'll stop 'm, we'll sock 'em, we'll put 'em to shame.
>> We know they're a tough club, but we'll win that game.
>> We've got the men to spoil their stuff—with passes and runs we'll call their bluff.
>> We're going to win on New Year's Day—California here we come.

17

"Pretty good ball club, Coach"

Stanford players were in good shape in terms of injuries except at fullback. Standlee was still limping but would play. Backup Milt Vucinich appeared out of the game after hurting his knee in the last practice at Stanford. "Personally, I think he's out," said team physician Fritz Roth. "He may come around by game time, but I doubt it."

Vucinich's loss concerned Shaughnessy. "We'll need every man, because I know any team Biff Jones coaches is bound to be tough. We'll have to play better than we did in the Washington game, and that was our best game." As it turned out, Vucinich did not play; neither did Lindskog's backup, Collin McClintock, who was suffering from a shoulder injury.

With Vucinich out and Standlee limping, more of the fullback duties would have to fall on Rod Parker, the 5-foot-8-inch, 188-pounder who filled in so well in the Oregon State game but had played only 32 minutes spread out over three games during the season. The Indians were bolstered by the return of tackle Jack Warnecke and end Hank Norberg, who had been injured most of the season. Warnecke, like Banducci, would have to wear a leather halter that prevented him from raising his arm above his shoulder.

On the Nebraska side, quarterback Roy "Cowboy" Petsch, who wore the number 13 on his jersey like his counterpart Albert, had cracked ribs and was uncertain whether he would be 100 percent. "I'm strictly a 2 o'clock player," Petsch said. "When game time rolls around I'll be ready." And he was.

The more experienced Nebraskans had eight seniors and three juniors on their first team, while Stanford had three seniors, four juniors, and four sophomores, the second-year men all on the line.

The day before the game, Nebraska alumnus and *Times* sportswriter Al Wolf predicted Stanford would win 20–14. He missed by 1 point on each team's score.

Also a day before the game, the Huskers received a treat: a Lincoln packing company sent sixty-five choice Nebraska beefsteaks by air express to their luncheon at the Vista del Arroyo Hotel in Los Angeles.

Almost ninety-two thousand attended the game, including Herbert Hoover. Sportswriter Cy Sherman wrote in the *Lincoln Star* that the former president had proven instrumental in getting Stanford to accept Nebraska as its opponent. Stanford had sought Michigan and its sensational halfback Tom Harmon, but it ran into the same problem as it had in trying to line up Minnesota. Hoover then stepped into the picture and swung the decision in the Cornhuskers' favor.

Just before the Cornhuskers took the field, Jones had his assistant coaches lead the players in "For Your Country and My Country," the official American military recruiting song. In keeping with the military aspects of football, the players were marching to do battle on the field. Among the words were, "Come a running boys, don't you hear that noise? Like the thunder in the sky."

The Huskers wore red jerseys, the Indians white. That was a

switch from the tradition that the home team always chose the darker jerseys. In fact, some fans were confused by the switch of colors and found themselves rooting for the wrong team early on.

As the Huskers took the field they heard the Stanford yell, "Give 'em the ax, the ax, the ax" thundering throughout the stadium. Team captains Standlee, Gallarneau, and Graff, the first-string seniors, and Nebraska captains George Knight and Petsch met at midfield for the coin toss. Nebraska won and chose to receive the ball.

The game started poorly for the Indians, just as predicted by Dick Hyland, *Los Angeles Times* columnist and Stanford alumnus. Four days before the game, Hyland said that a lack of physical contact because of illness, fear of injury, poor weather, and a long layoff since the Cal game might allow the Huskers to get an early jump on the Indians. And that's just what happened.

Vike Francis fielded Albert's low kickoff on the 25 and returned it to the Indians' 47. After Harry Hopp lost 3 yards, Francis took the pass from center, faked a reverse to Butch Luther, then ran behind superb blocking to the Indians' 35. The Huskers had found a weak spot in the Indians' defensive line. When Nebraska's guard would pull out to lead a running play, Stanford guard Chuck Taylor had a clear shot into the Huskers' backfield. "We didn't even have to block him," center Fred Meier said in an interview years later. "He'd charge like a damn bull. . . . That left a big hole in the defensive line. There was nobody there to tackle our fullback. He made ten yards every time we touched the ball." That was an exaggeration, but the Huskers marched steadily down the field.

Taylor remembered that first drive this way: "My technique was that I was always kind of an aggressive guard and always got across the line of scrimmage. Under certain circumstances this can be good, but under others it can be a little dangerous with all the traps the single-wing used in those days, and boy, they really wiped me out on a number of occasions on traps. I think I probably caused the first touchdown they made."

Shaughnessy had prepared his team to stop the Huskers' reverses that wingback Butch Luther had run so successfully in his three years at Nebraska. "In order to protect ourselves against these reverses, which nearly always went outside the defensive tackle, we instructed our weakside tackle to play off the outside shoulder of the weakside end," Shaughnessy said. "That left a big hole between our tackle and guard on the weak side. Our guards were supposed to compensate for this by splitting a little wider than normal to help fill this hole. In the excitement of the early moments of the game, habit took control of them and they lined up just the way they had been doing most of the season."

On the next play Francis faked to Luther and again charged over center for 12 yards to the 23. Francis, on the next down, handed to Luther, who ran down the sideline until Kmetovic wrestled him out of bounds at the 9. Stanford called a time-out. On the next down Francis picked up 2, Luther ran for 5 on a reverse, and then Francis pushed it into the end zone from the 2.

"We ran fullback half-spinners and full-spinners and marched right down the field," said second-string halfback Allen Zikmund, who coached Kearney State College in Kearney, Nebraska, to eleven conference championships from 1955 to 1971. "This is going to be great," he said. "Because we moved down [the field] just like we did all year long, you know, and it looked like, it's going to be our day."

Tackle Forrest Behm remembered thinking, "We were going to win the game. No questions about it. We marched right down the field; we moved the ball well, and . . . we handled the thing quite well."

It also seemed apparent that Shaughnessy's decision to avoid practice scrimmages leading up to the game because of injuries and the flu was showing its effects. Stanford had been in that position before. The Indians seemed to start slow but rallied once they got into the flow of the game.

After scoring in the first 3 minutes, the Huskers had every right to be confident. Any team other than Stanford might have folded under that early charge.

After the game Shaughnessy admitted that it looked bad for Stanford when Nebraska scored so quickly. "But I can't say I was particularly worried. These boys of mine have a way of getting their touchdowns and I figured they'd get started.

"But I sort of expected we'd run into trouble early from Nebraska's running attack because we just haven't had enough scrimmage work preparing for the game. We haven't enough reserves and I couldn't take too many chances getting any of the regulars injured."

Shaughnessy saw the problem right away, but because of substitution rules forbidding a player to return to the field until the next quarter, he was reluctant to make a change even to send in instructions. He wanted to keep his best eleven players on the field early in the game.

Shaughnessy noted that before the game, the Indians were very confident of winning. "The boys were very sure of themselves before the game, kidding and skylarking," Shaughnessy said. After the Nebraska touchdown they realized their perfect season was on the line. "Albert called a huddle and said, 'Well, just eleven yellow palookas lying down together; and I'm the worst. Let's go get 'em.'"

Gallarneau returned the Nebraska kickoff from his 12 to the 39, but the Indians were unable to move the ball much past midfield. Albert punted into the end zone and the Huskers got the ball on the 20. If Stanford's defense was to stiffen, this was the time. A second straight touchdown march might have been too much to overcome.

After one play and with the ball on the 18, Hopp quick-kicked the ball out of bounds on the Stanford 42. On the second play Albert threw a long lateral across the field from his 40 to his 38 to Kmetovic, who gathered in the ball and galloped 20 yards. The play had worked beautifully because Nebraska's left end failed to cover Kmetovic when he went in motion, and the left-side linebacker was too far away to stop the shifty Kmetovic once he picked up speed.

At the Nebraska 38 Kmetovic took an Albert pass that was almost another lateral 15 yards to the 23. Albert slipped going to pass on first down and fell at the 28 for a 5-yard loss. Standlee then burst through the line only to fumble. Nebraska center Bob Burruss recovered at the 24.

Shaughnessy relented on his decision not to substitute, sending in end Clem Tomerlin for Stan Graff with instructions for the team to revert to the defense Stanford had been using all year. That change enabled the Indians to send their defensive backs to better protect against the reverse while stopping the runs up the middle. The Huskers had picked up 50 yards rushing on that first drive; they would end the day with just 56 total yards gained rushing.

After two losses put the Huskers at their 18, Hopp punted from his 12 to Kmetovic, who caught it on the Stanford 39 and ran it back 14 yards to the Nebraska 47.

Stanford then began a drive that tied the game. In the huddle Albert told his teammates, "We didn't come all the way here to get [actress] Ann Sheridan's autograph. But I've got a friend who'll toss it in for the guy who plays some ball. That'll be you, Pete. Let's go." (Kmetovic did indeed get an autograph after the game from actress Jean Parker, but it is unlikely the boastful Albert had anything to do with it.)

On first down Albert faked a handoff to Gallarneau and gave the ball to Kmetovic on a quick opener over right tackle, with Banducci and Meyer scissor-blocking the Nebraska left end and left tackle. Kmetovic danced through the hole, picked up blocks from Standlee and Taylor, and slithered down the sideline until he was knocked out of bounds at the Nebraska 18. The Huskers looked confused by fakes and handoffs.

On the next play the Indians sought better field position by sending Gallarneau on a run toward the center of the field, but Nebraska anticipated the play. Gallarneau lost 2 yards, only the third time all season he had lost yardage; the other two times were for 1 yard each.

On second down at the 20, Albert called on Kmetovic again, who burst over right tackle to the 11-yard line. With Nebraska in a five-man line, Standlee and Kmetovic faked right at the snap to Albert, who reversed his pivot and handed the ball to Gallarneau. Duke cut through the bewildered line at a forty-five-degree angle and slipped into the end zone untouched. It was the counterplay again. Stanford had scored with 1:45 left in the first quarter. Davis J. Walsh, a writer for the *Los Angeles Examiner*, called Gallarneau's run "one of the most spectacular plays of this season, or any other." Albert's conversion tied the score.

Hopp, one of Nebraska's biggest stars, had played virtually no role in the first quarter and sat out the entire second quarter. Herman Rohrig replaced him. After the kickoff Nebraska found itself with third down and 5 yards to go. Rohrig quick-kicked from his 26, but Lindskog blocked it. The ball rolled to the 15, where Nebraska recovered. Because the kick came on third down, the Huskers got a second chance. Rohrig then punted to the Stanford 34, where Albert fielded the ball, returning it to the 45. Albert led the Indians to the Huskers' 9-yard line, but they were stopped there. Albert tried a field goal from the 16 but missed badly.

The Huskers took over on their 20, but two downs gained only a yard, so Rohrig punted just out of the reach of the charging Lindskog. The punt soared over Kmetovic's head, and as he raced backward to catch it over his shoulder, he fumbled. Zikmund recovered on the Stanford 33. The next down Rohrig dropped back to his 40 to pass; eluded Meyer, Graff, and Banducci; and heaved the ball toward Zikmund on the left sideline at the 9, two steps past Gallarneau. Zikmund pulled in the pass and fell into the end zone with Gallarneau hanging onto him. On the extra point attempt, Taylor broke through the line and blocked the kick. Nebraska 13, Stanford 7.

Shaughnessy said Gallarneau had underestimated Zikmund's speed. "A great money player, Gallarneau was burned up over his mistake," Shaughnessy said. Gallarneau stamped his feet and looked beseechingly toward Albert. "I knew that whenever he was in that frame of mind he was dynamite, and something was due to happen," Shaughnessy said.

After the touchdown a sub ran off the field with a message from Albert to Shaughnessy. "Frankie told me to tell you, Coach, to keep your chin up, he's got something up his sleeve."

It didn't take long for Stanford to gain the lead. Rohrig's kick-off went out of bounds on the Stanford 35. On first down Stanford threw a twist at the Huskers. Without the ball, Albert pulled back from center and Lindskog snapped the ball to Standlee, who passed to Gallarneau for 10 yards. Two more plays gained a yard. On third down and nine for a first down, Albert faked a pass and then followed Gallarneau, Kmetovic, and Standlee around left end for 7 yards to the Nebraska 47.

The Indians faced fourth and two and seemed likely to punt. But Albert gambled, sending Gallarneau off tackle for 5 yards and a first down.

Shaughnessy said he wasn't nervous when Albert elected to go for the first down at midfield. "I have confidence in anything Frankie elects to do when he's running the ball club. He's in charge out there on the field."

Albert knew that others thought he was taking a chance on that play call, "but I didn't think so. We were behind then and I wanted to keep possession of the ball. Anyhow, we haven't had much trouble all season when it came to making yards in mid-field. But I suppose it would have looked bad if we'd failed to have made a first down."

After a 2-yard gain by Kmetovic put the ball in the center of the field on the 40-yard line, Albert called on Gallarneau again.

Shaughnessy said the Indians noticed that the Huskers were playing a 5-2-2-2 defense. That left no one playing deep down the middle. "A man loose in there would be gone," Shaughnessy said. Albert wanted to give Gallarneau a chance to atone for his mistake in failing to cover Zikmund. "He knew that Gallarneau, in the frame of mind he was in, couldn't miss a pass if there were a ghost of a chance for completion," the coach said.

Assistant coach Jim Lawson, sitting in the press box, spotted a weakness in the Nebraska defense. Lawson relayed a message to Shaughnessy, who called for Albert to run the "63 flare pass, 23." Gallarneau went in motion to his left, which pulled in a defensive back to guard against a run around that end. The Indians sent their two ends down field and then had them each run toward opposite sidelines.

Gallarneau took off downfield, splitting the defensive backs in the middle of the field. Albert dropped back to his 48 and threw a wobbly pass about 30 yards to Gallarneau at the 18 in full stride. Rohrig and Zikmund had a shot at stopping Gallarneau, but a burst of speed put him into the end zone. As Gallarneau scored, Albert looked up to the press box, raised his left hand, and gave the OK sign to Lawson. It was the T formation in perfect form.

Albert's conversion gave the Indians a lead, 14–13, they would not relinquish. Albert came off the field and whispered to Shaughnessy, "Pretty good ball club, Coach, huh?"

Nebraska was not done yet. Zikmund fielded Albert's kickoff at the 15, picked up some blocks, and rambled to the Stanford 39, where Kmetovic and Albert knocked him out of bounds. Zikmund fractured his left ankle on the return but stayed in the game.

On first down Graff dropped Zikmund for a 14-yard loss. Zikmund went to the sideline, unable to continue on his injured ankle. Jones asked him if he could run. Zikmund ran down the sidelines without a problem. "Gee, it felt good," he said. "But when I turned to come back, no way. So I came back and said, 'Coach, I'm sorry. I can run straight ahead, but I can't turn.' That was it for me."

The Huskers moved the ball to the Indians' 30, where George Knight attempted a field goal from the 37 (the goal-post crossbar was over the goal line in those days). The kick was woefully short, rolling dead at the 7. The first half ended not much later, and Stanford went into the locker room with the psychological edge of a 1-point lead. "Our team had regained its composure," Shaughnessy said.

The Indians needed the halftime break. They had used virtually every sub they had, more than in any other game, hoping to keep fresh against a Nebraska team whose first and second strings were almost equal. In fact, the Huskers' second team played the entire second quarter. Jones's first team would be fresh in the second half.

Halftime featured the schools' marching bands on the field. Nebraska's band wore white shoulder coats, red trousers, and white cockade hats, just the reverse of Stanford's red coats and white pants. Card stunts included a waving U.S. flag; portraits of players, including Albert and Standlee; and a happy Indian eating an ear of corn.

Nebraska kicked off to Stanford, but the Indians couldn't do much with the ball. With it on the 31, Albert lofted a 68-yard quick kick that rolled into the Nebraska end zone. "There had been criticism of the T on the grounds that we couldn't quick kick, and Albert asked permission to demonstrate that it could be done," Shaughnessy said.

The Huskers took over on their 20. Stanford held again, and after Albert returned a Hopp kick 14 yards to the Stanford 23, the Indians began another drive. Stanford moved to the Nebraska 1-yard line, with the biggest gain a 43-yard run by Kmetovic. At the 17 Perfect Pete took a lateral from Albert at the 22 and rolled forward until a touchdown-saving tackle by Luther stopped him at the 1.

First down and one looked like a sure touchdown from the Indians, but after four plays Stanford was no closer to scoring, as Nebraska put up a tremendous goal-line stand. Two quarterback sneaks by Albert gained nothing, a plunge by Hoot Armstrong came up short, and another by Parker yielded no gain. If the Huskers were excited by their tenacious defense, fans couldn't tell by their body language. Unlike today's more emotional players, the Huskers went quietly to their huddle, where they called their play after taking over on downs.

Of the Huskers' goal-line stand, Albert said the Indians had a light backfield in the game "and that Nebraska line was awfully tough. We could have used Gallarneau and Chief Standlee at the time." Said Banducci, "Those Huskers were awfully big and tough and that [Royal] 'King Kong' Kahler can make anybody's ball team. They had quite an edge on us in weight."

With the ball on the 1, the Huskers decided to punt. Hopp, standing deep in his end zone, punted to Kmetovic at the Nebraska 39. With what Shaughnessy called the most savage blocking he had seen in either the college or pro ranks, Kmetovic headed left, reversed his field, and headed for the right sideline. The Huskers' would-be tacklers were "sent flying like rag dolls." One block along the way by Dick Palmer knocked Francis into a backward somersault that raised a gasp from the crowd. (Francis was knocked unconscious and had to be carried from the field. He later returned, however.)

Kmetovic sprinted down the sideline, and at the 5 one last Husker had a chance to tackle him, but Meyer hit Luther a glancing blow that knocked him off balance, and Kmetovic ran across the goal line untouched. Albert again kicked the extra point. Stanford 21, Nebraska 13.

Of Kmetovic's touchdown, Jones said, "I don't believe I saw a Nebraska man on his feet when that Kmetovic made his touchdown run against us." Backfield coach Glenn Presnell called it "the greatest play I've ever seen." For Kmetovic's part, he said his return was more of a "run from fright" than anything else. "I had no place to go. We didn't have set punt return plays in those days and we didn't set up well. Because we were going both ways we didn't have time to spend working on special return plays. I just happened to pick up everyone on the way back across the field. Albert blocked in both directions on that play."

Albert took little credit. "They said I got two great blocks on the play. Actually I got blindsided both times. Boy, that Kmetovic could go. He was a player."

With 4 minutes to go in the third quarter, the game was all but over. With the exception of one series of plays in the fourth quarter that got the Huskers 2 yards across midfield, they didn't drive into Stanford's territory again.

Shaughnessy said only one more play in the second half was significant. That was a tackle made by left tackle Ed Stamm on an Albert pass attempt to Kmetovic that George Abel intercepted. Abel had a clear field ahead of him to the end zone. Stamm's job was to protect the left sideline in case of just such an interception. Abel sprinted down the sideline, but Stamm knocked him out of bounds at the Nebraska 38.

"I got a kick out of it when Big Ed got up, glanced over at me with a significant grin and never said a word, took it in stride," Shaughnessy said. "That was merely the way to play football—the way those boys played football. They did the job because they loved it and loved to do it right."

Stanford threatened to score when it took over on the Nebraska 15 after Lindskog blocked a Rohrig punt. Lindskog had noticed the ends left a gap between the tackles, so he slipped through to block the punt with his chest. "The ball seemed to stick right with me," he said. In a rare show of emotion, Lindskog clapped his hands after recovering the ball. Nebraska held, taking over at its 20.

Fullback Bob Crane intercepted a Rohrig pass and returned it 2 yards to the 31, but again Stanford couldn't get into the end zone. The rest of the game was a defensive struggle.

In the end the Huskers had a difficult time determining who had the ball, so tricky were the Indians, and when they did, they couldn't keep up with the speed of Stanford's backfield. Jones said his team couldn't get back in the game in the second half because his "boys were too tired from chasing Kmetovic and Gallarneau."

Here's how the *Los Angeles Times* recapped the game:

Like specters on the loose, Stanford's white-clad ball carriers sped and slid past Nebraska's stubborn, scarlet-shirted stalwarts in the Rose Bowl yesterday and when they finished their work they had earned a 21–13 victory in one of the greatest football games ever played in the classic blossom basin.

Strong men fainted, women screamed wildly and the others of that capacity crowd of 91,500 roared with ceaseless enthusiasm as the Pacific Coast Conference champions came from behind to defeat the powerful Cornhuskers from the midland.

Never has there been a more ideal setting for the annual classic, played in a bowl bathed by a warm winter sun, with the purple Sierra Madres standing off as a picturesque background to the flower-festooned field of battle.

Jones tried to cross the field to congratulate Shaughnessy and Albert, but Stanford fans were carrying them off on their shoulders. "Hey, Coach," Albert said, "how does it feel to win ten straight games?" Jones later congratulated Shaughnessy in the locker room.

"My, my," Shaughnessy said. "I just can't understand these boys. They came from behind again and they'll go down in my book as just what they are—champions. I'm very proud of the boys. You can't beat champions. Nebraska proved to be a tough team just as we figured and proved themselves fine, clean sports throughout the game. Whew, I'm glad that one is over. This has been a season, hasn't it?"

Years later the game was considered one of the most memorable college football games of all time. AthlonSports.com ranked it No. 3. Collegefootballnews.com put it at No. 53 of college football's greatest games. The book *College Football's Most Memorable Games, 1913 through 1990* listed it as one of fifty-four "history-making contests."

The Nebraska coaches had nothing but praise for the Indians. "Well, they were all everybody said—and maybe we weren't although I thought it was a pretty fair ball game until that Kmetovic kicked over the traces," Jones said. "Go tell Clark Shaughnessy I'll buy him 120 acres of fine corn land if he'll tell me where we can get a Frankie Albert. That kid's got too much pass, too much kick, too much noodle for us."

"We came west hopefully," Jones said, "and for 20 minutes or more it looked like our chance to win was better than Stanford's. After that, it was too much Albert and Kmetovic."

Despite Stanford's success with the T, Jones had no plans to switch to the new formation. "But we may steal a play or two. We have no excuses. Stanford simply was a grand team." He refused to say Stanford was the best team Nebraska had played. "Don't forget that we played Minnesota," he said. "And say, I'll pay scalpers' prices to see the Indians play the Gophers next week. See if you can fix it up," he told sportswriters. (What a matchup that would have been: the No. 1 and No. 2 teams playing each other with former teammates Shaughnessy and Bierman as the head coaches.)

Nor would Shaughnessy say Nebraska was the best team the Indians had faced, but he conceded the Huskers were one of the toughest: "Great club, the toughest we met this year. My boys just have a habit of going out and getting their touchdowns no matter how tough a team they're up against."

Line coach Link Lyman called Stanford the smartest defensive team he had seen that year. "They closed up their secondary to stop our running, those linebackers knifing through something fierce to clutter up our reverses. But when we spread 'em, they read our minds and got back there in a hurry," he said.

Even the hometown Nebraska newspaper got in on the praise. *Lincoln Star* sportswriter Cy Sherman said, "The wreck of Nebraska's hopes was due to Stanford's possession of that pair of backfield wizards—Albert and Kmetovic."

Accurate final statistics were difficult to come by. Different newspapers had different totals. In those days sportswriters kept their own statistics. Today university sports departments keep "official stats." The most accurate seem to be that Stanford ran 73 plays to Nebraska's 47, for total yardage of 352 to 128. Stanford gained 254 yards on the ground to Nebraska's 56. The Indians picked up 98 yards passing to the Huskers' 72. Nebraska managed to complete only three passes in fourteen attempts while having four intercepted. In nine regular season games, the Huskers had only eight passes picked off. The Indians were seven for fourteen through the air with one interception. Stanford fumbled six times but recovered four of them. Kmetovic was the leading ground gainer with 129 yards on fourteen carries, followed by Gallarneau with 84 on seventeen carries. Francis led the Huskers with 51 yards on nine rushes.

Kmetovic was selected the most valuable player in the game, for which he received a seventy-five-dollar wristwatch and a kiss from actress Jean Parker. Some sportswriters had said before the game that Luther was a faster, shiftier runner than Kmetovic, but the Stanford halfback seemed to prove otherwise.

The United Press correspondent Henry McLemore wrote of Kmetovic, "Do me a favor, will you? Take all the All American teams that did not honor Pete Kmetovic with a halfback position, wrap them carefully in a cement slipover and drop them in the river with the last batch of ring-tailed cats."

Despite the loss the Husker players were still heroes in their home state. Two sets of the game films were shown throughout Nebraska from January 3 to 15 to avid moviegoers and football fans.

After the game the Huskers were the guests of Nebraska-born movie star Robert Taylor at the MGM Studio. They had lunch with Taylor, Ann Rutherford, Laraine Day, Mary Howard, and Ann Morris. Later they met Lana Turner, Judy Garland, Robert Montgomery, and Leo Carrillo.

"It's been a swell trip," Jones said, "and we wouldn't mind playing Stanford again tomorrow if they would just keep Pete Kmetovic out of there."

Said Curly Grieve, a sportswriter for the *San Francisco Examiner*, "That hocus-pocus which is called the T formation made [91,500] spectator converts and seemed definitely to signal the arrival of a new era in college football. The day of the tug-of-war is out—Clark Shaughnessy and his Stanford Indians have definitely killed it."

Los Angeles Times columnist Paul Zimmerman was convinced that Shaughnessy's team was better than any other Stanford Rose Bowl team, including the vaunted Vow Boys. "None of them had the heart, the determination, the speed, the power or the deception of the magicians who worked miracles at the expense of a great Nebraska aggregation."

They were indeed the Wow Boys.

18

The Legacy

It would be difficult to equal Stanford's 1940 success, but Shaughnessy was hopeful of another undefeated season when practice began the following fall. It was not to be. In addition to the graduation of Norm Standlee, Hugh Gallarneau, and Stan Graff, Pete Kmetovic and Vic Lindskog, who Shaughnessy said were vital to the T formation's success, missed many minutes with injuries. Kmetovic was hurt in a shutout loss to Oregon State, the eventual Rose Bowl representative, and the team that the Indians said best defended against the T the previous year. Perhaps there was more than a loss of personnel to graduation and injuries; the possibility can't be overlooked that the defenses may have caught up with the T.

The Indians ended the season losing to Washington State and Cal. They finished the season 6-3 with victories over Washington, Santa Clara, USC, Oregon, UCLA, and USF.

"Clark overcoached," Albert said years later. "It wasn't so bad the first year, when he put in the T formation sparingly. By the second year he had given us so many tools—heck we had seven different ways to hit a hole on the same play—that it became too complex. He was thinking football by pro standards, where guys have nothing else to do but concentrate on the game, since it's their living. But our kids were also thinking about girls, studies, good times."

Statistically, Albert had a better season in 1941 than in the undefeated season. He finished with 775 total yards compared with 704 in 1940 and completed fifty passes for 709 yards compared with thirty-six passes for 648 yards. His pass completion percentage also climbed from .364 percent to .442 percent.

Rumors cropped up that Shaughnessy might leave Stanford for Yale, Maryland, or some other university. On March 12, 1942, Shaughnessy ran into *Los Angeles Times* columnist Paul Zimmerman at the Biltmore Hotel in Los Angeles. "You know," he told Zimmerman, "when I came west to Stanford I was sure that at last I had found the place where I could remain the rest of my life and just coach football. I'm not a young man anymore, and I must have job security. But I want active coaching, too.

"We are at war now and that changes the aspect of everything out here on the Coast. I might become a service team coach. But my age is against me. I'd like to do that. Now that chances of continuing to have security and coach football are jeopardized in the West, I'm at a loss to know what to do. Stanford has been good to me and if I decide to go elsewhere I hope the public will understand I'm not running out."

Then on March 20, 1942, Shaughnessy announced he was leaving Stanford to become athletic director and coach at Maryland. He told Stanford officials he feared Stanford might abandon football because of the war and he wanted to continue coaching. Stanford named Jim Lawson to succeed him, but then Lawson went into the navy and Marchie Schwartz took over. The next year Stanford dropped football until 1946.

Sure enough, Shaughnessy was accused of running out on Stanford, but if Stanford officials were unhappy, they must have been satisfied that he left $350,000 in the school's athletic coffers. And he left the triumph of the only team in Stanford football history to go undefeated and untied.

The T formation's success in the Indians' win in the Rose Bowl coupled with the Bears' NFL championship victory was Shaughnessy's legacy. He is the only coach in football history to have a direct hand in winning the Rose Bowl and the NFL title in the same year.

Shaughnessy later called the Rose Bowl victory one of the twelve greatest games in football history. "The 1941 Rose Bowl game was an important one in the course of football because that was the game that sold the T formation—the modern T style of offense to school and college football. Before this game, the system had been regarded as too intricate and too complicated for use by school and college teams. . . . The performance by the Stanford boys in their first year with this system proved it could be worked. Then everybody accepted it. That's why I contend this was an important game—one of the most important games of modern football."

Jeff Davis wrote in his biography of George Halas, "From that moment on [the Rose Bowl game], everything else in football was obsolete. In the space of three weeks, George Halas and the Chicago Bears and Clark Shaughnessy at Stanford launched a football revolution with their T-formation attack."

In a 1953 letter to football historian Allison Danzig, Halas wrote, "The rush to get on the T bandwagon following the sensational success of the Bears and the Stanford Indians of Shaughnessy in 1940 marked one of the big turning points in offensive football."

In 2002 ESPN rated the shift to the modern T formation as the No. 2 sports innovation of all time, right behind baseball's free agency.

Esteemed *Los Angeles Times* columnist Bob Oates said Shaughnessy was one of the five "most important and inspiring figures" in football in the twentieth century. The others were Vince Lombardi, Knute Rockne, Bill Walsh, and Walter Camp—select company indeed.

After the Rose Bowl victory, Shaughnessy predicted that many college teams would shift to the T formation during the next season. Shaughnessy was besieged with requests to lecture on the T at coaching seminars during the summer of 1941. For example, as many as five hundred Texas high school coaches signed up to hear him talk about the T during a one-week coaching school in August 1941.

New Army coach Red Blaik got permission from George Halas for the Bears' quarterback Sid Luckman to come to West Point to teach the cadets the T. Blaik had been Luckman's high school coach. Two years later Frank Leahy, coach of Notre Dame, abandoned the box formation for the T.

Shaughnessy's T formation led to many variations designed to stay one ahead of the defense. Lou Little of Columbia invented the wing T, Don Faurot of Missouri the split T, while others developed the slot T, the double-wing T, the I, and the pro spread.

Within ten years 250 of the 350 top college teams across the nation had adopted the T. Some variation of the T remains in effect today, with new wrinkles, of course, but the basic premise is intact.

Why did so many teams adopt the T formation? No doubt because it had proved successful, but Shaughnessy had another reason. "It's a matter of self-preservation," he said. "Coaches get fired when they lose, and even when they win sometimes. So they just follow the line of least resistance and go with the pack. If a coach dares try something new and it flops, he gets fired because he's a screwball and only a stupid person would attempt such a thing. But if he tries something successful with another team and it fails, he's got a perfect out. He can blame it on the material, and keep his job, particularly if he's a good apple-polisher."

Still, the T formation had its skeptics. Paul Zimmerman in his book, *A Thinking Man's Guide to Pro Football*, wondered whether the T really was the reason the Bears dominated the Redskins in the 1940 championship game. "The answer to that 73–0 mystery is probably a lot more basic than the T formation and the counter plays off the man-in-motion and the hundreds of other playbook explanations that fans have been bored with for years. It comes down to personnel—and emotion." Zimmerman is no doubt right. The Bears' defense was at least as responsible for the lopsided score as was the offense. In addition to holding the Skins to the 3 yards rushing, the Bears intercepted eight passes, three of which were returned for touchdowns. That can't be attributed to the T.

Certainly, Shaughnessy agreed that it takes more than a formation to provide a winning team. He knew without a doubt that his backfield—which he called the best he had ever seen—was as responsible for the T's success as the formation itself. "It's often been said that the T formation was a godsend to the Wow Boys, who were tremendously talented but didn't really fit into any orthodox system," he said. "This is true—but it wasn't a one-way street; the personnel did a lot for the T. It might have had a very short life without them."

Halas recognized that talent at Stanford as well. He drafted several of that Stanford team to play for the Bears. Among them were Albert—although he never played for the Bears—Standlee, Gallarneau, and Vucinich.

Pop Warner remarked in 1951 that the Bears and the Indians "would have been just as successful if they had used most any other modern formation, because both teams that year had much better material than their opponents."

Shaughnessy agreed. Writing in *Esquire* magazine, he said, "Every football coach knows that it doesn't make much difference what formations you are committed to. The material and how it is used makes the offense."

Part of the success of the Stanford team was that its players were smart, off the field and on. Most had come to Stanford on academic scholarships and played football as a school activity.

No one had visions of playing professional football after graduation, although a handful did. "The boys on our 1940 team had the ability to adjust their tactics to meet the situation as it developed on the field," Shaughnessy said. "They were able to revise their assignments either during time out or during the 25 seconds between plays. What else? Those boys were combative and confident. They were a very spirited team. They were Westerners and proud of it. You could not browbeat them, lie to them, or teach them one unsportsmanlike thing."

Too little also has been said about the psychological impact of the T on the players. Shaughnessy noted that in the wing formations too often players were no more than blockers, and perhaps only one or two players touched the ball. With the T, several players got into the ball-handling action.

Publicly, Shaughnessy downplayed his contributions to development of the modern T, saying, "The Bears had won their share of championships, and were usually either on top or crowding the leader for many, many years before I collaborated with George Halas."

Indeed, Halas minimized Shaughnessy's role. "Papa Bear" had been experimenting with the modern T since the late 1920s. "What the Bears did was to put the T and the man in motion together and then gradually add refinements, such as the signal system and counter plays and spread," Halas said. "This was a period of evolution spanning almost twenty years and was the product of the Bears' organization rather than of one individual." Although Halas acknowledged Shaughnessy's contribution, he said in his autobiography, "For Bears' victories after 1930, I must credit Ralph Jones, the intelligent Ralph Jones, who created our modern T formation with man-in-motion, the strategy now used by almost every team in the country."

One telling moment came during a league meeting in 1934 when some members wanted to make a dropped lateral a live ball, which eventually became fact, but not that year. Halas was adamantly opposed, saying it would hamper the T, which called for a lot of laterals, especially to men in motion. "You gentlemen will destroy me and the modern T formation," he said. "You are taking away my bread and butter." He broke down in tears. The league didn't change the rules that year.

Stanford's successful use of the T gave it much broader attention than did the Bears' simply because the college game was far more popular than the professional game. The fact that both teams proved so successful with the T only added to the aura that it was the formation of the future.

In his later years Shaughnessy expressed some bitterness about not getting enough credit for his innovations in the T. *Smithsonian* writer William Barry Furlong noted that Shaughnessy confided in him that he had long brooded about the fact that Halas had received most of the credit for his ideas.

While there is little question that three or four coaches contributed to the modern T, there's no doubt that Shaughnessy was the first to successfully reapply it to the college game, which many people thought couldn't happen because it was too complicated for young players. At the very least, he helped shake football out of the "doldrums of fixed and worn-out systems of attack."

New York Times sportswriter Arthur Daley wrote, "There is no way of separating the part played in [the T formation's] development by Shaughnessy of Stanford and George Halas of the Chicago Bears. They were its archpriests." No matter who deserves the credit, the T formation changed football forever.

The year 1940 "is of crucial importance to the game's development," according to the Professional Football Researchers Association. The association said the Bears' one-sided win over the Redskins "led to the eventual triumph of the T formation in all its guises as the premier attacking system." While most teams began switching to the T, some teams held out, including the Pittsburgh Steelers, who operated the single wing until 1952. But by the end of the war in 1945, "the T had clearly become the dominant method of moving a football," the association said.

The Bears' Luckman was the first professional quarterback to star behind the T. He was followed by Slinging Sammy Baugh of the Redskins, who became a convert. The T may have been considered too intricate and complicated for college students, yet Luckman broke down in tears trying to run the T early on. Baugh said he hated the T at first, but then came around. Paul Christman of the Cardinals and Tommy Thompson of the Eagles followed them.

Leading up to the 1940 championship game, many of the teams in contention were playing inconsistently, the PFRA said. "The Bears were equally erratic, occasionally exploding with scoring binges but struggling on other days. To a large extent, the Halasmen relied on defense until they got their tricky T formation running smoothly," the association said. "On December 8, it ran perfectly."

Stanford's success with the T also may have led to changes in the substitution rules in 1941. It wasn't long before teams used separate defensive and offensive squads, allowing more players to use specific skills. In 1940 Albert was a quarterback, defensive back, punter, and place kicker. Today four different players usually hold those jobs.

Oates wrote, "The two-platoon revolution, which disrupted the defense-dominate mindset that still hobbles soccer and other sports, revised football into a series of contests between offensive and defensive experts, between, for example, fast and talented contingents of wide receivers and defensive backs—the kinds of athletes who had rarely had the size to fit in anywhere on a one-platoon football team."

In 1999 Oates called the free substitution change "the most influential single rule change in the last fifty years—in any sport."

Shaughnessy recognized that move would come about early on, primarily because teams needed stronger defenses with better athletes to defend against the T. "The T formation this fall [1941], in addition to the boom that would naturally attend its publicity, will be the popular system because it is so adaptable to the abilities of so many players," he said. Shaughnessy pointed out that the basic value of the T is that more players of limited capabilities can be used. "It is simply, clearly, definitely and completely a breakaway from the old power game based on blocking, power blocking. That is the key point that is never, or seldom ever, brought up."

Getting away from the power game also made the match more exciting. Instead of something like a rugby scrum, the T relied on more passing and now-you-see-it, now-you-don't deception with the football. "This type of play," Shaughnessy said, "literally opens up the play . . . making it very difficult, if not impossible, for a wide front of fixed position [the line] to be held effectively." He added, "Another thing: a player who has some leeway on the field, who feels some individual responsibility, rather than being just a robot moved about here and there from the sidelines, gains confidence, confidence in himself, which multiplied by the entire team means team confidence."

Shaughnessy also may have been given too little credit for his genius on the defensive side of the ball both in college and professional football. Stanford was heralded for its offense, but the Indians managed to score slightly fewer than 20 points a game. Their defense, however, held opponents to 8.5 points a game and never gave up more than two touchdowns in a game. They shut out their first two opponents. "Our own defense was pretty good," Shaughnessy said, "as it was bound to be with that kind of personnel, and it didn't have the same problems as our opponents; we were facing more orthodox offenses with which we were familiar."

Pop Warner also gave a great deal of credit to Stanford's defense. "I think a team's strength can be judged by its defense as well as its offense, and this Stanford team has bottled up the offenses of every team it has met."

19

Epilogue

In a poll of sportswriters, Clark Shaughnessy was ranked the No. 2 comeback sports figure of 1940 behind baseball's Jimmy Wilson. The memorable coach's stay at Stanford was short lived, however. Shaughnessy quit after the 1941 season to take a job at Maryland, then he moved to Pittsburgh and back to Maryland. The Associated Press dubbed him "football's man in motion." After he left Stanford, Shaughnessy's record was 7-2 at Maryland in 1942, 10-17 at Pittsburgh from 1943 to 1945, 3-6 at Maryland in 1946, and 1-8-1 at Hawaii in 1965.

In 1948 he became the head coach of the Los Angeles Rams but held that position for only two years. During that time Shaughnessy developed the pro set, which still is in use today. That formation put three receivers into the passing game. The Rams had Elroy "Crazy Legs" Hirsch, a good runner who Shaughnessy thought could be a better receiver. Because he already had two excellent receivers in Tom Fears and Bob Shaw, Shaughnessy moved Hirsch to flanker, and the Rams won the Western Conference title in 1949.

Shaughnessy also made important contributions on the defensive side of the line in pro football. "It disturbs me that Clark Shaughnessy is not in pro football's Hall of Fame," said Sid Gilman, former San Diego Chargers coach and a Hall of Famer. "Everyone talks of Shaughnessy's offensive contributions, but he contributed just as much on defense. Much of defense is terminology, and they are still using Shaughnessy terminology today. He's a man who definitely deserved to be called a football genius."

Shaughnessy was a finalist for the Hall of Fame in 1970, 1975, and 1976, each time falling short of the votes needed to induct him at Canton, Ohio.

Bob Oates, the longtime sports columnist for the *Los Angeles Times* who votes for the Pro Football Hall of Fame, said, "One of those still improbably on the outside is Clark Shaughnessy, the intellectual who made Hall of Fame contributions on each side of the line of scrimmage. He is the only coach who ever did. In Hall of Fame voting, I measure every new candidate against [Red] Grange, [Joe] Namath, and [Jerry] Rice. And Shaughnessy." As a professional coach, Oates pointed out, Shaughnessy was responsible for disarming the shotgun established in 1961 by Red Hickey of the San Francisco 49ers. Stuck with three ordinary talents at quarterback—John Brodie, Bill Kilmer, and Bobby Waters—Hickey devised a system in which each quarterback took one play on each first down series of plays. Waters might pass or run on first down, Kilmer could do the same on second down depending on yardage needed for a first down, and the slow-footed Brodie, a Stanford alumnus, was simply a third-down and long passer.

On successive Sundays the 49ers routed two title contenders, the Detroit Lions 49–0 and Los Angeles Rams 35–0. When they faced the Bears, for whom Shaughnessy was a technical coaching adviser from 1951 to 1962, he was on the sidelines. He came up with a defensive scheme that had the Bears winning 31–0. "I want to tell you that you have to be lucky to shut down the shotgun," he said. "It's different, and in football, anything that's different is

tough to handle, anything at all. And that's the most original offense in the last quarter century—since George Halas opened up
the T." It might be expected that Shaughnessy would praise Halas
at this time, since he was working for the legendary coach. "We
were lucky to beat the shotgun because our linemen executed their
possum assignments perfectly," Shaughnessy continued. "We faked
out the offense instead of letting the offense fake us. Our middle
linebacker, Bill George, was a perfect possum in that game. He
lined up head-on the snapper, playing possum, but just before the
snap he jumped one yard to the left, or one yard to the right. The
blocker assigned to George couldn't find him.

"We were in what appeared to be a six-man line. They all played
possum until just before the snap. Sometimes they jumped away
at the moment of the snap. You can do that against the shotgun
because a shotgun play never starts as fast as a T play. That's the
weakness of the shotgun. The reason the 49ers couldn't block us
was they couldn't find us." The offense had no idea when and
where the Bears would blitz. They also would drop back five pass
defenders to match the five receivers the 49ers sent downfield.

The shotgun in Hickey's form had a short life. However, many
teams used the formation in third-down situations. Shaughnessy
predicted that back in 1961. "You'll see a lot of shotgun football in
this league from now on," he said, "not on every down, maybe—
but there are a lot of downs when it will be the best offense."

Shaughnessy was called the architect of the standard NFL defense still in use today. After he left the Rams, Halas hired him to
defend, of all things, the T formation. Shaughnessy created the 5-
3-3 defense that gave the linemen the job of plugging holes between tackles, freeing the outside linebackers to watch for an end
run and passes into the flat, while the middle linebacker moved
from side to side at the point of attack. Later, as the pro set became more popular, he shifted the defense into a four-man line,
inserting another pass defender. Shaughnessy also expanded the
way in which the defense blitzed the quarterback. No longer was

just the "red dog," a single rusher, used to attack the passer. Linemen were taught loops and stunts to get into the offensive backfield. Shaughnessy liked to say, "It doesn't make a heck of a lot of difference what you do. Just make it new."

He also recognized the importance of a quarterback on defense. While an assistant coach for the Bears in 1954, he spotted a defensive genius in a linebacker named Bill George. He had a knack for recognizing offenses, so Shaughnessy and Halas allowed him to call defensive sets and audibles. Shaughnessy told Halas that the middle linebacker could define the defense much like the quarterback defined the offense in the T formation. It was the start of a string of Hall of Fame middle linebackers for the Bears, including George, Dick Butkus, and Mike Singletary, and the current All Pro Brian Urlacher.

Shaughnessy died May 15, 1970, in Santa Monica, California, at the age of seventy-eight. In his will he left Halas a collection of his good plays and formations. "One formation looks especially promising," Halas wrote in his 1979 autobiography.

Assistant coach Marchie Schwartz took over for Shaughnessy in 1942 and coached one year, until Stanford suspended football for the duration of the war. Schwartz tended to a family business in the Midwest for a year, then returned to Stanford, where he coached until he retired after the 1950 season. He went into the title insurance business thereafter. His six-year record at Stanford was 28-28-4. He is in the College Football Hall of Fame for his All-American years at Notre Dame as a halfback when the Irish won the national title in 1930. In 1962 a panel of sportswriters and broadcasters named Schwartz to the backfield of the all-time Notre Dame team. He died April 18, 1991, in Danville, California, at the age of eighty-two.

Stanford assistant coach Phil Bengston eventually became an assistant coach for the Green Bay Packers under the legendary Vince

Lombardi. He became head coach when Lombardi stepped down after the 1967 season. Following in the footsteps of an icon was a difficult task at best. He coached the Packers from 1968 to 1970, compiling a 20-21-4 record. He died December 18, 1994, in San Diego, California, at the age of eighty-one.

Frankie Albert led Stanford to a 6-3 record in 1941, when he again was selected the All-American first-team quarterback and was the runner-up for the Heisman Trophy. He appeared on magazine covers and starred in a largely fictional movie about his college career called *The Spirit of Stanford*, for which he received six thousand dollars. Lloyd Bridges and Forrest Tucker appeared in the film. "It was a typical football movie, some screenwriter's idea of what happened in my career. It took 14 days to make, and that's not enough time to make a good one," Albert said.

The Bears drafted Albert in the first round in 1942, but after graduating he served three years in the navy during World War II. Upon discharge Albert signed for ten thousand dollars to play for the San Francisco 49ers in their first season in 1946 in the American Football Conference. He brought his same game to the 49ers, passing for 29 touchdowns in 1948 and surpassing Sid Luckman's record. He also ran for 8 touchdowns in fourteen games. In his ninety-game career with the 49ers, Albert threw 1,564 passes and completed 831 for a 53.1 percent completion rate. He compiled 10,795 passing yards and threw for 115 touchdowns and ninety-eight interceptions.

Albert, Shaughnessy, and Schwartz were reunited in 1950 when Schwartz, Stanford's head coach, hired his former boss and the Wow Boys' star to help coach spring practice. Albert retired from quarterbacking in 1952.

He coached the 49ers for three years, from 1956 to '58. He almost won a championship when the 49ers led the Detroit Lions 24–7 at halftime in the Western Conference championship but lost 31–27. "I don't think I was too well suited for coaching," Albert said. "I enjoyed the relationships with the players, but I'm very emotional. Maybe I was too keyed up. I was happy to get out of coaching. I've been a good fan, that's about it."

He became a team part owner with a 5 percent interest of the 49ers. He worked in real estate, sold automobiles, and invested in apartments and restaurants. His three daughters went to Stanford, where one became nationally ranked in tennis.

When he was inducted into the College Football Hall of Fame in 1956, he said, "Everything I have I owe to Stanford University, Clark Shaughnessy and the T formation."

He died September 4, 2002, at the age of eighty-two from complications of Alzheimer's disease in Palo Alto.

The Bears drafted Norm Standlee in the second round after he graduated in 1941. He helped the team win another NFL championship. He then went into the army, where he served as a captain in the Corps of Engineers in India. In 1946 he joined the 49ers, where he was captain for several years. His career statistics with the Bears and 49ers showed he played in thirty-three games and rushed 111 times for 510 yards and six touchdowns. He came down with polio in 1952, which forced him out of football.

At one time Standlee confided to friends that he never got over the fact that Albert made All American in 1940 and thereby received all the attention on the team. He told them that if he had not been injured, he would have made All American.

He became a part owner of a liquor store that went bankrupt, and his wife divorced him. He fought the ravages of alcoholism and was confined to a wheelchair in his later years. He was found dead at the age of sixty-two on January 3, 1981, in a motel in Mountain View, California.

After the 1942 season the Philadelphia Eagles drafted Pete Kmetovic in the first round, but he became a chief petty officer in the navy until 1945. He played with the Eagles in 1946 and the Detroit Lions in 1947. He coached football for a year at San Bernardino High School in California, then became freshman football coach at the University of San Francisco in 1949.

In 1950 he became backfield coach under former teammate Chuck Taylor, who was coaching Stanford. Kmetovic spent thirty-three years as a football coach, rugby coach, and manager of operations at Stanford until he retired in 1984. He died Feb. 8, 1990, of pneumonia at the age of seventy at his home in Palo Alto.

Chuck Taylor was named an All American after the 1942 season, then spent three years in the navy. He played for the Miami Seahawks in the American Football Conference until he returned to Stanford in 1948 as freshman football coach for a year. He then became an assistant coach with the 49ers from 1949 to 1950.

Stanford named Taylor head coach in 1951. In his first year the Indians were 9-0, earning the nickname "The How Boys," another play on words. But the Indians lost to Cal in the Big Game and to Illinois in the Rose Bowl. They still ended the year ranked No. 7 in the country. At the age of thirty-one, Taylor was the youngest man to be named national Coach of the Year. His record was 40-29-2 in seven years at Stanford. From 1963 to 1971 Taylor was Stanford's athletic director, one of two people with the distinction of being a player, a coach, and an athletic director at the same school. He was named to the College Football Hall of Fame in 1984. He died May 7, 1994, at the age of seventy-four in Palo Alto.

The Bears drafted Hugh Gallarneau in 1941 in the fourth round because of his familiarity with the T. He played with Standlee for the 1941 championship Bears. The next year Duke joined the marines, where he became a major. In 1946 he returned to the Bears, where he was named All Pro that year. He gained 1,421 yards on 343 carries in five seasons, scoring twenty-six TDS. He scored his first pro touchdown on a pass from Sid Luckman over the rookie defensive back Herman Rohrig, an ex-Cornhusker. Gallarneau said Rohrig looked at him in the end zone and said, "You again."

Gallarneau became an executive with Marshall Field's and Hart, Schaffner, and Marx in Chicago, his hometown. He retired as a vice president in 1985. He also broadcast a radio show, *On the Spot*, and did an NBC-TV show, *Touchdown*, while in Chicago.

He was inducted into the College Football Hall of Fame in 1982. He died July 14, 1999, at the age of eighty-two.

The Eagles drafted Vic Lindskog in the second round in 1942, and he became an All Pro in his last year, 1951. He played center at 6-foot-1-inch tall and 203 pounds, relying on superior quickness instead of strength. On defense he was a linebacker, where he intercepted four passes that he returned for 112 yards, including a 65-yard TD against the Brooklyn Tigers in 1944.

He was an assistant coach under head coach Jim Trimble from 1952 to 1954. He coached the British Columbia Lions of the Canadian Football League from 1955 to 1959. He also coached at Bakersfield Junior College, where he was line coach of the Junior Rose Bowl Championship team of 1960. He later became offensive line coach under Bob Waterfield and Hamp Pool for the Los Angeles Rams. He ended his coaching career in 1968 and became an NFL scout until he retired in 1985. He died February 28, 2003, at age eighty-eight.

The Eagles drafted Bruno Banducci in the sixth round in 1943. He played professional football for twelve seasons with the Eagles, the 49ers, and the Toronto Argonauts of the Canadian Football League. He was elected to the Helms Hall of Fame. He died September 15, 1985, in Sonoma, California, at the age of sixty-four.

The Bears drafted Milt Vucinich in the fifth round in 1943. He played one year—1945—in three games as a center and linebacker. He later became an insurance executive. He carried the insurance on the San Francisco Giants when Bob Lurie owned the team. Vucinich lives in San Mateo, California.

After graduating in 1941, Jack Warnecke enrolled in Harvard's architectural school. He completed the three-year course in one year, then worked as a draftsman for his father's architectural firm until 1947, when he opened his own firm in San Francisco. He became a world-renowned architect.

He designed the pedestrian mall in front of the White House, the memorial of John F. Kennedy at the Arlington National Cemetery, the Hawaiian State Capitol, the American embassy in Thailand, and libraries at the U.S. Naval Academy, Stanford, and the Universities of California at Berkeley and Santa Cruz. He also designed the basketball floor at Stanford's Maples Pavilion and a two-thousand-seat auditorium at UCLA. He is still active today in San Francisco.

Notes

Accounts of the plays of the ten Stanford football games in the 1940 season come mainly from Cyclone Covey's *The Wow Boys: The Story of Stanford's Historic 1940 Season, Game by Game* published in 1957. Covey painstakingly recorded every play from game films, most of which are no longer available. Other research came from play-by-play accounts published in the *San Francisco Chronicle* and the *Lincoln Star* as well as game stories from those newspapers and the *Los Angeles Times*. In addition, the author reviewed films of the 1941 Rose Bowl game.

Preface
"In 1936 Stanford's Angelo 'Hank' Luisetti": Migdol, *Stanford: Home of Champions*, 94.
"While war and the economy": *Stanford Daily*, September 27, 1940.

Introduction
"We'd been reading": Fimrite, "Melding of Men," 95.
"Just then, a tall, slim man": *San Diego Union-Tribune*, September 13, 2002.
"Now, I have a formation": Durant and Etter, *Highlights of College Football*, 148.
"He remembered the first chalk talk": Pope, *Football's Greatest Coaches*, 222.
"Other players were skeptical": Leckie, *Story of Football*, 128.
"But the players knew": Merrick, *Down on the Farm*, 144.
"What Shaughnessy had discovered": Shaughnessy, *Football in War and Peace*, 69.

1. From Power to Finesse
"One evening in 1935": Halas, *Halas by Halas*, 157.
"After a loss to Green Bay": Dunscomb, "Shaughnessy Behind," 66.
"Halas, who would go": Halas, *Halas by Halas*, 157.

"We passed the evening": Halas, *Halas by Halas*, 157.

"Halas had first come across": Davis, *Papa Bear*, 39.

"What Jones brought": Davis, *Papa Bear*, 93.

"I did a good bit": Dunscomb, "Shaughnessy Behind," 66.

"In 1935 Shaughnessy joined the Bears": Halas, *Halas by Halas*, 157.

"That same year": Davis, *Papa Bear*, 135.

"When Shaughnessy began": Zimmerman, *Thinking Man's Guide*, 187.

"In a 1942 *Esquire* article": Shaughnessy, "Football for Morale," 160–61.

"Shaughnessy also compared the T": Shaughnessy, Jones, and Halas, *Modern "T" Formation*, iii.

"By using the man in motion": Dunscomb, "Shaughnessy Behind," 66.

"Before we began collaborating": Dunscomb, "Shaughnessy Behind," 66.

"Football is a science": Shaughnessy, "Football for Morale," 160.

2. A Surprise Choice

"It came as no surprise": *Fremont Argus*, November 19, 1997.

"After the Vow Boys graduated": Merrick, *Down on the Farm*, 138.

"Gallarneau, who went": Merrick, *Down on the Farm*, 151.

"Bud Spencer": Pope, *Football's Great Coaches*, 221.

"Critics began calling": *Stanford Daily*, November 13, 1940.

"Dartmouth coach Earl 'Red' Blaik": *New York Times*, November 29, 1939.

"During the Dartmouth game": Fimrite, "Melding of Men," 94.

"As the players, coaches, and alumni": Liebendorfer, *Color of Life*, 71.

"Thornhill may have known": *San Francisco Chronicle*, November 11, 1939.

"Frankie Albert showed some promise": Grothe, *Great Moments*, 35.

"Before the Big Game": *San Francisco Chronicle*, November 10, 1939.

"Sportswriters had high hopes": *San Francisco Chronicle*, November 27, 1939.

"Thornhill refused to resign": *San Francisco Chronicle*, December 16, 1939.

"Not long after the search": *Stanford Daily*, January 12, 1940.

"DeGroot's undefeated 1939 Spartans": *San Francisco Chronicle*, November 25, 1939.

"Not long after the search": Liebendorfer, *Color of Life*, 74.

"Among his losses in 1939": Oriard, *King Football*, 113. Oriard uses a quotation about the disastrous season that was printed in the November 26, 1939, *Chicago Tribune*.

"Shaughnessy was set up to lose": Davis, *Papa Bear*, 135.

"Shaughnessy gave Berwanger jersey number 99": Pennington, *Heisman*, 13.

"In trying to field": *Stanford Daily*, January 12, 1940.

"On October 24 the University of Chicago newspaper": *Los Angeles Times*, October 25, 1939.

"Shaughnessy recognized he wasn't getting the job done": Shaughnessy, "Football for Morale," 160.

"Shaughnessy became the fall guy": Watterson, *College Football*, 195.

"At the end of the year": Quoted in Watterson, *College Football*, 193.

"I did not de-emphasize": Fimrite, "Melding of Men," 92.

"The *Daily Maroon* editor": Quoted in Watterson, *College Football*, 195.

"An alumnus wrote that he was sending his son": Quoted in Watterson, *College Football*, 195.

"Hutchins was steadfast": Covey, *Wow Boys*, 19.

"Although Shaughnessy was no longer football coach": Pope, *Football's Great Coaches*, 219.

"Football was Shaughnessy's life": Parrott, "Clark Shaughnessy," 10.

"Almost three years later": *Los Angeles Times*, March 22, 1942.

"Shaughnessy was born": Pope, *Football's Greatest Coaches*, 226.

"In 1943 he listed": Shaughnessy, *Football in War and Peace*, 10.

"That game eventually": Pope, *Football's Great Coaches*, 226.

"The following year he made the team": Dunscomb, "Shaughnessy Behind," 68.

"I was scared stiff": Dunscomb, "Shaughnessy Behind," 68.

"In the summer of 1911": Dunscomb, "Shaughnessy Behind," 68.

"Minnesota's 1914 yearbook": Pope, *Football's Great Coaches*, 226.

"After graduation Shaughnessy stayed": *Stanford Daily*, September 20, 1940.

"He was in for a shock": Pope, *Football's Great Coaches*, 227.

"Shaughnessy began showing his coaching genius": Pope, *Football's Great Coaches*, 227.

"From 1915 to 1926 Shaughnessy ran": Pope, *Football's Great Coaches*, 228.

"Shaughnessy surprised his new players": Pope, *Football's Great Coaches*, 228.

"In 1928 Loyola traveled": Pope, *Football's Great Coaches*, 228.

"When he was hired at Chicago": *Los Angeles Times*, April 4, 1939.

"Not long after he was out of a job": Pope, *Football's Great Coaches*, 219.

"Stanford president Ray Lyman Wilbur had watched": Covey, *Wow Boys*, 21.

"Athletic director . . . Al Masters had sought": Covey, *Wow Boys*, 22.

"Jim Lawson, an assistant coach": *Los Angeles Times*, January 14, 1940.

"The next day Shaughnessy left Los Angeles": Liebendorfer, *Color of Life*, 75.

"So bad was his cold": *Los Angeles Times*, May 8, 1940.

"The last stop on the tour": Liebendorfer, *Color of Life*, 75.

"That got me": Pope, *Football's Great Coaches*, 220.

"He sought advice from Dr. Albert Boles": Dunscomb, "Shaughnessy Behind," 63.

"Shaughnessy caught a plane": Dunscomb, "Shaughnessy Behind," 64.

"Shaughnessy knew that abolishing football": Shaughnessy, "Football for Morale," 96.

"Not long after Shaughnessy arrived": *Stanford Daily*, January 16, 1940.

"When Stanford announced his appointment": *San Francisco Chronicle*, January 12, 1940.

"In 1977 *Sports Illustrated*": Fimrite, "Melding of Men," 92.

"Said Prescott Sullivan": Quoted in Fimrite, "Melding of Men," 94.

"Not all the press": *San Francisco Chronicle*, January 14, 1940.

"Shaughnessy almost immediately raised more doubts": Davis, *Papa Bear*, 136.

"One *Chronicle* headline": *San Francisco Chronicle*, January 12, 1940.

"Even so, alumni were less than thrilled": Fimrite, "Melding of Men," 94.

"The *Stanford Daily* noted": *Stanford Daily*, January 12, 1940.

"Hampton Pool, who coached": *Stanford Daily*, January 12, 1940.

"Jack Warnecke, a tackle on the team": Warnecke, "How a Nazi," 16.

"Even coaches from across": *Los Angeles Times*, January 14, 1940.

3. Installing the T

"For example, on March 7": *Stanford Daily*, March 8, 1940.

"Back home he watched game films": *Stanford Daily*, March 8, 1940.

"Masterson, a Nebraska alumnus": *Los Angeles Times*, December 21, 1940.

"Before he chose his assistants": Liebendorfer, *Color of Life*, 76.

"Shaughnessy had not used": This quotation came from an article, "Cranking Up the Model 'T.'" A copy of the article was given to the author by former Wow Boy Milt Vucinich, who did not know where or when it was published. The author has been unable to track down the original source.

"If sportswriters, alumni": Cavalli, *Stanford Sports*, 14.

"Warner's reaction": Shaughnessy, "Football for Morale," 162.

"Shaughnessy often used military allusions": Shaughnessy, "Football for Morale," 162.

"For the T formation to work": Shaughnessy, "Football for Morale," 162.

"Certainly, any football player": Covey, *Wow Boys*, 18, 26.

"The psychology came": Shaughnessy, "Football for Morale," 161.

"The offense was a game": Shaughnessy, "Football for Morale," 160.

"Shaughnessy noted": Shaughnessy, "Football for Morale," 161.

"In Albert, Shaughnessy saw": Dunscomb, "Shaughnessy Behind," 19.

"Albert had played": *Alumni Almanac*, 20. This undated article came from a collection of articles about Albert in Stanford's Athletic Department files.

"Shaughnessy said Albert": Shaughnessy, "Football for Morale," 69.

"Albert perfected the bootleg": Cavalli, *Stanford Sports*, 16.

"Albert chose to wear": Spencer, "He Clowns," 83.

"When Shaughnessy became coach": "Albert Reflects on the Beginning of an Era." This undated article from an undetermined publication came from a collection of articles about Albert in Stanford's Athletic Department files.

"Teammates were in awe": *Fremont Argus*, November 19, 1997.

"Albert showed extraordinary leadership": Cavalli, *Stanford Sports*, 14.

"Shaughnessy noted that Albert": Covey, *Wow Boys*, 27.

"Fullback Norm Standlee": Shaughnessy, *Football in War and Peace*, 70.

"Shaughnessy called Standlee": Shaughnessy, "Football for Morale," 70.

"Despite his praise": Shaughnessy, *Football in War and Peace*, 70.

"Said Albert": *San Jose Mercury*, January 14, 1981.

"Halfback Pete Kmetovic": "Cranking Up the Model 'T.'"

"That proved true in the double wing": "Cranking Up the Model 'T.'"

"Vucinich said Kmetovic threw": Interview with the author.

"In the T his elusive change": Shaughnessy, *Football in War and Peace*, 70.

"The fourth player": From an obituary sent to the Stanford Athletic Department when Gallarneau died on July 14, 1999.

"He had been a blocking back": Covey, *Wow Boys*, 29.

"He was a typical": Shaughnessy, *Football in War and Peace*, 73.

"What made these players": Shaughnessy, *Football in War and Peace*, 73.

"Chuck Taylor, another San Jose native": Liebendorfer, *Color of Life*, 75.

"Vic Lindskog was twenty-four": Dunscomb, "Shaughnessy Behind," 64.

"Years later Albert said": Grothe, *Great Moments*, 39.

"California sportswriters had dubbed": Leckie, *Story of Football*, 128.

"Team morale": *Stanford Daily*, April 4, 1940.

"He told a *Stanford Daily*": *Stanford Daily*, September 20, 1940.

"It was like dying": *Fremont Argus*, November 19, 1997.

"Stanford publicist Don Liebendorfer": *Los Angeles Times*, May 8, 1940.

"Albert called Shaughnessy 'the great craftsman'": Covey, *Wow Boys*, 22.

"Bengston remembered": "T-Formation Ushers in the Modern Era." This undated article from an undetermined publication came from a collection of articles about the 1940 team in Stanford's Athletic Department files.

"Albert quickly became a believer": "Albert Reflects on the Beginning of an Era."

"Substitute halfback John Casey": *Los Angeles Times*, April 24, 1940.

"Shaughnessy told his players": *Fremont Argus*, November 19, 1997.

"The players approached": *Fremont Argus*, November 19, 1997.

"Shaughnessy had brought in Masterson": *Los Angeles Times*, December 21, 1940.

"When Masterson first met Albert": Spencer, "He Clowns," 85.

"Once he told a reporter": Spencer, "He Clowns," 20.

"I never saw anything": Spencer, "He Clowns," 85.

"Marchie Schwartz determined": Spencer, "He Clowns," 85.

"The team was slow": Liebendorfer, *Color of Life*, 76.

"Tackle Jack Warnecke said Shaughnessy was right": Warnecke, "How a Nazi," 17.

"But Shaughnessy stuck": *Fremont Argus*, November 19, 1997.

"I didn't tell anyone": Walt Gammage, "Sport Shorts," *Palo Alto Times*, no date.

"We scrimmaged the freshmen": *Fremont Argus*, November 19, 1997.

"They beat the hell out of us": *Fremont Argus*, November 19, 1997.

"However, Albert saw": *Fremont Argus*, November 19, 1997.

"The *San Francisco Chronicle*'s": *San Francisco Chronicle*, June 2, 1940.

"As time got closer": Dofflemyer, *Stanford Wow Boys*, 14.

"Jeffrey remembered running": Dofflemyer, *Stanford Wow Boys*, 15.

"Shaughnessy was in his element": Fimrite, "Melding of Men," 96.

"Three weeks before the season": *Los Angeles Times*, September 7, 1940.

"He was still holding": *Stanford Daily*, September 20, 1940.

"Bill Leiser wrote that Stanford": *Los Angeles Times*, August 8, 1940.

"Columnist Dick Hyland": *Los Angeles Times*, September 20, 1940.

4. "This stuff really works"

"Packing lunches": Valli e-mail to author.

"Sixty-four years later": *Hayward Daily Review*, March 25, 2004.

"In fact, no one expected": *Los Angeles Times*, September 14, 1940.

"No one knew what to expect": Dofflemyer, *Stanford Wow Boys*, 17.

"Assistant coach Marchie Schwartz": Covey, *Wow Boys*, 42.

"Shaughnessy wasn't so sure": *Los Angeles Times*, September 21, 1940.

"At a rally on campus": *Stanford Daily*, September 27, 1940.

"On Friday the Dons": *San Francisco Chronicle*, September 27, 1940.

"The two players": *San Francisco Chronicle*, September 27, 1940.

"The *San Francisco Chronicle* sports editor": Quoted in Fimrite, "Melding of Men," 96.

"Shaughnessy wasn't much": *Hayward Daily Review*, March 25, 2004.

"When the Indians trotted": Cavalli, *Stanford Sports*, 15.

"Vucinich said one": Interview with the author.

"He wasn't disappointed": *Fremont Argus*, November 19, 1997.

"Shaughnessy was always concerned": Shaughnessy, *Football in War and Peace*, 26.

"Hey, this stuff": Fimrite, "Melding of Men," 97.

"Albert would find himself": Dunscomb, "Shaughnessy Behind," 19.

"Albert often said": Covey, *Wow Boys*, 35.

"*Sports Illustrated* writer Ron Fimrite": Fimrite, "Melding of Men," 97.

"I remember Stanford": Valli e-mail to author.

"They kept changing guards": Fimrite, "Melding of Men," 97.

"Vucinich said Albert's ball handling": Fimrite, "Melding of Men," 98.

"We put Kmetovic in motion": Merrick, *Down on the Farm*, 145.

"This type of football": Quoted in Fimrite, "Melding of Men," 98.

"Mac Speedie": Merrick, *Down on the Farm*, 144.

"The Indians weren't through": Liebendorfer, *Color of Life*, 77.

"Because of the relative ease": *San Francisco Chronicle*, September 29, 1940.

"In a classic understatement": "Coach Shaughnessy, Victory-Starved at

Chicago, Leads Hungry Stanford Toward the Rose Bowl Table," *Newsweek*, November 4, 1940, 44.

"Shaughnessy said the team astounded": *San Francisco Chronicle*, September 29, 1940.

"After looking at game films": Covey, *Wow Boys*, 46.

"Santa Clara coach": Covey, *Wow Boys*, 46.

"Oregon coach Tex Oliver": Fimrite, "Melding of Men," 98.

"Overlooked because": Covey, *Wow Boys*, 43.

"Standlee could be heard": *San Francisco Chronicle*, September 29, 1940.

"What made college football": Horowitz, *Campus Life*, 119.

"University of Nebraska historian": Quoted in Oriard, *King Football*, 7.

"A 1951 article": Quoted in Oriard, *King Football*, 7.

"Even the smallest": Oriard, *King Football*, 5.

"As author Michael Oriard": Oriard, *King Football*, 2.

"He writes that out of 113": Oriard, *King Football*, 11.

"Big-time college football": Oriard, *King Football*, 24.

5. A Confidence Builder

"The odds of 2 to 1": *San Francisco Chronicle*, October 5, 1940.

"We went into a five-man": *San Francisco Chronicle*, October 6, 1940.

"As was typical": *San Francisco Chronicle*, October 5, 1940.

"Years later Stan Graff": Dofflemyer, *Stanford Wow Boys*, 22.

"Until I see a better team": *Los Angeles Times*, October 7, 1940.

"Shaughnessy wasn't satisfied": Covey, *Wow Boys*, 5.

6. Shaugnessy the Man

"Football obsessed Shaughnessy": Fimrite, "Melding of Men," 93.

"One of his daughters": Cavalli, *Stanford Sports*, 14.

"There's a lot of satisfaction": Zimmerman, *Thinking Man's Guide*, 187.

"Shaughnessy seemed to be more preoccupied": Fimrite, "Melding of Men," 93.

"Stanford's Chuck Taylor": Fimrite, "Melding of Men," 93.

"Milt Vucinich, then": Interview with the author.

"Backup quarterback Ray Hammett": Telephone interview with the author.

"Shaughnessy was often so deep": Cavalli, *Stanford Sports*, 16.

"Assistant coach Marchie Schwartz": Fimrite, "Melding of Men," 93.

"Shaughnessy had a poor": Fimrite, "Melding of Men," 93.

"The world lost": Pope, *Football's Great Coaches*, 230.

"Nonetheless, his Stanford": Dunscomb, "Shaughnessy Behind," 19.

"We all respected him": Fimrite, "Melding of Men," 98.

"He wrote in a 1942": Shaughnessy, "Football for Morale," 22.

"What is there about": Shaughnessy, *Football in War and Peace*, 5.

"William Barry Furlong": Furlong, "How the War," 130.

"Shaughnessy found fault": Shaughnessy, "Football for Morale," 161.

"Shaughnessy told Furlong": Furlong, "How the War," 130.

"Shaughnessy said he had studied": Furlong, "How the War," 133.

"Shaughnessy discovered that Guderian's tactics": Furlong, "How the War," 134.

"On a certain T-formation play": Pope, *Football's Great Coaches*, 224.

"Shaughnessy wasn't alone": Leckie, *Story of Football*, 126.

"By 1943 former Stanford": Shaughnessy, *Football in War and Peace*, 53.

"There are many reasons": Shaughnessy, "Football for Morale," 22.

"Tackle Jack Warnecke reflected": Warnecke, "How a Nazi," 19.

7. The Scrappy Broncos

"The word on": *Palo Alto Times*, October 8, 1940.

"He was unhappy": *San Francisco Chronicle*, October 8, 1940.

"And he wasn't": *San Francisco Chronicle*, October 8, 1940.

"Shaw was into 'coach-speak'": *San Francisco Chronicle*, October 8, 1940.

"The Broncos' depth": *San Francisco Chronicle*, October 8, 1940.

"Years later Albert": Covey, *Wow Boys*, 60.

"Shaw said after the game": *San Francisco Chronicle*, October 15, 1940.

"Stanford threatened": *Stanford Daily*, October 14, 1940.

"As the game ended": Covey, *Wow Boys*, 82.

"Albert, Standlee, and Taylor": *San Francisco Chronicle*, October 15, 1940.

"Shaughnessy praised Santa Clara": *San Francisco Chronicle*, October 15, 1940.

"After the game Shaw said": *San Francisco Chronicle*, October 14, 1940.

"Shaw told sportwriters": *San Francisco Chronicle*, October 15, 1940.

"To celebrate the victory": Liebendorfer, *Color of Life*, 78.

8. The White Ghosts

"Twelve hundred cheering": *Stanford Daily*, October 18, 1940.

"Commercial air travel": *Hayward Daily Review*, March 25, 2004.

"The plane flew": Http://www.aerodyn.orgHistory/dc-3.html.

"Train travel": *Spokesman-Review* (Spokane WA), October 18, 1940.

"The thirty-seven Indians": *San Francisco Chronicle*, October 19, 1940.

"The long, boring ride": *San Francisco Chronicle*, October 19, 1940.

"While O'Brien held": *San Francisco Chronicle*, October 21, 1940.

"While the Indians were traveling": *San Francisco Chronicle*, October 19, 1940.

"Not Pop Warner": *Stanford Daily*, October 18, 1940.

"Shaughnessy told the press": *Spokesman-Review* (Spokane WA), October 18, 1940.

"Bill Leiser": *San Francisco Chronicle*, October 18, 1940.

"Stanford's assistant coach Jim Lawson": *San Francisco Chronicle*, October 15, 1940.

"The Cougars made Shaughnessy": *San Francisco Chronicle*, October 18, 1940.

"At their three hundredth game": *Spokesman-Review* (Spokane WA), October 20, 1940.

"Stanford wore all-white": *San Francisco Chronicle*, October 20, 1940.

"Shaughnessy called the game": *San Francisco Chronicle*, October 21, 1940.

"Hollingbery called Stanford": *San Francisco Chronicle*, October 22, 1940.

9. Recruiting

"For example, former Stanford": Merrick, *Down on the Farm*, 139.

"USC also recruited Albert": Spencer, "He Clowns," 85.

"Milt Vucinich, a star": Interview with the author.

"Ray Hammett, a backup": Telephone interview with the author.

"Bill Mannon, a tackle": Telephone interview with the author.

"Woody Strode, one of the first": Strode and Young, *Goal Dust*, 27.

"Some friends of the school": Strode and Young, *Goal Dust*, 29.

"They gave me one hundred": Strode and Young, *Goal Dust*, 26.

"Strode said he had to earn": Strode and Young, *Goal Dust*, 27.

"In late 1937, when Frankie": *Los Angeles Times*, January 17, 1938.

"Apparently the Pacific Northwest": Neuberger, "Purity League," 64.

"The conference winner": Neuberger, "Purity League," 66.

"Investigator Edwin N. Atherton": *New York Times*, January 3, 1940.

"After looking at the report": *Los Angeles Times*, January 6, 1940.

"Atherton's main job": *Los Angeles Times*, February 12, 1940.

"We intend to have": *Los Angeles Times*, April 6, 1940.

"One guideline that caused": *Los Angeles Times*, February 12, 1940.

"In mid-July Atherton": *San Francisco Chronicle*, September 4, 1940.

"One recruit, Johnny Petrovich": Neuberger, "Purity League," 18.

"Stanford, which did not": *Los Angeles Times*, September 15, 1940.

"Apparently Atherton looked": *San Francisco Chronicle*, May 10, 1941.

"Stanford accepted the decision": *San Francisco Chronicle*, May 13, 1941.

"Atherton recognized the unfairness": *Los Angeles Times*, May 11, 1941.

"In June the conference": *Los Angeles Times*, June 14, 1941.

"The PCC wasn't the only": Watterson, *College Football*, 197.

"The major problems": Watterson, *College Football*, 197–98.

"The problem the NCAA": Watterson, *College Football*, 198–99.

10. "Pop" Comes Around

"Shaughnessy told his players": Warnecke, "How a Nazi," 21.

"Bill Leiser, the incredibly": *San Francisco Chronicle*, October 25, 1940.

"The Indians attended": *Stanford Daily*, October 25, 1940.

"A crowd of more than sixty thousand": *Stanford Daily*, October 25, 1940.

"In preparing for the game": *Los Angeles Times*, October 25, 1940.

"Assistant coach Phil Bengston": *San Francisco Chronicle*, October 22, 1940.

"Shaughnessy played down": *Los Angeles Times*, October 26, 1940.

"Vern Landreth, who was going": *Los Angeles Times*, November 4, 1940.

"Stanford had a potent": *San Francisco Chronicle*, October 23, 1940.

"USC scout Bob McNeish": *Los Angeles Times*, October 23, 1940.

"The Trojans took the train": *Los Angeles Times*, October 25, 1940.

"Again the two teams": Fimrite, "Melding of Men," 98.

"Albert said seeing the plays": Cavalli, *Stanford Sports*, 18.

"We won several games": Grothe, *Great Moments*, 38.

"Shaughnessy later sent in": *San Francisco Chronicle*, October 29, 1940.

"The crowd roared": *San Francisco Chronicle*, October 27, 1940.

"Vic Lindskog, for example": Dofflemyer, *Stanford Wow Boys*, 33.

"During halftime": *Stanford Daily*, October 31, 1940.

"Shaughnessy also found": *New York Times*, January 28, 1941.

"USC's defense": Merrick, *Down on the Farm*, 147.

"Assistant coach Jim Lawson": *San Francisco Chronicle*, October 27, 1940.

"The ball was now": Spencer, "He Clowns," 86.

"A play later": Spencer, "He Clowns," 86.

"Shaughnessy substituted": *Los Angeles Times*, October 27, 1940.

"'Oh, me,' Shaughnessy said": *San Francisco Chronicle*, October 27, 1940.

"When a friend told": Covey, *Wow Boys*, 120.

"Jones called Stanford": *Los Angeles Times*, October 27, 1940.

"That's about as smartly": *Los Angeles Times*, October 28, 1940.

"Peoples said": Dofflemyer, *Stanford Wow Boys*, 89.

"He also noted": *Los Angeles Times*, October 28, 1940.

"Five days after the victory": *Los Angeles Times*, October 31, 1940.

11. Meeting Jackie Robinson

"Earlier, on September 20, 1940": *Stanford Daily*, September 20, 1940.

"This wasn't just the work": *San Francisco Chronicle*, November 3, 1940.

"*Los Angeles Times* headlines": *Los Angeles Times*, November 9, 1940.

"Michael Oriard points out": Oriard, *King Football*, 298.

"Oriard noted that": Oriard, *King Football*, 314–15.

"UCLA was a friendly place": *Daily Bruin*, November 4, 1999.

"In his autobiography": Strode and Young, *Goal Dust*, 26.

"Not until World War II": Strode and Young, *Goal Dust*, 9.

"Nonetheless, with elusive": *San Francisco Chronicle*, October 30, 1940.

"Some called him": Tygiel, *Jackie Robinson Reader*, 25.

"The Bruins' coach Babe Horrell": *San Francisco Chronicle*, November 2, 1940.

"That didn't surprise": *San Francisco Chronicle*, October 31, 1940.

"Shaughnessy as usual": *Los Angeles Times*, November 1, 1940.

"Shaughnessy also noted": *San Francisco Chronicle*, November 2, 1940.

"With each game Albert": Spencer, "He Clowns," 20.

"Shaughnessy knew he would be in trouble": Pope, *Football's Great Coaches*, 223.

"Hundreds of Stanford fans": *Stanford Daily*, October 24, 1940.

"In Los Angeles they stayed": *Stanford Daily*, November 1, 1940.

"UCLA moved the ball": *Los Angeles Times*, November 3, 1940.

"Albert had been watching": Shaughnessy, *Football in War and Peace*, 70.

"About Robinson, Shaughnessy said": Covey, *Wow Boys*, 124.

"Our boys are very tired": *Los Angeles Times*, November 3, 1940.

"The Washington Huskies": Covey, *Wow Boys*, 144.

12. Closing In

"Never mind": *San Francisco Chronicle*, November 7, 1940.

"When he heard": *San Francisco Chronicle*, November 7, 1940.

"Phelan liked the role": *San Francisco Chronicle*, November 7, 1940.

"Worn out from their": *San Francisco Chronicle*, November 5, 1940.

"Shaughnessy downplayed": *Los Angeles Times*, November 9, 1940.

"He also talked": *Los Angeles Times*, November 9, 1940.

"The Indians might be playing": *Los Angeles Times*, November 9, 1940.

"The Huskies took over": Merrick, *Down on the Farm*, 148.

"Albert didn't seem particularly": Vucinich interview with author.

"Reserve guard John Kerman": Dofflemyer, *Stanford Wow Boys*, 46.

"Taylor had suffered": Merrick, *Down on the Farm*, 148–49.

"When Albert came back": Spencer, "He Clowns," 85.

"[Kmetovic's touchdown]": Dunscomb, "Shaughnessy Behind," 19.

"Albert had to rub": Spencer, "He Clowns," 86.

"Phelan would say": *San Francisco Chronicle*, November 10, 1940.

"From that time on": Dofflemyer, *Stanford Wow Boys*, 49.

"Gallarneau was the unsung hero": Dunscomb, "Shaughnessy Behind," 19.

"After the game a reporter": Pope, *Football's Great Coaches*, 223.

"After the game George Dunscomb": Dunscomb, "Shaughnessy Behind," 19.

"Vucinich told *San Francisco Chronicle*": *San Francisco Chronicle*, November 10, 1940.

"The boys were in high spirits": *San Francisco Chronicle*, November 10, 1940.

"Years later Kmetovic said": Dofflemyer, *Stanford Wow Boys*, 51.

"Asked to compare": *San Francisco Chronicle*, November 10, 1940.

"He told a reporter": *Stanford Daily*, November 11, 1940.

"As Stanford prepared": Parrott, "Clark Shaughnessy," 4.

13. Life on Campus

"Men wore slacks": *Stanford Daily*, October 25, 1940.

"And what did the *Stanford Daily*": *Stanford Daily*, October 31, 1940.

"One student who was seen": *Stanford Daily*, October 18, 1940.

"Like college students": *Stanford Daily*, May 3, 1940.

"That was during a time": Http://www.dmarie.com/timecap.

"The *Daily* also kept": *Stanford Daily*, April 10, 1940.

"The student newspaper also noted": *Stanford Daily*, May 29, 1940.

"As the presidential election": *Stanford Daily*, November 1, 1940.

"From the 1920s through the 1950s": Horowitz, *Campus Life*, 122.

"Frankie Albert joined": Spencer, "He Clowns," 20.

"He was active": Vucinich interview with the author.

"To help with living expenses": Spencer, "He Clowns," 86.

"Academics placed a demand": *Stanford Daily*, October 7, 1940.

"No college campus": *Los Angeles Times*, January 17, 1940.

14. Another Tough Matchup

"Assistant coach Phil Bengston": *San Francisco Chronicle*, November 12, 1940.

"Honestly, I think": *San Francisco Chronicle*, November 13, 1940.

"Stiner worked up": *San Francisco Chronicle*, November 15, 1940.

"osc's best player": *San Francisco Chronicle*, November 14, 1940.

"Stiner believed this was": *San Francisco Chronicle*, November 13, 1940.

"We'll score": *San Francisco Chronicle*, November 14, 1940.

"Albert continued to astonish": *San Francisco Chronicle*, November 12, 1940.

"In one respect": Grothe, *Great Moments*, 29.

"After the game Shaughnessy": *San Francisco Chronicle*, November 18, 1940.

"Lying on his side": Spencer, "He Clowns," 21.

"Parker, a senior": Dofflemyer, *Stanford Wow Boys*, 55.

"In all, Albert threw": Covey, *Wow Boys*, 193.

"Bill Leiser, the *San Francisco*": *San Francisco Chronicle*, November 18, 1940.

"Stiner had nothing": Covey, *Wow Boys*, 194.

"Albert credited": *San Francisco Chronicle*, November 18, 1940.

"Shaughnessy said Oregon State": *Oregonian*, November 19, 1940.

"Until last Thursday": *San Francisco Chronicle*, November 18, 1940.

"Stiner countered": *Los Angeles Times*, November 19, 1940.

"Albert was hoping": *Stanford Daily*, November 18, 1940.

"Shaughnessy was having": *San Francisco Chronicle*, November 19, 1940.

15. Big Game Fever

"Each school had": *Stanford Daily*, November 26, 1940.

"Stanford students painted": *Stanford Daily*, November 26, 1940.

"On the day before the game": *Stanford Daily*, November 29, 1940.

"Harry Shipkey": *Los Angeles Times*, November 24, 1940.

"The schools had agreed": *San Francisco Chronicle*, November 19, 1940.

"Stanford's appearance": *San Francisco Chronicle*, November 27, 1940.

"The extra week": *San Francisco Chronicle*, November 18, 1940.

"In fact, team physician": *Los Angeles Times*, November 27, 1940.

"A sportswriter asked": *Palo Alto Times*, November 24, 1940.

"Going into the Big Game": *San Francisco Chronicle*, November 23, 1940.

"On the Friday": *San Francisco Chronicle*, November 24, 1940.

"Allison, who held practices": *San Francisco Chronicle*, November 24, 1940.

"Assistant coach Marchie Schwartz": *San Francisco Chronicle*, November 24, 1940.

"Shaughnessy complained": Covey, *Wow Boys*, 201.

"Marchie Schwartz termed": *Palo Alto Times*, November 28, 1940.

"Mind you, I have yet": *San Francisco Chronicle*, November 27, 1940.

"Stanford was accused": *San Francisco Chronicle*, November 27, 1940.

"On game day": Covey, *Wow Boys*, 198–99.

"After putting on their uniforms": Pope, *Football's Great Coaches*, 224.

"Shaughnessy didn't say anything": Covey, *Wow Boys*, 198.

"The winner of the game": *Stanford Daily*, November 24, 1939.

"The Cal rooting section": *Stanford Daily*, November 29, 1940.

"In card stunts": "Feeling Fall," http://www.Stanfordalumni.org/news/magazine/1977 (accessed December 2, 2003).

"When Stanford ran": Dofflemyer, *Stanford Wow Boys*, 61.

"Later that night": Dofflemyer, *Stanford Wow Boys*, 60–61.

"After the game": *San Francisco Chronicle*, November 31, 1940.

"Shaughnessy was just happy": *San Francisco Chronicle*, November 31, 1940.

"Shaughnessy praised": Covey, *Wow Boys*, 202.

"Allison, of course": *San Francisco Chronicle*, December 1, 1940.

"About his Bears": *San Francisco Chronicle*, December 1, 1940.

"In the locker room": *Los Angeles Times*, December 4, 1940.

"When he was told": Spencer, "He Clowns," 20.

16. Bring on Nebraska

"The selection prompted": Liebendorfer, *Color of Life*, 84.

"Nebraskans hadn't": Liebendorfer, *Color of Life*, 84.

"The student newspaper": *Husker Century*, http://www.mgnptv.org.sportsFeat/pioneer/hc_events/hc_events/1940.html (accessed March 22, 2004).

"We were like a kid": *Hastings (NE) Tribune*, January 2, 2002.

"Said Wayne Blue": *Daily Nebraskan*, December 17, 2001.

"Nebraska coach Lawrence McCeney 'Biff' Jones": *Los Angeles Times*, December 10, 1940.

"The demand for": *Los Angeles Times*, December 3, 1940.

"The first day tickets": *Los Angeles Times*, December 12, 1940.

"Masters said he could": Liebendorfer, *Color of Life*, 84.

"Shaughnessy gave his team": Halas, *Halas by Halas*, 189.

"In studying the films": Danzig, *Oh, How They Played*, 354.

"Shaughnessy addressed the Bears": Dent, *Monster of the Midway*, 229–30.

"Nebraska coach": Halas, *Halas by Halas*, 189.

"It's not clear": Davis, *Papa Bear*, 165.

"A dropped pass": Whittingham, *Redskins*, 73.

"Shaughnessy also received": *New York Times*, December 4, 1940.

"Earlier in December": *New York Times*, December 4, 1940.

"Halfback Allen Zikmund": "Every Rose Has Its Thorn," *Husker Century*, http://www.mgnptv.org.sportsFeat/pioneer/hc_events/hc_events/1940.html (accessed November 28, 2004).

"Zikmund remembered walking": *Hastings (NE) Tribune*, January 2, 2002.

"When the players walked": *Hastings NE Tribune*, January 2, 2002.

"Knute Rockne": *Los Angeles Times*, December 3, 1940.

"When Masterson was asked": *Los Angeles Times*, December 21, 1940.

"The Cornhuskers watched": *Los Angeles Times*, December 21, 1940.

"On December 19 ten thousand": *Lincoln Sunday Journal and Star*, December 22, 1940.

"In Phoenix the Cornhuskers": *Lincoln Star*, December 24, 1940.

"Link Lyman, the Huskers' line coach": *Los Angeles Times*, December 18, 1940.

"Former Nebraska lineman": *Lincoln Star*, December 26, 1940.

"Lyman, who owned": *Los Angeles Times*, December 23, 1940.

"Fifteen to twenty Indians": *New York Times*, December 22, 1940.

"Nebraska players also came": *Los Angeles Times*, December 23, 1940.

"Stanford was an 11 to 5 favorite": *New York Times*, December 22, 1940.

"The *Times*' Wolf": *Los Angeles Times*, January 1, 1941.

"I've taught the boys": *Lincoln Star*, December 31, 1940.

"We are expecting": *Lincoln Star*, January 1, 1941.

"If Stanford had players": *Los Angeles Times*, December 29, 1940.

"Behm was badly burned": "Every Rose Has Its Thorn."

"There was no doubt": *Los Angeles Times*, December 29, 1940.

"On the train": Http://nebraska.statepaper.com.

"In an interesting sidelight": *Los Angeles Times*, July 12, 1940.

17. "Pretty good ball club, Coach"

"Vucinich's loss": *New York Times*, December 27, 1940.

"On the Nebraska side": *Lincoln Star*, December 31, 1940.

"The day before the game": *Los Angeles Times*, December 31, 1940.

"Also a day before the game": *Lincoln Star*, December 23, 1940.

"Almost ninety-two thousand attended": *Lincoln Star*, December 28, 1940.

"Just before the Cornhuskers": *Grand Island (NE) Independent*, December 31, 2001.

"The Huskers wore red": Liebendorfer, *Color of Life*, 84.

"The game started poorly": *Los Angeles Times*, December 29, 1940.

"We didn't even": Http://www.huskerpedia.com/interviews/fred-meier090202.hmt (accessed September 18, 2004).

"Taylor remembered": Merrick, *Down on the Farm*, 154.

"Shaughnessy had prepared": Shaughnessy, *Football in War and Peace*, 47.

"We ran fullback half-spinners": *Hastings (NE) Tribune*, January 2, 2002.

"After the game": *Los Angeles Times*, January 2, 1941.

"Shaughnessy noted that before": Shaughnessy, *Football in War and Peace*, 47.

"Shaughnessy relented": *Los Angeles Times*, January 2, 1941.

"Stanford then began": Spencer, "He Clowns," 21.

"Davis J. Walsh, a writer": Shaughnessy, *Football in War and Peace*, 48.

"Shaughnessy said Gallarneau": Shaughnessy, *Football in War and Peace*, 49.

"After the touchdown": Spencer, "He Clowns," 21.

"Shaughnessy said he wasn't nervous": *Los Angeles Times*, January 2, 1941.

"Albert knew that others": *Los Angeles Times*, January 2, 1941.

"Shaughnessy said the Indians": Shaughnessy, *Football in War and Peace*, 49.

"Albert wanted to give Gallarneau": "T-Formation Ushers in the Modern Era." This undated article written by Art Rosenbaum from an undetermined publication came from a collection of articles in Stanford's Athletic Department files.

"Albert's conversion": Pope, *Football's Great Coaches*, 224.

"On first down": "Every Rose Has Its Thorn," *Husker Century*, http://
www.mgnptv.org.sportsFeat/pioneer/hc_events/hc_events/1940.html (accessed November 28, 2004).

"Our team had regained": Shaughnessy, *Football in War and Peace*,
50.

"There had been criticism": Shaughnessy, *Football in War and Peace*,
50.

"Of the Huskers' goal-line stand": *Los Angeles Times*, January 2,
1941.

"Of Kmetovic's touchdown": Merrick, *Down on the Farm*, 157.

"Albert took little credit": Merrick, *Down on the Farm*, 159.

"I got a kick": Shaughnessy, *Football in War and Peace*, 50.

"Stanford threatened to score": *Los Angeles Times*, January 2, 1941.

"In the end the Huskers": *Los Angeles Times*, January 2, 1941.

"Here's how the *Los Angeles Times*": *Los Angeles Times*, January 2,
1940.

"Hey, coach": Shaughnessy, *Football in War and Peace*, 53.

"My, my": *Los Angeles Times*, January 2, 1941.

"Well, they were all": Merrick, *Down on the Farm*, 159.

"We came west": *Lincoln Star*, January 2, 1941.

"Despite Stanford's success": *Los Angeles Times*, January 2, 1941.

"Line coach Link Lyman": *Los Angeles Times*, January 2, 1941.

"Even the hometown": *Lincoln Star*, January 2, 1941.

"The United Press correspondent": *Los Angeles Times*, January 2,
1941.

"It's been a swell trip": *Los Angeles Times*, January 3, 1941.

"Said Curly Grieve": Quoted in Fimrite, "Melding of Men," 92.

"*Los Angeles Times* columnist": *Los Angeles Times*, January 3,
1941.

18. The Legacy

"Clark overcoached": *Tacoma News Tribune*, December 29, 2002.

"Rumors cropped up": *Los Angeles Times*, February 19, 1942.

"On March 12, 1942": *Los Angeles Times*, March 22, 1942.

"Then on March 20": *Los Angeles Times*, March 21, 1942.

"The 1941 Rose Bowl game": Shaughnessy, *Football in War and Peace*,
47.

"Jeff Davis wrote": Davis, *Papa Bear*, 165.

"In a 1953 letter": Danzig, *Oh, How They Played*, 401–3.

"Esteemed *Los Angeles Times* columnist": Oates, *Football in America*, 51.

"After the Rose Bowl victory": *New York Times*, January 28, 1941.

"Shaughnessy was besieged": *Los Angeles Times*, January 14, 1941.

"Within ten years": Quoted in Fimrite, "Melding of Men," 92.

"It's a matter of self-preservation": Zimmerman, *Thinking Man's Guide*, 191–92.

"Still, the T formation": Zimmerman, *Thinking Man's Guide*, 188.

"It's often been said": "Cranking Up the Model T."

"Pop Warner remarked": Danzig, *Oh, How They Played*, 336.

"Writing in *Esquire*": Shaughnessy, "Football for Morale," 159.

"The boys on our 1940 team": Dunscomb, "Shaughnessy Behind," 64.

"Too little also has been said": Shaughnessy, "Football for Morale," 161.

"Publicly, Shaughnessy downplayed": Dunscomb, "Shaughnessy Behind," 66.

"What the Bears did": Danzig, *History of American Football*, 77.

"Although Halas acknowledged": Halas, *Halas by Halas*, 156.

"One telling moment": Halas, *Halas by Halas*, 323.

"In his later years": Furlong, "How the War," 138.

"While there is little question": Shaughnessy, *Football in War and Peace*, 2.

"New York Times sportswriter": *New York Times*, February 23, 1950.

"The year 1940 'is of crucial importance': "1940: The Triumph of the T," Pro Football Researchers Association, http://www.footballresearch.com/articles (accessed March 14, 2004).

"The Bears' Luckman": Zimmerman, *Thinking Man's Guide*, 187.

"Stanford's success with the T": Oates, *Football in America*, 58.

"The T formation this fall": Shaughnessy, "Football for Morale," 159.

"Shaughnessy pointed out that the basic value": Shaughnessy, "Football for Morale, 160.

"Getting away from": Shaughnessy, "Football for Morale," 162.

"Our own defense was pretty good": "Cranking Up the Model T."

"Pop Warner also": *San Francisco Chronicle*, November 28, 1940.

19. Epilogue

"The Associated Press dubbed": Quoted in Danzig, *History of American Football*, 362.

"It disturbs me": *Fremont Argus*, November 19, 1997.

"Bob Oates, the longtime": Oates, *Football in America*, 310.

"On successive Sundays": Oates, *Football in America*, 220–24.

"The shotgun in Hickey's form": Oates, *Football in America*, 224.

"Shaughnessy liked to say": *Tacoma News Tribune*, December 29, 2002.

"He also recognized": Davis, *Papa Bear*, 281.

"One formation": Halas, *Halas by Halas*, 324.

"Frankie Albert led": *Alumni Almanac*. This undated article came from a collection of articles about Albert in Stanford's Athletic Department files.

"Albert retired": "Albert Reflects on the Beginning of an Era." This undated article from an undetermined publication came from a collection of articles about Albert in Stanford's Athletic Department files.

"When he was inducted": Cavalli, *Stanford Sports*, 16.

"He scored his first": *Dayton Daily News and Journal Herald*, February 30, 1987, 28.

Bibliography

Babcock, Michael. *Go Big Red: The Complete Fan's Guide to Nebraska Football*. New York: St. Martin's Griffin, 1998.

Cavalli, Gary. *Stanford Sports*. Palo Alto CA: Stanford Alumni Association, 1982.

Covey, Cyclone. *The Wow Boys: The Story of Stanford's Historic 1940 Football Season, Game by Game*. New York: Exposition Press, 1957.

Danzig, Allison. *The History of American Football*. Englewood Cliffs NJ: Prentice-Hall, 1956.

———. *Oh, How They Played the Game*. New York: MacMillan, 1971.

Davis, Jeff. *Papa Bear: The Life and Legacy of George Halas*. New York: McGraw-Hill, 2004.

Dent, Jim. *Monster of the Midway*. New York: Thomas Dunne Books, 2003.

Dofflemyer, Robert T. *The Legend of the Stanford Wow Boys*. Lemon Cove CA: Dry Crik Press, 1993.

Dunscomb, George. "Shaughnessy behind the Eight Ball." *Saturday Evening Post*, November 1, 1941, 18–19, 61, 63–64, 66, 68.

Durant, John, and Les Etter. *Highlights of College Football*. New York: Hastings House, 1970.

Eisenhammer, Fred, and Eric B. Sondheimer. *College Football's Most Memorable Games, 1913 through 1990*. Jefferson NC: McFarland and Company, 1992.

Falkner, David. *Great Time Coming*. New York: Touchtone, 1995.

Fimrite, Ron. "A Melding of Men All Suited to a T." *Sports Illustrated*, September 5, 1977, 91–100.

Finney, Pete. *The Father of Modern Football: Shaughnessy Fit Game to a T*. Nashville TN: Athlon, 1989.

Fuller, James. *Biographical Dictionary of American Sports: Football*. Westerly CT: Greenwood Press, 1987.

Furlong, William Barry. "How the War in France Changed Football Forever." *Smithsonian*, February 1986, 125–38.

Grothe, Pete, ed. *Great Moments in Stanford Sports*. Palo Alto CA: Pacific Books, 1952.

Halas, George. *Halas by Halas: The Autobiography of George Halas*. New York: McGraw-Hill, 1979.

Horowitz, Helen Lefkowitz. *Campus Life: Undergraduate Cultures for the End of the Eighteenth Century to the Present*. New York: Alfred A. Knopf, 1987.

Kaye, Ivan N. *Good Clean Violence: A History of College Football*. New York: Lippincott, 1973.

Leckie, Robert. *The Story of Football*. New York: Random House, 1965.

Liebendorfer, Don E. *The Color of Life Is Red*. Palo Alto CA: Stanford Athletic Department, 1972.

MacCambridge, Michael. *America's Game: The Epic Story of How Pro Football Captured the Nation*. New York: Random House, 2004.

Merrick, Fred. *Down on the Farm*. Huntsville AL: Strode Publishers, 1975.

Migdol, Gary. *Stanford: Home of Champions*. Champaign IL: Sports Publishing, 1997.

Neuberger, Richard L. "Purity League." *Collier's*, November 18, 1940, 63–64, 66.

Oates, Bob. *Football in America: Game of the Century*. Coal Valley IL: Quality Sports Publications, 1999.

Oriard, Michael. *King Football*. Chapel Hill: University of North Carolina Press, 2004.

Parrott, Harold. "Clark Shaughnessy: From Out of the Frying Pan into the Rose Bowl." *This Week*, December 30, 1940, 10, 12.

Pennington, Bill. *The Heisman: Great American Stories of the Men Who Won*. New York: Regan Books, 2004.

Perrin, Tom. *Football: A College History*. Jefferson NC: McFarland, 1987.

Pope, Edwin. *Football's Great Coaches*. Atlanta: Tupper and Love, 1955.

Rader, Benjamin G. *American Sports: From the Age of Folk Games to the Age of Televised Sports*. Englewood Cliffs NJ: Prentice-Hall, 1996.

Roberts, Howard. *The Chicago Bears*. New York: Putnam, 1947.

Robinson, Ray. *Rockne of Notre Dame: The Making of a Football Legend*. New York: Oxford University, 1999.

Samuelson, Rube. *The Rose Bowl Game*. New York: Doubleday, 1951.

Shaughnessy, Clark. "Football for Morale." *Esquire*, August 1942, 159–62.

———. *Football in War and Peace*. Clinton SC: Jacobs Press, 1943.

Shaughnessy, Clark, Ralph Jones, and George Halas. *The Modern "T" Formation with Man-in-Motion*. Chicago: May and Halas, 1941.

Spencer, Emerson L. "He Clowns to Touchdowns." *Saturday Evening Post*, September 27, 1941, 81–86.

Strode, Woody, and Sam Young. *Goal Dust, an Autobiography*. Landam MD: Madison Books, 1990.

Sullivan, John. *The Big Game*. New York: Leisure Press, 1982.

Tygiel, Jules, ed. *The Jackie Robinson Reader*. New York: Dutton, 1997.

Warnecke, John Carl. "How a Nazi General Changed Stanford Football." *Sandstone and Tile*, published by the Stanford Historical Society (Summer/Fall 2002): 16–21.

Watterson, John Sayle. *College Football*. Baltimore MD: The John Hopkins University Press, 2000.

Weland, Alexander M. *The Saga of American Football*. New York: Macmillan, 1955.

Whittingham, Richard. *Redskins: An Illustrated History*. New York: Simon and Schuster, 1990.

Zimmerman, Paul. *A Thinking Man's Guide to Pro Football*. New York: Dutton, 1971.